The Day Begins With Christ

By

Adríenna Dionna Turner

authorHOUSE

AuthorHouse™
1663 Liberty Drive
Bloomington, IN 47403
www.authorhouse.com
Phone: 833-262-8899

This book is a work of non-fiction. Unless otherwise noted, the author and the publisher make no explicit guarantees as to the accuracy of the information contained in this book and in some cases, names of people and places have been altered to protect their privacy.

All Scripture quotations and explanations are derived from King James Version, New Living Translation, New International Version, Life Application Study Bible, NKJV, New King James Version Holy Bible: Woman Thou Art Loosed edition, and Nelson Study Bible, NKJV.

Published by AuthorHouse 08/24/2020

ISBN: 978-1-4389-1901-0 (sc)
ISBN: 978-1-4634-5416-6 (e)

Print information available on the last page.

Dream 4 More Literary Consulting Firm
Website: www.dreams4more.com
Email: dream4more@earthlink.net

Author Site: http://www.adriennaturner.webs.com

Editor: Kathleen Jackson
Developmental Editor and Copyediting: Harriet Wilson (VIP Editing)
Associate Editor (proofread): Adrienna Dionna Turner

Foreword

Congratulations, today you will be starting your 50-day journey that will lead you down your spiritual path with God. *Day Begins with Christ* is designed to build a closer relationship with God, where you let your Day Begin with Jesus Christ.

This book will not only explain God's plan for your life, also how you will grow as a believer day-to-day. It will also challenge your personal relationship with God with daily activities, questions, and review portions that will strengthen you not only as a Christian, but will direct your path to God's will for your life.

This is a daily inspirational, devotional-meditation book to gain divine wisdom from God's Holy Word.

The Day Begins With Christ

Introduction

The *Day Begins with Christ* is an inspirational, non-fiction book to help followers of Jesus Christ mature as believers by seeking spiritual growth through guidance and direction from our Heavenly Father. Additionally, this book is for all who seek the gospel, seek the truth, and want to know how to follow Christ daily until He returns.

Many people are indecisive about their spirituality and religion, as others are lukewarm. *Lukewarm believers* are neither hot nor cold. In other words, they still want to dip into worldly functions, and then go to church, trying to represent themselves as believers of Jesus Christ. We have also broken the lines of communication with our Creator, where we are unable to hear His voice.

Jesus is a good shepherd. His sheep are able to hear His voice. No one can comprehend God,[5] but through the guidance of the Holy Spirit, believers have insight into some of God's plans, thoughts, and actions. We can obtain the *mind of Christ* through the Holy Spirit. We can begin to know God's thoughts, talk with Him, and expect His answers to our prayers.

Are you spending enough time with Christ to have His Spirit living inside of you? To have an intimate relationship with Christ comes only from spending time consistently in His presence and in His Word (see *Philippians 2:5*).[6] However, we are continuing to entertain in unrighteousness behavior, instead of seeking repentance. Overall, our constant focus is to resist the Devil and his evil tactics to destroy humanity.

> *Revelation 14:6, KJV: "...the everlasting gospel to preach unto them that dwell on the earth, and to every nation, and kindred, and tongue, and people."*

Some believe a final worldwide appeal is to spread the gospel of God's Word to all people. Others will see signs and wonders as God's judgment. Everyone will have their chance to proclaim their allegiance to God. Our final judgment will not be put off forever. Have you confessed your sins and trusted in Jesus Christ? Have you received Jesus Christ's good news in your life and applied it? After reading this book, hopefully you will change your life and follow the footsteps of Jesus Christ!

---

[5] Romans 11:34
[6] Life Application Study Bible, NKJV, 1996.

Day Begins 1: God's Laws Intended For Man And Woman

The Purpose For Following God's Laws: The Ten Commandments

At the foot of Mount Sinai, God showed His people the true lifestyle and beauty of His laws. Initially, the *Ten Commandments* were created to lead Israel to a life of holiness. Eventually, Israelites were able to see the nature of God and His plan. God's commands and guidelines were intended to direct the community to meet the needs of each individual in a loving and responsible manner.

People argue not to abide to the Old Testament laws, only obey the New Testament laws because Jesus has fulfilled the prophecies of the Old Testament. Some refer to what Jesus was asked in the Bible: "What laws are we commanded to follow?" Jesus' responded with the two greatest commandments:

> *Matthew 22:37-40, NKJV: "Jesus said to him, 'You shall love the Lord with all your heart, with all your soul, and with all your mind. This is the first and great commandment. And the second is like it: 'You shall love your neighbor as yourself.' On these two commandments hang all the Law and the Prophets."*

Are we still responsible to fulfill God's ultimate law of love? As the body of Christ, we are the descendants of Abraham, who is the Father of Generations (Nations). Through Abraham's bloodline, we are able to abide to the laws of God. Additionally, Moses was a prophet whom freed the Israelites from four hundred years of Egyptian rule through the inspiration and miracles of God. We are the continuation from godly bloodlines. We can equally apply the Old Testament's *Ten Commandments* with the New Testament today.

Ten Commandments Chart:
Old Testament

Commandment 1: Exodus 20:3	*"You shall have no other gods before Me." – NKJV*
Commandment 2: Exodus 20:4, 5-6	*"You shall not make yourself a carved image..." – NKJV* *4: "You shall not make yourself an idol in the form of anything in heaven above or on the earth beneath or in the waters below." -- NIV* *5: "You shall not bow down to them or worship them; for I, the Lord, your God, am a jealous God, punishing the children for the sin of the fathers to the third and fourth generation of those who hate me." -- NIV* *6: "But showing love to a thousand*

	generations of those who love Me and keep My commandments." – NIV
Commandment 3: Exodus 20:7	*"You shall not take the name of the Lord your God in vain..." -- NKJV* *"You shall not misuse the name of the Lord your God, for the Lord will not hold anyone guiltless who misuses His name." – NIV*
Commandment 4: Exodus 20:8, 9-10	*"Remember the Sabbath day, to keep it holy." -- NKJV* *9: "Six days you shall labor and do all your work." -- NIV* *10: "But the seventh day is a Sabbath to the Lord, your God. On it you shall not do any work, neither you, nor your son or daughter…nor the alien within your gates." – NIV*
Commandment 5: Exodus 20:12	*"Honor your father and your mother, so that you may live long in the land the Lord your God is giving you." -- NIV*
Commandment 6: Exodus 20:13	*"You shall not murder." – NKJV*
Commandment 7: Exodus 20:14	*"You shall not commit adultery." – NKJV*
Commandment 8: Exodus 20:15	*"You shall not steal." – NKJV*
Commandment 9: Exodus 20:16	*"You shall not give false testimony against your neighbor." – NIV*
Commandment 10: Exodus 20:17	*"You shall not covet (or desire) your neighbor's house. You shall not covet (or desire) your neighbor's wife (or husband)…or anything that belongs to your neighbor." – NIV*

Jesus Viewpoint on the Ten Commandments in New Testament

Commandment 1: Matthew 4:10 Luke 4:8	*"…Worship the Lord, your God, and serve Him only.'" – NIV*
Commandment 2: Luke 16:13	*"No servant can serve two masters…" – NKJV*
Commandment 3: Matthew 5:34	*"But I tell you, Do not swear at all: either by heaven, for it is God's throne." – NIV*
Commandment 4: Mark 2:27, 28	*"…The Sabbath was made for man, and not man for the Sabbath. Therefore, the Son of Man is also the*

	Lord of the Sabbath." – NKJV
Commandment 5: Matthew 10:37-39	*"He who loves father or mother more than Me is not worthy of Me. And he who loves son or daughter more than Me is not worthy of Me." -- NKJV* *38: "And anyone who does not take his cross and follow Me is not worthy of Me."--NIV* *39: "Whoever finds his life will lose it, and whoever loses his life for My sake will find it." – NIV*
Commandment 6: Matthew 5:22	*"...Whoever is angry with his brother (or sister) without a cause shall be in danger of the judgment." -- NKJV* *21: "...Do not murder, and anyone who murders will be subject to judgment." -- NIV* *22: "But I tell you that anyone who is angry with his brother (or sister) will be subject to judgment...But anyone who says, 'You fool!' will be in danger of the fire of hell." – NIV*
Commandment 7: Matthew 5:28	*"But I tell you that anyone who looks at a woman (or man) lustfully has already committed adultery with her (or him) in her (or him) heart." – NIV*
Commandment 8: Matthew 5:40	*"If anyone wants to sue you and take away your tunic, let him have your cloak also." – NKJV*
Commandment 9: Matthew 12:36-37	*"But I tell you that men will have to give account on the day of judgment for every careless word they have spoken." -- NIV* *37: "For by your words you will be acquitted, and by your words you will be condemned." – NIV*
Commandment 10: Luke 12:15	*"..Take heed and beware of covetousness..." -- NKJV* *"Then He said to them, 'Watch out! Be on your guard against all kinds of greed; a man's life does not consist in the abundance of his possessions.'" – NIV*

Consequently, some argue that they do not see *God's wonders* or *miracles* anymore. Miracles only occurred in the Old Testament such as the parting of the Red Sea for the Israelites to walk across to escape from their enemies; the burning bush that Moses could hardly glaze at; and Moses throwing his staff down, of which turned into a cobra, swallowing the other snakes produced by Egyptian conjurers. If we trust and believe in God with all our heart, mind and soul, we will be able to see His wonders work in our lives now.

When you are in painful situations, such as wondering how God will provide *a way of escape*. You realize there has to be a God who governs over His creations. According to God's promise to Abraham, He sent two angels to Sodom and Gomorrah to see if anyone was worthy to spare their lives from His wrath.[7] God heard the outcry of the people in Sodom and Gomorrah. Citizens of Sodom and Gomorrah became lovers of themselves. Homosexuality was widely practiced and greatly accepted. This included idolatry and other activities that God did not approve.

Lot, Abraham's nephew, allowed two strangers in his home when they arrived at the gateway of Sodom and Gomorrah. Later, the men in the town learned about the new visitors. Lot was familiar with Sodom and Gomorrah's customs of engaging in homosexual sexual acts and orgies. Lot offered his two virgin daughters in the place of his visitors. You have to realize that Lot was not aware that these two men were actually angels to do God's bid by destroying these two cities. In addition, these were the same two angelic figures sent down to speak to Abraham earlier.[8]

After bearing in mind Lot's kindness, these angels informed Lot to take his belongings, his wife and daughters out of the city of Sodom and Gomorrah. Lot was told not to look back. His wife was inquisitive about what was happening to her homeland. She turned around to glance at the city, Sodom and Gomorrah, and changed into a pillar of salt.[9] Alternatively, Lot and his daughters were able to see her body transfigure into a pillar of salt. They kept moving and did not turn back, regardless of what happened to their loved one.

Do you think you would be strong enough not to look back? Would you simply be curious that you had to see what was going on behind you? The only logical reason to risk it all, by looking back, is the fear of what lies ahead. Maybe Lot's wife could not picture herself in a new land, new lifestyle, and adapting to her new surroundings.

God had brought Lot and his daughter out. Similarly, it is up to you to have a great desire to follow God and what He commands you to do. Some of us do not desire to follow God's laws or commands. We continue to make excuses and are not willing to change our lifestyle. We are conditioned to believe what our society presents to use instead of turning to the Creator. Please do not end up like Lot's wife.

---

[7] Genesis 18:20-33
[8] Genesis 19:1-11
[9] Genesis 19:26

We need to seek and read the Word that He has laid out for us, before the foundation of the world. We need to ask Him for guidance in all that we do. It may be an adjustment for some, but remember that Jesus left the heavens to become like man and bare such a huge burden for us, so we can be with Him in heaven for eternity.

Abraham came from a family who relied on guidance and direction from many gods or idols. He yearned for more and desired to hear from the one and only God. From the first time Abraham heard God's voice in the midst, he knew that he had to obey God's command regardless of what others would think or say. God spoke to Abraham's heart, touched his spirit, and longed for Abraham to worship Him—the one and true living God. He also allowed God to direct his path and guide him during his travels. To proceed with God's request, Abraham had to remove familiarity and negativity to follow God wholeheartedly.

Are you wiling to do the same? Will you go out on the limb and do God's will? Are you willing to leave the familiarity? Are you ready to leave the negativity and people of bad influences? Can you seek the true and living God who has a plan for your life? Do not look or turn back once God speaks to your heart. Get up and leave!

Deuteronomy 4:8, NIV: "And what other nation is so great as to have such righteous decrees and laws as this body of laws I am setting before you today?"

Deuteronomy 4:9, NIV: "Only be careful, and watch yourselves closely so that you do not forget the things your eyes have seen or let them slip from your heart as long as you live. Teach them to your children and to their children after them."

Deuteronomy 4:2, NIV: "Do not add to what I command you and do not subtract from it, but keep the commands of the Lord, your God, that I give to you."

In *Deuteronomy 4:2*, to presume you can make changes to God's law is to assume a position of authority over God, who gave the laws. As believers of Jesus Christ, we are consciously aware that text cannot be added or omitted from God's Word. However, many religions and many denominations of religions create their own perception of the Bible, by rewriting God's Word into their own translation. They may include their own writings to coincide with the Bible. Consequently, as followers of Jesus Christ, not only are we to read and study the Bible, but we are also to pray to the Lord for understanding and wisdom.

God loves us and wants to protect us. God created these laws for us. Moreover, we are to be careful of false religions and false prophets that appear in sheep clothing. Their intentions are not of God. The Bible refers to these false prophets as wolves, ready to devour lost souls and weak believers. Their true mission is to seek you and have you follow their doctrine, belief system, or religious practices? They do not have any light in them and no truth in their writings or books. Jesus said, "I am the light, I am the truth, and I am the way." Ask God for discernment to show you the difference between falsehood and truth. Seek God to speak to your heart and mind to have clarity of these false teachings and confirmation.

Lastly, in *Deuteronomy 4:9*, Moses wanted to make sure that the people did not forget all they had seen God do. Therefore, Moses urged parents to teach their children about God's miracles. Parents are to remember God's faithfulness and share stories recounting God's greatness. It is easy to forget the miraculous acts God has worked in the lives of His people. You can remember God's great acts of faithfulness by telling your children, friends, or associates what you have seen Him do in your life.

Some argue that God's laws only applied to the Israelites. God's laws were devised to guide all people towards lifestyles that are healthy, upright, and devoted to God. The purpose was to point out sin, actual or potential sins, and to show the proper way to deal with sin. Therefore, the *Ten Commandments*, also known as the heart of God's laws, are just as applicable today as they were over three thousand years ago because they proclaim a lifestyle endorsed by God. They are the perfect expression of who God is and how He wants people to abide by them.

God gave other laws besides the *Ten Commandments*. You may be wondering if these laws are just as important and the answer is simple. God never issued a law that did not have a purpose. However, many of the laws we read in the Pentateuch (Jewish doctrine) were directed specifically to people of that time and culture. For example, no one practices sacrificing animals to cover our sins since Jesus Christ sacrificed himself as the 'Lamb' that removes our sins. Jesus also tells us, "Go on your way. From now on, don't sin."[10]

The New Testament refers to the death and resurrection of Jesus Christ. All the prophecies in the Old Testament have been fulfilled once Jesus Christ came and died for our sins. In other words, the Old Testament laws help us recognize our sins and correct our wrongdoings. Jesus Christ takes our sins away. Jesus is our primary example to follow because He alone, perfectly obeyed the law and modeled its true intent.

---

[10] John 8:11, Message Bible

~Let Your Day Begin With Christ, Day 1~

Let your Day Begin Activity: Following God's *Ten Commandments*. We need to reflect how we can spend more time alone with God. Do you want to be a living example for Christ? Jesus informs us through His message, *"if you love me, you will follow my commandments."* In addition, do we need to forgive someone to move forward on God's plans and focus on our walk with God? Make a list of those who you need to forgive, and do it to release your burdens onto God. Second, assign one day of the week to set aside to spend time with God, by turning off the television, radio, and computer to spend time with Him. Reflect on His Word and promises, even if it is praying, meditating, reading the Bible, or reading other devotional book(s). Keep your focus on loving God, spend at least one hour with God on this day of choice. Make God first and do not interrupt His time.

Today's Questions:

> What laws are we commanded by God to follow?
> - Read Matthew 22:37-40; Mark 12:28-33; Romans 13:8-10; Galatians 5:14; John 14:15, 21, 23; Leviticus 19:18; Deuteronomy 6:5; 10-12; 30:6.

> What did Jesus say to the Pharisees and Sadducees (Deuteronomy 12)?

Review to Begin your Day with Christ:

> The two greatest commandments are to love the Lord and to love your neighbor: Do we fulfill God's ultimate law of love? If not, give some explanations on how we can change to fulfill God's law of love. If we are, do we share God's Word with others? God also commands us to make disciples of Jesus Christ; however, we have to become disciples first before spreading the message to others. [My upcoming book, *Counsel Me Lord to be a Vessel for Christ* discuss friendships, discipleship, and leadership]

> Those that followed God no matter what their circumstances were, we can look at prophets such as *Job* (Job 1:20-22); *David* (Psalm 27:4; 63:1, 8); *Shadrach, Meshach, and Abednego* (Daniel 3:16-18). Are we willing to do the same as these prophets in the Bible? Are we willing to make sacrifices to please Jesus Christ despite man's laws even if it can cost your precious life?

Day Begins 2: First Commandment

A Deeper Look At The Ten Commandments: Inside And Out

The first four Commandments involve our relationship with God and the remaining six Commandments involve our relationship with others.

First Commandment History

The *First Commandment* focuses on loving God.[11] God exists in three spirits and/or persons: God, the Father, Jesus Christ, who came as man on Earth and ascended back to Heaven, and the Holy Spirit. These three spirits and/or persons are also called the *Trinity* (Father, Son and Holy Spirit). They are set of three entities that form a unity.

God created everyone with the capacity to worship. Everyone worships someone or something. However, God commanded us to worship only Him, and to serve no other gods before Him, who is worthy of all praise and worship. There are ways to guard ourselves against having other gods before the True God: seek first the Kingdom of God by making God your first priority; set your affections on things above; stay away from idols viewed as substitutes to God; and study and read your Holy Bible to know the true God.[12]

In the Old Testament, the Israelites where enslaved in a land of many idols and gods under Egyptian rulership. Egyptians worshipped the Sun God, and each god represented a different aspect of life. It was accepted as a normal form of worship, to serve many gods to receive blessings. When God told His people to worship and believe in Him, Israelites had to remove all Egyptians rules and forms of worship from their way of living.

Ultimately, the Israelites assumed that God was just another god to serve and worship. Even though God commanded the Israelites to have no other gods before Him, it was difficult for them to accept. God led the Israelites out of bondage, escaping Egypt's stronghold and its rulership under Pharaoh to delete all confusion from the Israelite's religious assimilation. Therefore, God clarified 'no other gods before me' as His *First Commandment*. This can be viewed as God's number one rule to be carried out among His people and is emphasized more than the other Commandments.

There are three main categories of religion: monotheism, polytheism, and pantheism. All three of these religions were practiced before God engraved the Ten Commandments on stone tablets.

---

[11] Exodus 20:3

[12] Malone, Julius. *Introduction to the Ten Commandments*, Sermon at New Testament Church (Milwaukee, WI) notes taken by author, 2004.

Monotheism is the doctrine or belief that there is only one God. *Polytheism* is the belief in or worship of more than one god. *Pantheism* is the belief in and worship of all gods. This is also the belief that God is in everything and everything is God.

Moreover, tribes throughout the Bible also worshipped idol gods: Philistines (also known as Dagon*)*; Amorites (also known as Molech*)*; Moabites (also known as Chemosh); Babylonians (also known as Marduke); and Canaanites (also known as Baal*).* Egyptians served many gods such as Sun God. The Egyptian community also worshipped the Pharaoh. Greeks had nearly thirty thousand gods to avoid missing one 'Unknown God.'[13] Romans worshipped and followed many gods, and they persecuted those that worshipped the one and only true God. Some view the Romans as atheists. Today, most Romans are under the Roman Catholic Church. They do not only worship Jesus Christ, but believe they have to speak to the Virgin Mary (idol statue form) to get their prayers to Jesus.

The New King James version states that God was not excusing other nations for their idol worshipping. God explains in His Word. While judgment was delayed for those other nations, it would be swift and complete for Israel since they knew God's laws. We must remember that idol worshipping is not just keeping statues around the house. Ideally, *idol worshipping* is a commitment to the other qualities, beliefs and practices, or to strengths and attributes of humanity. We are *idol worshipping* when our focus is on the creation of or the evolution of the animal kingdom. We are *idol worshipping* when the orderliness of stars is revered without reference to God, who created them.[14]

What does it mean to me?

What are other gods? *Gods* or *idols* are any person, place, or thing that one loves more than our Heavenly Father. Other examples of these idols are making our families, friends, careers, homes, cars, boats, trucks, jewelry and anything else that causes us to lose sight of God. What is higher than any worldly possession? What is higher than anything on earth? It is our Heavenly Father, Yahweh.

God is the one that blessed us with our husband or wife, with our children or those dear to us. We forget and overlook who gave us our spiritual gifts. Who will you serve? Who do you love? Will you put God first in your daily functions and put aside all the other things that you once thought was greater than life itself?

Today, many of us rank other things as more important than spending time with God. Our roles, careers, or jobs may take up all our time and energy, and we forget about God. For example, someone might view his or her elder, pastor, reverend or bishop as a 'man of God,' and never seek God. In other words, you view a 'prophet of God' as a god. If we concentrate too much on them, whether it is for personal identity or self-gratification to fit in a social organization (church), it becomes our *gods* or *idols*.

---

[13] Acts 17:23
[14] Life Application Study Bible, New King James Version, 1996.

Some believe they are worshipping God by going to every church function held. However, any time we devote more time to people or things, it ultimately controls our thoughts and energies, not allowing God to hold the central place in our lives.

~Let Your Day Begin With Christ, Day 2~

Let your Day Begin Activity: God requires us to worship Him. He is our Creator. He is a Jealous God. Write down different forms of worship. How can you worship and give Him praise today? Put an hour aside out of the day to praise Him for what He has created (e.g., praise dance, sing a song to Him, write a poem), and let God fill your heart with His Spirit.

Today's Questions:

Name some idols or gods that the Israelites worshipped.

Who is God to you?

What have you done for God lately?

How can I schedule God's time in to be more fruitful, not busy? (Acronym for BUSY: Being Under Satan's Yoke)

Review to Begin your Day with Christ:

First Commandment: God commanded us to worship only Him and to serve no other gods before Him, who is worthy of all praise and worship (Revelation 4:10-11; 5:9-14; 22:8-9). What are the ways to guard ourselves against having other gods before the True God?
- Seek first the Kingdom of God, by making God your first priority (Matthew 6:33).
- Set your affections on things above (Colossians 3:2; 1 John 2:15-17).
- Stay away from idols viewed as substitutes to God (1 John 5:21).
- Study and read your Holy Bible to know the true God (John 17:3; Jeremiah 9:23-24; Philippians 3:7-10).

Day Begins 3: Second Commandment

The *Second Commandment* refers to idolatry. There was a constant problem among the Hebrews, which led to the enslavement of Babylonian captivity.[15] God informed Abraham ahead of time that his nation would be held captive under Egypt jurisdictions and laws for four-hundred years.[16] Moreover, the *Second Commandment* is a prohibition against worshipping idols in reference to God.

Some examples are Aaron building a golden calf to represent God;[17] and Jeroboam made two calves of gold, placed one in Bethel and the other in Dan.[18] Aids to worship can become objects of worship;[19] many pictures in Tabernacle;[20] pictures in the temple built by Solomon;[21] and even now there are pictures of the Triune God, which can be found in some artwork as a Rock, Fortress, Shield, Shelter, Shade, Shepherd, a mother hen, Eagle, Lion, Lamb, Consuming Fire, Wind, etc. Additionally, the Roman Catholics have statues, images, and pictures in their church.[22]

The *Second Commandment* is because God is a jealous God.[23] Those being disobedient against God and rebellious can be shown as hating God. In contrast, God blesses those that are obedient,[24] and those desiring to take advantage of God's mercy. The definition of *mercy* means we do not receive justice or get what we deserve. *Grace* means we receive what we do not deserve. *Justice* means we receive what we deserve. *Justice* also refers to God's compassion.[25]

Images limit God. No artificial image can represent the true God. God cannot be captured into an image.[26] The reason we cannot place God into an image, or why images limit God, is that God is *omnipotent;*[27] God is *omniscient;*[28] and God is *omnipresent.*[29] In the *Roget's 21st Century, omnipotent* means all-powerful, almighty, divine, godlike, mighty, supreme, unlimited, and unrestricted. It also states that *omniscient* means all-knowing, all-seeing, almighty, infinite, knowledgeable, panosophical, preeminent, and wise. In the *Webster's College Dictionary, omnipresent*

---

[15] Jeremiah 25:1-11

[16] Genesis 11

[17] Exodus 32:1-6

[18] 1 Kings 12:25-33

[19] Numbers 21:4-9; John 3:14-15; 2 Kings 18:1-5

[20] Exodus 25:1-31

[21] 1 Kings 6:21-35

[22] Malone, Julius. *Introduction to the Ten Commandments.* Sermon at New Testament Church. Milwaukee, 2004.

[23] Deuteronomy 4:24; Zechariah 1:14

[24] Deuteronomy 28:1-14; John 13:17

[25] Psalm 103:10; 130:3; Ezra 9:13

[26] Isaiah 40:18-25; Exodus 15:11; John 4:24; 1 Kings 8:27; Jeremiah 23:24; Acts 17:29; Romans 1:22-23; 1 Timothy 1:17

[27] Jeremiah 32:17; Psalm 93:4

[28] Psalm 139: 2-4

[29] Psalm 139:7-12

means God is present in all places at the same time. Rejoice that God is everywhere. God is too high and holy to be captured in an image, idea, or object. God is too wide and wise to be comprehended.[30]

---

[30] Malone, Julius. *Introduction to the Ten Commandments*. Sermon at New Testament Church. Milwaukee, 2004; Job 11:7; Romans 11:33

~Let Your Day Begin With Christ, Day 3~

Let your Day Begin Activity: Idolatry. Take a piece of paper and make a list of all things that you idolize. Be very honest with yourself because you can only improve your life with God. No matter if it is money, cars, clothes, women, whatever the case may be and start today by getting rid of those things. After making this list, arrange them from easiest to hardest to do and eliminate one thing off that list every week. Foremost, God comes first in your life, not the things we idolize. Knowing this may take some time, put this list in a secure place and get rid of everything that you put before God.

Today's Questions:

What are the other gods or idols we devote most of our time, energy, and strength?

How important is it to make God most important in your life, is it worth all these things that you will be giving up?

Review to Begin your Day with Christ:

Review in this chapter some of the graven images. Write them down and check the ones you have idolized, asking God for forgiveness.

Second Commandment: What are some of the reasons for God creating the second commandment?

Day Begins 4: Third Commandment

The *Third Commandment* is to avoid taking God's name in vain. First, the word *vain* is a translation of the Hebrews word *shav*. In Hebrews and English *Lexicon of Brown, Driver, and Briggs*, *shav* means emptiness, nothingness, worthlessness, and vanity. Second, *vain* means to take, carry, or bear the Lord's name in vain, to use His name thoughtlessly, irreverently or carelessly, and according to *Lexicon of Brown, Driver and Briggs*, to use 'to no good purpose.' Lastly, *to take the Lord's name in vain*, means to bring dishonor to the Lord by one's lips, by one's lifestyle, by one's words, or by one's walk. In other words, anything that is said or done that brings dishonor or disrespect to the name of God.[31]

The Descriptions Of Taking The Lord's Name In Vain

The descriptions of taking the Lord's name in vain is when it is used in profanity, swearing, filthy, or corrupt speech. William Ward said, "Profanity is the use of strong words by weak people."[32] In addition, one can take the Lord's name in vain when it is emptied of its majesty, glory, honor, respect, and reverence to His name.

God's name can also be taken in vain when used in such expressions as shock, surprise, anger, amazement, disappointment, pain, etc. Examples are 'Oh my God (OMG)!' 'Good Lord!' 'Jesus Christ!' Think before we speak out thoughtlessly when using these names of *God* or *Jesus*. Additionally, the Lord's name in vain is expressed thoughtlessly in worship or Christian expressions such as 'hallelujah' or 'praise the Lord.' Another saying is 'God bless you' when someone sneezes.

Jesus spoke of people honoring Him with their lips, but their hearts were far away from Him.[33] There is a difference between speaking about God carelessly, versus speaking about God prayerfully and reverently. Please start to take the time to be aware of using His name in vain, or bad habits that cause you to use His name in vain. Try to replace them with other words that do not refer to the Lord's name. If you find it difficult to do at first, pray to the Lord and ask for forgiveness, and God will show you the way to break this habit.

Another way to take the Lord's name in vain is by using euphemisms used in place of God such as gosh or golly. In addition, to take the Lord's name in vain is when it is used for personal gain by preachers, politician, and other businessmen (or women), and through ill-gotten gains. God commands us to pray for our pastors, politicians, and officials or leaders in command, and those who have a wide influence over others that are not taking the Lord's name in vain for gain. Lastly, failure to keep a promise, pledge, or vow made in God's name.[34]

---

[31] Romans 2:21-24
[32] Ephesians 4:29 and Colossians 3:8
[33] Matthew 15:8
[34] Matthew 5:33-37; James 5:12

Dangers Of Taking The Lord's Name In Vain

The dangers of taking the Lord's name in vain will not go unpunished.

Exodus 20:7, NKJV: "You shall not take the Lord, your God, in vain, for the Lord will not hold him guiltless who takes His name in vain."

The *Third Commandment* refers to the sanctity of God's name.[35] Those that use the Lord's (Yahweh) name in vain involves trivializing His name by regarding it as insignificant such as in horror movies that would make jesters like 'Holy crap,' 'Oh my God,' or 'Jesus Christ!' They are simply using God's name in vain for evil purposes by coaxing God in violation to His character and purposes. Yet, punishment is usually not immediate.[36] However, no one can hide from God.[37] Conversely, those who take God's name in vain are not fulfilling the purpose for which they were created.[38]

God's name demonstrates His character, His mercy, and His greatness. Throughout the Bible, prophets and prophetesses names were associated with their character. Today, we try to get all fancy and unique with our children's names, which have no true meaning, or relates to their character when they mature. Or we do not know where our children's names derived from, or the definition of their names.

For instance, the name *Abram* means 'exalted father,' which later was changed to *Abraham*, 'father of a multitude.'[39] The name *Esau* means red or hairy. *Jacob* stands for 'heel catcher, trickster, deceiver,' later was changed to *Israel*, which means prince with God, one who struggles with God.[40]

A person who overcomes by faith, amidst terrible circumstances, will receive hidden manna to eat. *Manna* is angel's food. Therefore, the hidden manna to eat and new name are all prospective rewards for faithfulness to God. The *hidden manna* is the food from heaven that sustained Israel in the wilderness,[41] a portion of which was placed inside the ark as a memorial.[42] The *hidden manna* also suggests special intimacy with Christ.[43] Over-comers are promised supernatural sustenance in the resurrected state to enable them to function effectively as co-rulers in Christ's kingdom.

In John's day, *white stone* signified acquittal from legal charges. However, it seems best to relate to the Greek athletic games of giving a white stone to the victor in a contest, or to gladiators at the Roman games who had won the admiration of the

---

[35] Nelson Study Bible, NKJV.
[36] Ecclesiastes 8:11
[37] Psalm 139:7-12; Proverbs 15:3; Jeremiah 23:24; Daniel 5:23; Acts 17:28; Hebrews 10:31
[38] Isaiah 43:7, 21; Matthew 5:16; 1 Corinthians 10:31; Revelation 4:11
[39] Genesis 17:1-6
[40] Genesis 25:21-26; 32:24-30
[41] Exodus 16:4, 14, 15, 31; Exodus 16:32, 33
[42] Hebrews 9:4
[43] Luke 14:7-11; 22:28-30

public, and had been allowed to retire from future combats. This symbolization of victory over the enemies of God cannot be separated from a new name, which identifies the obedient believer regarding his or her distinctive character. How wonderful will that be?

Defenses Against Taking The Lord's Name In Vain

Some of the defenses against taking the Lord's name in vain are to guard your heart or mind by being careful at what you look or listen or engage in, being anointed with the Holy Spirit of God, or develop clean words to express emotions without God's name being a part of the expression. We can practice using God's name reverently or respectfully because God is holy. We are to live a life that glorifies God's name. What are in the name of the Lord are victory, healing, safety, protection, and salvation.

~Let Your Day Begin With Christ, Day 4~

Let your Day Begin Activity: God's name in vain. Make a list of all phrases or words you have used loosely in which puts God's name in vain. You know you have done it, whether it was today or in the past, write it down. Throughout the day, any time you say the Lords name in vain, say 5 positive things about the Lord that He has done for you. Repent for it. Ask God to help you not to speak such words from your lips. Tell others not to use these words in your presence, for you are honoring God.

Today's Questions:

What are some things we can do to break our habits of using God's name in vain?

What are some movies you have watched that uses God's names in vain? Music? TV Shows? Ask yourself, is God pleased with it?

What can be some dangers for continuing using God's name in vain? In the ancient times, they were stoned to death as one form of punishment.

Review to Begin your Day with Christ:

We can please God with words of praise, worship, and glorifying His holy name. Try to break our habits of foul language and putting God's name in vain for at least thirty days, and replace it with glorifying words to our Father.

Some defenses against taking God's name in vain:
- Guard your heart or mind by being careful at what you look at, or listen to, or engage in (Psalm 119:37; Proverbs 4:23; Mark 7:21-23; Luke 6:45; Ephesians 4:29; Colossians 3:8; 4:6; Philippians 4:8; 1 Timothy 6:20).
- Be filled with the Holy Spirit of God (Ephesians 5:18-20; Galatians 5:22-23).
- Develop some clean words to express surprise, etc. without God's name being a part of the expression.
- Practice using God's name reverently or respectfully (Matthew 6:9; Psalm 111:9). God's name is holy because He is holy.
- Live a life that glorifies God's name (Psalm 29:2; Matthew 5:16).
- Remember what is in the name of the Lord: victory, healing, safety, protection, and salvation.

✦ Remember and respect the names of God. Refer to the many names of God can be found in *Day Begins 49: Glorify the Lord and Keep it Holy.*

Day Begins 5: Fourth Commandment

The *Fourth Commandment* is the most controversial of the *Ten Commandments*.

Reasons God Gave Sabbath To Man And To The Jews

In the beginning of time, when Adam and Eve explored their paradise home, the scenery was breathtaking and beyond description. As beautiful as the world that God created and completed, the greatest gift that God gave to the newly created couple was the privilege of a personal relationship with Him. Therefore, God gave them the *Sabbath*, a day of special blessing, fellowship, and communion with their Creator. The Sabbath is central to our worship of God. It reveals the reason God is to be worshipped: for He is the Creator, and we are His creatures.

The Sabbath lie at the very foundation of divine worship, for it teaches this great truth in the most impressive manner and no other institutions does this. The true grounds of divine worship are found in the distinction between the Creator and His creation. This great fact can never be obsolete and must never be forgotten.[44] It was to keep this truth forever before the human race that God established the Sabbath.

In examining these texts, we find that, according to the *Fourth Commandment*, God set aside, or made holy on the seventh day of the week, the day we call Saturday.

1. God rested on the Sabbath.
2. God blessed the Sabbath.
3. God sanctified the Sabbath.

The reasons God gave the Sabbath to the Jews: need for rest and to be refreshed;[45] remember the Sabbath day; and God rested on the seventh day. First, the need for rest comes from the English word *Sabbath,* and the Greek word *Sabbaton*, later translated into the Hebrews word *Shabbat*, which means to rest, cease, and inactivity.

Second, the *Fourth Commandment* states that Seventh-Day Adventist contest that the Sunday observance is the first day of the week. Many other religions are worshipping the 'Sun God,' also worshipped by ancient Egyptians, which reverence Sunday as the day of the Sabbath. Remember the Sabbath is to a day of rest and worship God on the seventh day, which falls on Saturday.[46]

Then *Luke 24:1* says that the day Jesus rose from the grave was the first day of the week. However, the Bible speaks about a three-day sequence: the day before the

---

[44] Seventh-Day Adventists Believe: A Biblical Exposition of 27 Fundamental Doctrines.
[45] Exodus 20:8-10; 31:17
[46] Malone, Julius. *Introduction to the Ten Commandments*. Sermon at New Testament Church. Milwaukee, 2004.

Sabbath (the day Jesus died); the Sabbath; and the first day of the week (the day Jesus rose from the dead). Everyone in the world is able to recognize Good Friday as the day Jesus died. The entire world recognizes Easter Sunday as the day He rose to life. In the New Testament, it refers to this day as the Sabbath.[47]

God rested on the seventh day, not because he was weary, but because the work of creation was completed.[48] In addition, God rested because He expected humans to rest. He set an example for human beings to follow.[49] God not only made the Sabbath, He blessed it. According to *Ibid*, "the blessings on the seventh day implied that it was thereby declared to be a special object of divine favor, and a day that would be blessings to His creatures."

Last, but not least, God sanctified the Sabbath. To *sanctify* something means to make it sacred or holy, or to set it apart as holy and for holy use, to consecrate it. People, places (church, sanctuary or temple), and time can be sanctified. The fact that God sanctified the seventh day means that this day is holy, that He set it apart for the lofty purpose of enriching the divine-human relationship.[50] God blessed and sanctified the seventh day Sabbath because He rested on this day from all His works. He blessed and sanctified it for humanity, not for Himself. His personal presence brings to the Sabbath God's blessing and sanctification.[51]

The Sabbath And The Law

Sabbath observance is an antidote for idolatry. Keeping the Sabbath then becomes the sign of our allegiance to the true God -- a sign that we acknowledge His Sovereignty as Creator.[52] The *Sabbath Commandment* is the seal of God's law. Additionally, the *Fourth Commandment* is the only one of the Ten Commandments that identifies the true God by giving His name: the Lord our God; His title: the One who made it as the Creator; and His territory: the heavens and the earth.[53] Humans require physical rest to refresh their bodies, so God basis this Commandment as a day of rest on the Sabbath.

The Meanings Of The Sabbath

1. *Memorial of Creation:* The fundamental significance of the *Ten Commandments*, referring to the Sabbath, it memorializes the creation of the world.[54] It is linked

---

[47] Luke 23:54
[48] John 4:24; Psalm 121:4; Isaiah 40:28
[49] Exodus 20:11
[50] Seventh-Day Adventists Believe: A Biblical Exposition of 27 Fundamental Doctrines, p. 250.
[51] Seventh-Day Adventists Believe: A Biblical Exposition of 27 Fundamental Doctrines, p.250.
[52] Seventh-Day Adventists Believe: A Biblical Exposition of 27 Fundamental Doctrines, p.251.
[53] Exodus 20:10, 11
[54] Exodus 20:11, 12

inseparably to the act of Creation, the institution of the Sabbath, and the command to observe it.

2. *Symbol of Redemption:* Memorial deliverance in *Deuteronomy 5:15: "Remember that you were slaves in Egypt, and that the Lord, your God, brought you out of there with a mighty hand and an outstretched arm. Therefore the Lord, your God, has commanded you to observe the Sabbath day."* Sabbath rest stands out as a special symbol of redemption. The greatest burden we carry is the guilt of our disobedience. The Sabbath rest, by pointing back to Christ's rest in the tomb, the rest of victory over sin, offers to the Christian a tangible opportunity to accept and experience Christ's forgiveness, peace, and rest.

3. *Sign of Sanctification:* The Sabbath is a sign of God's transforming power, a sign of holiness or sanctification. In addition, Christ's blood sanctified for believers.[55] The Sabbath is also a sign of the believer's acceptance of His blood for the forgiveness of sins. Just as God has set the Sabbath aside for a holy purpose, so He has set His people apart for a holy purpose to be His special witnesses. Their communion with Him on the Sabbath day leads to holiness, where they learn to depend, not on their own resources, but on the God who sanctifies them. *True sanctification* is harmony with God, oneness with Him in character. It is received through obedience to those principles that are the transcript of His character. In addition, the Sabbath is the sign of obedience. He who from the heart obeys the *Fourth Commandment* will obey the whole law. He is sanctified through obedience.

4. *Sign of Loyalty:* Scripture reveals before the Second Coming, the whole world will be divided into two classes: those who are loyal and keep the commandments of God and the faith of Jesus, and those who worship the beast and his image.[56] God's truth will be magnified before many. It will be clear to all who practiced obedient observance of the Seventh-Day Sabbath that Scripture gives evidence of divine loyalty to the Creator.

5. *Time of Fellowship:* For a higher level of companionship, God gave the man and woman to each other.[57] However, Sabbath was a gift to humanity, offering the highest form of companionship -- companionship with God. Sabbath is experiencing God's presence among us. Without the Sabbath, all would be labor and sweat without end. The arrival of the Sabbath, however, brings hope, joy, meaning, and courage. It provides time to commune with God through worship, prayer, song, the study of and meditation on the Word, and through sharing the gospel with others. The Sabbath is our opportunity to experience God's presence.

6. *Sign of Righteousness by Faith:* Followers of Jesus Christ recognize that through the guidance of an enlightened conscience, the Holy Spirit can lead non-believers who honestly search for truth to an understanding of the general principles of God's law.[58] Alternatively, a true Christian does not keep the

---

[55] Hebrews 13:12
[56] Revelation 14:12, 9
[57] Genesis 2:18-25
[58] Romans 2:14-16

Sabbath to make him or her righteous. Instead, he or she can share the message with others. Those that keep the Sabbath in this way are not a legalist, for the outward keeping of the seventh day betokens the believer's inner experience in justification and sanctification. Moreover, one will rest on the Sabbath because he or she loves God, and wants a closer fellowship with Him.

"The spirit of true Sabbath keeping reveals a supreme love for Jesus Christ, the Creator and Savior, who is making us into new people. It makes the keeping of the right day in the right way a sign of righteousness by faith."

7. *Symbol of Resting in Christ:* The Sabbath was a memorial of God's delivering Israel from Egypt, distinguished the redeemed of that time from the surrounding nations. It is a sign of deliverance from sin to God's rest, setting the redeemed apart from the world.

"The rest is a spiritual rest: a rest from our 'own works,' a ceasing from sin. It is into this rest that God calls His people, and it is of the rest that both the Sabbath and Canaan are symbols."

God's original purpose of offering that rest to humanity remains unchanged.

"The observance of the Seventh-Day Sabbath thus testifies, not only to faith in God as the Creator of all things, but also to faith in His power to transform the life and qualify men and women for entering that eternal 'rest' He originally intended for the inhabitants of this earth."

Hebrews 4:9, NIV: "There remains, then, a Sabbath-rest for the people of God."

"One must first enter, by faith, into His spiritual rest, the rest of the soul from sin and from its own efforts at salvation. All who have entered this rest --- the saving grace received by faith in Jesus Christ -- have ceased every effort to achieve righteousness by their own works."[59]

Reasons For Change In Corporate Worship From Saturday Sabbath Day To The Sunday Lord's Day

The change in corporate worship from Saturday to Sunday was not made by the Pope, the Catholic Church, Christians in Rome, nor Constantine. The early Christians were worshipping on Sunday before the Pope and the Catholic Church, and the Romans did not have a Sabbath day. Constantine made Sunday a legal holiday in 321 A.D. since Christians was already worshipping on Sunday. There are several reasons for the change.

---

[59] Seventh-Day Adventists Believe: A Biblical Exposition of 27 Fundamental Doctrines, pp. 249-258.

The first reason is that Jesus rose from the dead on Sunday, which is the first day of the week.[60] In other words, Saturday Sabbath commemorated God's rest, and Sunday commemorated Jesus' resurrection. The second reason is the appearances of Jesus after His resurrection were on Sunday, the first day of the week.[61] The third reason is the appearance of Jesus to John on the Island of Patmos was on Sunday.[62] The early Christians called Sunday, *The Lord's Day*.[63] The fourth reason is the Holy Spirit descended and the early church was born and believers were added to the Church on the Day of Pentecost, which was on Sunday.[64] The fifth reason was that the early Church met for corporate worship on Sunday.[65] According to the Jews, Sabbath is sundown Friday until sundown Saturday. For the Romans, Sabbath is at midnight on Sunday until midnight on Monday. The sixth reason is freedom regarding the day of worship.[66] [67]

Since the Sabbath plays a vital role in the worship of God as Creator and Redeemer, it is not be surprising that Satan has waged an all-out war to overthrow a sacred institution. Surprisingly, nowhere in the Bible authorizes a change from the day of worship God made in Eden and restated on Mount Sinai.

Subsequently, Catholic Cardinal James Gibbons wrote, "You may read the Bible from Genesis to Revelation, and you will not find a single line authorizing the sanctification of Sunday. The Scriptures enforce the religious observance as Saturday."

A.T. Lincoln, a Protestant, admitted: "It cannot be argued that the New Testament itself provides warrant for the belief that since the Resurrection, God appointed the first day to be observed as the Sabbath."

If there is no biblical evidence that Christ or His disciples changed the day of worship from the seventh day, then how did Christians come to accept Sunday in its place? The change from Sabbath to Sunday worship came gradually. There is evidence that by the middle of the second century, some Christians were voluntarily observing Sunday as a day of worship, not a day of rest. The Church of Rome is mainly Gentile believers,[68] led in the trend toward Sunday worship. In Rome, strong anti-Jewish sentiments arose, becoming stronger as time passed. Christians tried to distinguish themselves from the Jews, which trended away from the veneration of the Sabbath and moving towards the exclusive observance of Sunday.

---

[60] Matthew 28:1-10; Mark 16:1-8; Luke 24:1-12; John 20:1-9
[61] Matthew 28:1-10; Mark 16:9-14; Luke 24:13-43; John 20:19-29
[62] Revelation 1:10

[64] Acts 2:1-47
[65] Acts 20:7; 1 Corinthians 16:2
[66] Romans 14:5-8; Galatians 4:9-10; Colossians 2:16-17
[67] Malone, Julius. *Introduction to the Ten Commandments*. Sermon at New Testament Church. Milwaukee, 2004.
[68] Romans 11:13

From the second to the fifth centuries, while Sunday was rising in influence, Christians continued to observe the Seventh-Day Sabbath nearly everywhere throughout the Roman Empire. The fifth-century, historian Socrates wrote: "Almost all the churches throughout the world celebrate the sacred mysteries on the Sabbath of every week. Yet, the Christians of Alexandria, and at Rome because of some ancient tradition, have ceased to do this."

Ask yourself: Why did those who were turning from worship on the seventh day, choose Sunday and not another day of the week? Some believe since Christ was resurrected on Sunday, it was alleged that He had authorized worship on that day. Because of the popularity and influence of the Sun God, pagan worship was practiced by Babylonians, and later the Romans, recorded Sunday as a day of worship. Sun worship played an important role throughout the ancient world. It was one of the oldest components of the Roman religions. Eastern cults, from the early part of the second century A.D., the cult of Sol Invictus was dominant in Rome and in other parts of the Empire. The popular religion made its affect on the early church through the new converts. Christian converts from paganism were constantly attracted toward the veneration of the Sun.

During the fourth century, Constantine saw the opportunity to Sunday laws. First Sunday laws of a civil nature were issued, later known as *religious character*. The emperor Constantine decreed the first civil Sunday law on March 7, A.D. 321. Because of Sunday's popularity among the pagan sun worshipers and the esteem with many Christians, Constantine hoped that by making Sunday a holiday, he could ensure the support of these two constituencies for his government. Several decades later, the church followed this example such as the Council of Laodicea (A.D. 364) issued the first ecclesiastical Sunday law. Christians honor Sunday. In A.D. 538, was the year marked as the beginning of the 1260-year prophecy. The Roman Catholic Third Council of Orleans issued a law even more severe than that of Constantine.[69]

Change Prophesized In Daniel

The Bible reveals the observance of Sunday as a Christian institution that had its origin in "the mystery of lawlessness."[70] Yet, when we focus on the prophecy of *Daniel 7*, God revealed His foreknowledge of the change of the day of worship. Daniel's vision depicts an attack on God's people and on God's law. A *little horn* symbolizes a great apostasy within the Christian church. Arising from the fourth beast, and becoming a major persecuting power after the fall of Rome, the little horn attempts to change the times and law.[71] This apostate power will be successful at deceiving most of the world, but at the end of judgment, will decide against it.[72]

---

[69] Seventh-Day Adventists Believe: A Biblical Exposition of 27 Fundamental Doctrines, 258-260.
[70] 2 Thessalonians 2:7
[71] Daniel 7:25
[72] Daniel 7:11, 22, 26

During the final tribulation, God will intervene for His people and deliver them.[73] This prophecy fits only one power within the Christian population. There is, but one religious organization that claims to possess the prerogatives of modifying divine laws. Roman Catholic authorities, during A.D. 1400, Petrus de Ancharano have claimed: "the Pope can modify divine law since his power is not of man, but of God, and he acts in the place of God on earth, with the fullest power of binding and losing his sheep."

In contrast, Luther claimed that the Holy Scripture, and not the tradition of the church, was his guide in his life, which his slogan was *sola scriptura* -- "The Bible and the Bible only." John Eck, one of the defenders of the Roman Catholic faith, attacked Luther on his viewpoint, by claiming that the authority of the church was above the Bible.

The Sabbath day has been changed to the Lord's Day. The authority of the church changed it. In *Isaiah 56 and 58*, God calls Israel to a Sabbath reform. Isaiah is revealing the glories of the future gathering of the Gentiles into His fold.[74] Through their mission worldwide, it is especially directed to a class of people who profess to be believers, but who have in reality departed from His precepts.[75] He expresses their mission to those professed believers in these terms:

Isaiah 58:12-14, NKJV: "...You shall rise up the foundations of many generations; and you shall be called the Repairer of the Breach, the Restorer of Streets to Dwell In. If you turn away your foot from the Sabbath from doing your pleasure on My holy day and call the Sabbath a delight, the holy day of the Lord honorable, and shall honor Him, not doing your own ways, not finding your own pleasure, nor speaking your own words, then you shall delight yourself in the Lord..."

God's law changed when the little-horn power changed the Sabbath. *Revelation 14:6-12*, speaks of the everlasting gospel that accomplishes that work for restoring and magnifying the law. This message is to arouse the world, inviting everyone to prepare for judgment.[76]

Preparation For The Lord's Day

We can set a day aside throughout the week for Sabbath and make the preparations necessary to observe it in a manner pleasing to God. Be careful not to exhaust our energies. Since this day is a special communion with God, we are to avoid anything that tends to diminish its sacred atmosphere. We are to cease our secular work, and avoid all work done to earn a living, and all business transactions.[77] In other words, we are to devote this day to God, instead of pleasing ourselves. We tend to be

---

[73] Daniel 12:1-3
[74] Isaiah 56:8
[75] Isaiah 58:1, 2
[76] Seventh-Day Adventists Believe: A Biblical Exposition of 27 Fundamental Doctrines, 260-262.
[77] Nehemiah 13:15-22

more involved in secular interests such as conversations and thoughts with our significant other, or to be engaging in sports that would distract from communion with our Creator, and violate the sacredness of the Sabbath. We are to enjoy the blessings of the Sabbath.

Generally, the Sabbath begins at sunset on Friday evening, and ends at sunset Saturday evening.[78] Scriptures refers to the day before the Sabbath, which is preparation day. *Preparation day* is a day to prepare for the Sabbath, so that nothing will interrupt its sacredness.[79] Therefore, we prepare food for the Sabbath, so that during its sacred hours, we can rest from our labors.[80] When the hours of the Sabbath approaches, family members (or groups of believers) can get together on Friday evening to worship and invite the Spirit of Christ as a guest. We are to unite in worship requesting God's presence and guidance through the week.

The *Sabbath* is a day of delight, joy, and remembrance of our Holy Father. We are following the example of Christ, who regularly worshiped on the Sabbath, took part in the services, and gave religious instruction.[81] Jesus Christ did more than just worship, He also fellowshipped with others,[82] spent time outdoors,[83] and went about doing holy deeds of mercy. Wherever He could, He healed the sick and afflicted.[84] [85]

There are some things to put into practice on the Lord's Day. We are to rest the body, soul, and spirit. The *Sabbath principle* is to rest one day out of the seven days. This day of rest refreshes and restores us. Spiritual rest is found in God, and results in physical rest. This is a time to rejoice -- a balance between work and worship. Worship is to be a priority when serving God. We are to reflect on Jesus, who created man on the sixth day, and required us to rest on the seventh day. On the day of rest, we can spend time with our family, friends, and/or believers of Jesus Christ. Moreover, remember that God is the source of creation, salvation, and sanctification.[86]

Promises To Those Who Practice The Sabbath Principle

"You shall delight yourself in the Lord." [87]

We are to look forward to what we delight in. What is your main source of joy? These men found delight in God: David;[88] Asaph;[89] and Job.[90] God will promote you

---

[78] Genesis 1:5; Mark 1:32

[79] Mark 15:42

[80] Exodus 16:23; Numbers 11:8

[81] Mark 1:21; 3:1-4; Luke 4:16-27; 13:10

[82] Mark 1:29-31; Luke 14:1

[83] Mark 2:23

[84] Mark 1:21-31; Luke 13:10-17; John 5:1-15

[85] Seventh-Day Adventists Believe: A Biblical Exposition of 27 Fundamental Doctrines, 261-262.

[86] Malone, Julius. *Introduction to the Ten Commandments*. Sermon at New Testament Church. (Milwaukee, WI) notes taken by author, 2004.

[87] Isaiah 58:14; Psalm 37:4

once you delight in Him.[91] Next, God will provide your full share of the blessings He promises. For example, the promises He made to Jacob, to feast on his inheritance.[92] In addition, you will experience divine health.[93]

Fourth Commandment: Are We Breaking The Sabbath Day?

The *Fourth Commandment* stresses the word, "Remember." While most believers agree the other nine Commandments are still binding today, and will be binding throughout all eternity, they feel the *Fourth Commandment* was done away with. The word, *remember*, tells us that God knew people were going to have trouble with the commandment that they would be tempted to forget it.[94]

In *Luke 6:3-5*, the priests tried to accuse Jesus of breaking the Sabbath Day. On the contrary, the story of David elaborates on how David and his men ate consecrated bread, was a need greater than any ceremonial regulations.[95] Jesus demonstrates a parallel principle with the story of David that human need is more important than human regulations and rules. Another Scripture tells us about Jesus breaking the Sabbath day, it was after Sabbath sunset:

> *"At evening, when the sun had set, they brought Him all who were sick and those who were demon-possessed. Moreover, the whole city gathered at the door. Then, He healed many who were sick with various diseases, and cast out many demons, and He did not allow the demons to speak because they knew Him."[96]*

Although Jesus was criticized for His work of alleviating suffering, Jesus replied, "It is lawful to do well on the Sabbath."[97] Jesus' healing activities neither broke the Sabbath nor abolished it. God intended the Sabbath for humanity's spiritual refreshment and enrichment.

If your activities distract you from purpose, and turn the Sabbath into a holiday, make sure your intentions are proper according to God. The Lord of the Sabbath invites all to follow His example. Those who accept His call experience the Sabbath as a delight and spiritual feast -- foretaste of Heaven. Week by week, the seventh day comforts our conscience, assuring us that despite our unfinished characters, we stand

---

[88] Psalm 27:4
[89] Psalm 73:25
[90] Job 23:12
[91] Isaiah 58:14; Psalm 75: 6-7; 27:5; Proverbs 21:1; Habakkuk 3:17-19
[92] Isaiah 58:14, The Living Bible
[93] Exodus 15:26, Psalm 103:3
[94] Shelton, Danny. *The Forgotten Commandment: A Battle For Our Loyalty To Christ Or Man*, p. 7.
[95] 1 Samuel 21:1-6
[96] Mark 1:32-34
[97] Matthew 12:12

complete in Christ. His accomplishment at Calvary counts as our atonement. We enter His rest.[98]

This reflects the relationship between the Sabbath and Christ's work of salvation alluded in two Sabbath miracles: healing of the paralytic or someone paralyzed,[99] and healing of the blind man.[100] Christ's justification is expressed through a memorable statement: "My Father is working until now, and I am working."[101] What did Christ mean when He defended Himself against the charge of Sabbath-breaking by appealing to the 'working until now' of His Father? According to De Samuel Bacchiocchi, he shows that the 'working until now' of the Father and of the Son has historically received three basic interpretations:

1. Continuous creation
2. Continuous care
3. Redemptive activities

Traditionally, the adverbial phrase, *until now* has been interpreted as the continuous working of God, whether it be in creation, preservation or redemption, which allegedly overrides or rescinds the Sabbath law. However, the adverb, *until*, is used in Greek text, presupposes not constancy, but culmination. The use of the emphatic form is *even until now.*

> *John 9:4, NKJV: "I must work the works of Him who sent me, while it is day; night comes when no one can work."*

In this statement, the culmination of the divine and human working is explicitly designated as the 'night.' By virtue of the conceptual similarities between *John 5:17* and *John 9:4*, it seems legitimate to determine that the *night* is the culmination of both texts of which God rested on the Sabbath at the completion of creation because of sin. He has been 'working until now' to bring the promised Sabbath rest to fruition.

Jesus answered, "The work of God is this: to believe in the one He has sent."[102] Therefore, we have to believe that God sent Jesus to do the works of the Father, which the Father is in me and I am the Father according to Jesus explanation.[103] Christ appeals to the 'working' of His Father not to nullify, but to clarify the function of the Sabbath. To understand Christ's defense, one must remember that the Sabbath is linked to both the creation,[104] and redemption.[105]

---

[98] Seventh-Day Adventists Believe: A Biblical Exposition of 27 Fundamental Doctrines, p. 264.
[99] John 5:1-18
[100] John 9:1-41
[101] John 5:17; 9:4
[102] John 6:29
[103] John 10:37, 38; 4:34; 14:11; 15:24
[104] Genesis 2:2-3; Exodus 20:11
[105] Deuteronomy 5:15

While interrupting all secular activities, the Israelites were remembering the Creator God, by acting mercifully toward fellow-beings. They were imitating the Redeemer-God. For Jesus Christ, the Sabbath is the day to work for the redemption for the whole man. This comes from the fact that in both healings, Jesus looked for the healed men on the same day, and having found them, He ministered to their spiritual need.[106] Jesus opponents cannot perceive the redemptive nature of His Sabbath ministry because they judge by appearances.[107]

In the Sabbath healing of the blind man, recorded in *John 9*, Jesus extends His followers the invitation to become links of the same redemptive chain.[108] The *night* refers to the conclusion of the history of salvation, from the adverbial phrase, *until now*. To bring about the final Sabbath, the Godhead 'is working' for our salvation, but we must extend it to others. Following God's laws more than human principles and practices is far more important. The Bible, God's Word, is over the church and its fundamentals.

---

[106] John 5:14; 9:35-38
[107] John 7:24
[108] John 9:24

~Let Your Day Begin With Christ, Day 5~

Let your Day Begin Activity: Remember the Sabbath. Put aside a day every week to rest, this is to remember the Sabbath. No shopping, movies, concerts, or other entertaining events on this day. Only televised programs or movies about Jesus, Christian and Gospel songs, and read God's Holy Word. We need rest. Our bodies have to rest to get prepared for the following week and time away from the stressors of daily activities (e.g., work, school, and running errands).

Today's Questions:

Do you believe your rest day falls on Saturday, like the Jews and Seventh Day Adventist do? Or just one day a week is sufficient.

What happens to your mind, body, and spirit if you do not rest?

Why is the Sabbath Day so significant to God?

Review to Begin your Day with Christ:

Fourth Commandment: Preparation for the Lord's Day: Exodus 16:22-23; Matthew 27:62; Mark 15:42; Luke 23:54; and John 19:31.
- Rest the body, soul, and spirit. The Sabbath principle is rest one day out of seven (Exodus 20:9-10).
- Rest refreshes and restores.
- Spiritual rest is found in God and results in physical rest (Exodus 33:14; Psalm 23: 2-3; Matthew 11:28-30).
- Rejoice—a balance between work and worship. Worship is to be a priority (Exodus 20:9-10; Philippians 4:4; Nehemiah 8:10; Proverbs 17:22).
- Reflect on Jesus, the Lord of the Sabbath (Mark 2:27-28).
- Relate to family, friends, and believers (Hebrews 10:25; Acts 2:42).
- Remember God is the source of creation, salvation, and sanctification (Psalm 103:1-5; 24:1; Ephesians 2:1, 8-9; 1 Thessalonians 5:23).

Day Begins 6: Fifth Commandment

The *Fifth Commandment* is one of the first of the six involving horizontal relationship with others. This is how we learn to relate to others. Strong families equal strong churches, which equal strong communities, which equal strong countries. Originally, the command is to *honor father and mother*. *Honor* is derived from the translation of a Hebrews verb meaning, 'to be heavy or weighty.'[109] In other words, *honor* is to weigh someone down with respect, reverence, esteem, and significance. In addition, *to honor* means to 'place value on, to consider important.' In addition, we are commanded to give honor to which honor is due,[110] and to be honored always.[111]

Two Promises: Honoring Your Parents Or Guardians

There are two promises granted by following this Commandment.[112] One promise is to live longer on the earth if we obey our parents, and show honor to them.[113] For instance, reflecting on my great-grandmother, Gran, who lived until the age of 102. I believe that Gran honored her parents to live slightly over a century. She was born April 27, 1902, died on July 27, 2004. Alternatively, disobedient children in ancient times were stoned.[114] The second promise is that it may be well with you.[115] [116]

---

[109] Exodus 20:12
[110] Romans 13:7
[111] 1 Peter 2:13-17
[112] Exodus 20:23; Ephesians 6:2-3
[113] Exodus 20:12; Ezekiel 22:7; Ephesians 6:3
[114] Deuteronomy 21: 18-21
[115] Deuteronomy 5:16; Ephesians 6:3
[116] Malone, Julius. *Introduction to the Ten Commandments*. Sermon at New Testament Church. Milwaukee, 2004 and emphasis added by author.

~Let Your Day Begin With Christ, Day 6~

Let your Day Begin Activity: Honoring your parents. Take the time today to do something special for your parents. Even if it is calling them to tell them how special they are to you, buying flowers and balloons, or even a card (e-card too) that shares how you feel about them. Let them know that you truly love them and appreciate them.

Today's Questions:

Why should we honor (obey and respect) our parents?

What are some things we can do to honor our parents?

Ask our parents for forgiveness when we wrong them, list some of these things? Write them down in a journal and find time to discuss it your parent(s), also ask questions how you can make the parent-child relationship better. Are you willing to compromise and work it out?

Review to Begin your Day with Christ:

Today, children may be scolded or removed out of the household when they do not honor (respect) their parents. In ancient biblical times, children who disobeyed their parents were stoned to death. God promises us if we are obedient to our parents and respect them, we will live longer on earth. If we are disobedient, we will live lesser days on the earth. Think about it.

Fifth Commandment: We are commanded to honor them (Exodus 20:23; Leviticus 19:3; Deuteronomy 5:16; Matthew 15:4; Ephesians 6:2).

Day Begins 7: Sixth Commandment

The *Sixth Commandment* is the most misunderstood and misused since the Hebrew word *ratsach* or *rasah* in *Exodus 20:13* are translated 'kill' rather than 'murder.' In the Bible, all murder is killing, but not all killing is murder. According to the *Nelson's Illustrated Bible Dictionary*, *murder* is the unlawful killing of one person by another, especially with premeditated malice. Some examples of murder: *Homicide* is the unlawful killing of one human being by another.[117] *Suicide* is self murder.[118] Can a person who commits suicide go to heaven?[119] *Abortion* is the killing of the unborn in the womb. When does life began?[120] *Euthanasia* is a Greek word *Eu*, which means 'good,' and *Thanatos* means 'death.' *Euthanasia* literally means 'good death.' Other names are 'mercy killing' and 'doctor assisted suicide.'

How God Views Suicide: Can A Person Go To Heaven?

Pastor Julius Malone states that suicide is a violation of the *Sixth Commandment.* Over twenty-five thousand Americans commit suicide each year. More Americans die from suicide than homicide. Suicide is listed among the top ten causes of death in the U.S. The model age for attempting suicide is thirty-two for men and twenty-seven for women, and the succeeding age is fifty through fifty-four for men and women. Men kill themselves twice as often as women, but women attempt suicide twice as often as men do. There are over five thousand suicides among teenagers each year. Suicide is the second highest cause of death among young adults aged fifteen through twenty-four, surpassed as accidents.

Some reasons or motives for suicide are d*epression* -- usually severely depressed individuals are potential suicides. Those described in the Bible who wanted to die are Jonah[121] and Elijah.[122] Other reasons or motives for committing suicide can be *retaliation,* where many young people take their lives in an attempt to get at a family member, friend, or loved one. *Reunion* is another reason for suicide. Some people take their lives to be reunited with someone who has deceased or died. *Reincarnation* is where some people believe that after death they will return in a different condition. They hope to be reborn in a better condition and under better circumstances. Some Native American and African practices, rituals and beliefs, refer to reincarnation as a cycle of nature and life. *Retroflex* is killing of oneself in place of someone who is unreachable. One example in the Bible is Ahithophel.[123] *Retribution* is where some commit suicide in an effort to punish themselves. For example, Judas had strong feelings of guilt for what

---

[117] Numbers 35:15-18
[118] 1 Corinthians 6:19-20
[119] John 10:28-29; Romans 8:35-39; Judges 16:28-30
[120] Genesis 25:21-26; Exodus 4:11; Job 10:8-12; Jeremiah 1:5; Psalm 127: 3; 139:13-16; Matthew 18:10; Luke 1:41-44
[121] Jonah 4:1-3
[122] 1 Kings 19:1-4
[123] 2 Samuel 17:23

happened to Jesus Christ and his carcass hung from the tree.[124] *Rejection* can be such as divorce, separation, or rejection by peers, parents and other family members, work, etc. *Pain* can be physical, emotional, or mental, thinking it will never end.

Warning signs: One will usually talk about suicide, death, or dying. In addition, someone in a suicidal state of mind will talk about being helpless, hopeless, and show signs of self-worthlessness, including withdrawal and isolation from family, friends, co-workers, peers, and other social contacts. Other signs can be *loss of interest* such as hobbies, personal appearance, mood swings, behaving recklessly, giving away valued possessions and writing out wills. *Recent loss* are layoffs and involuntary terminations of employment, deceased loved ones, trivial disturbance in sleeping pattern, long periods of sadness, and drowning in drunkenness or getting high.

Please do not think suicide is your way of escaping your failure and half-forgotten dreams disappear by taking your own life. Moreover, taking your own life is a selfish, independent act that takes God out of the equation. Do not think suicide is the final answer. God can unleash your destiny if you just ask, seek, and knock.

Prevention of suicide: If you see the signs of a loved one or person thinking suicidal thoughts or actions, please do not leave them alone. They need to seek professional help. Through prayers, whether it is praying in private or interceding with others is another way to prevent someone committing suicide. We can show love, appreciation, and concern, including a willingness to listen by allowing the person to talk and express his or herself freely without judging or ridiculing. Criticism or making them feel guilty can make matters worse. It does not minimize the problem. We have to take it seriously and cautiously with love. They may say they are fine, but even if they say they are, we can find encouraging words to edify and lift them up. Find creative things that would help this person overlook their problems or troubles. Through love, we are displaying God's love for His creation, and He wants the best for us all and loves us. There is a time for healing in which we are to believe and trust in God.

Examples Of Suicide In The Bible: Motives, Warning Signs, And Preventive Steps

Those who are lost from God's presence: In an effort to escape a temporary problem, one may run to a permanent problem.[125] There is no problem greater than eternal torment in hell. Once we are in hell, there is no possibility of salvation after death.

The Philippians' jailor turned to Jesus.[126] There is rest in Jesus.[127] Suicide causes pain and shame for friends and family. For the saved, *suicide* is a violation of

---

[124] Matthew 27:3-5
[125] Luke 16:19-24
[126] Acts 16:27
[127] Matthew 11:28-30

the *Sixth Commandment*. Our life belongs to God, who is our Creator and Redeemer.[128] Suicide is not a part of God's plan for a life.[129] Suicide dishonors God.[130] Loss rewards will be suffered at the Judgment Seat of Christ.[131]

If you are having suicidal thoughts, do not isolate yourself from others.[132] We are to rest in the sovereignty of God;[133] and to seek God's grace.[134] Some argue that Christian music can be both uplifting and depressing.[135] However, we can sing songs from the heart,[136] speak the Word in our lives, and give thanks to the Lord.[137]

When dealing with a suicide, one is concerned about the deceased. Some believe that suicide is the only unpardonable sin because it cannot be repented after one has taken one's life. The *unpardonable sin* is to die without Jesus Christ, after reaching the age of accountability.[138] All other sins can be forgiven. Murderers who were forgiven: Moses[139] and David.[140] *Salvation* is by grace through faith.[141]

One relationship with Christ determines one's destiny, not the last thing that one did before death. God's grace saved us. The meaning of justification, sanctification and glorification is found in *Romans 3:21-28*. *Justification* is deliverance from the penalty of sin -- past, present and future.[142] *Justification* is also a declaration of righteousness because of what Jesus did on the cross.[143] There are no degrees of justification. *Sanctification* is proof of justification.

Justification is the result of predestination.[144] *Sanctification* is deliverance from the power of sin.[145] *Glorification* is deliverance from the presence of sin.[146] [147]

---

[128] Psalm 24:1; Romans 14:7-8; 1 Corinthians 6:19-20; Ephesians 2:10; 1 Peter 1:18-19
[129] Jeremiah 29:11; John 10:10; Revelation 4:11
[130] 1 Corinthians 10:31; Revelation 4:11
[131] Romans 14:10-12; 1 Corinthians 3:11-15
[132] 1 Kings 19:3; Hebrews 10:24-25
[133] Psalm 37:7; 40:1-4
[134] 2 Corinthians 12:9-10
[135] 1 Samuel 16:14-23
[136] Psalm 34:1; 42:5; 103:1-5
[137] 1 Thessalonians 5:18
[138] John 14:6; Acts 4:12; Romans 1:20-23
[139] Exodus 2:11-15
[140] 2 Samuel 12:9-14
[141] Ephesians 2:8-9
[142] Romans 6:23
[143] Isaiah 53:5-6; Romans 3:21-28; 2 Corinthians 5:21; Romans 10:1-4; Philippians 3:7-14
[144] Romans 8:28-30
[145] Philippians 2:12-13; 1 Thessalonians 4:3
[146] Romans 13:11
[147] Malone, Julius. *Introduction to the Ten Commandments*. Sermon at New Testament Church (Milwaukee, WI) notes taken by author, 2004.

Terms In The Bible About Suicide

The verb *is passed*, is the Greek word, *Metabebeken.*

John 5:24, NKJV: Jesus says, "Most assuredly, I say to you, he who hears My word and believes in Him who sent Me has everlasting life, and shall not come into judgment, but has passed from death into life."

Everlasting life is living forever with God, which begins when you accept Jesus Christ as your Savior. At that moment, new life begins in you.[148] It is a completed transaction. You will face physical death, but when Christ returns, your body will be resurrected to live forever.[149]

The verb, *perish*, the Greek word, *apolovtai.*

John 10:28, NKJV: Jesus says, "And I give them eternal life, and they shall never perish; neither shall anyone snatch them out of My hand."

A shepherd protects his sheep.[150] Jesus protects His people from eternal harm. While believers can expect to suffer on earth, Satan cannot harm their souls or take away their eternal life with God. There are many reasons to be afraid here on earth because this is the devil's domain.[151] However, if you choose to follow Jesus, He will give you everlasting safety.

In *Jeremiah 31:3*, nothing can separate a true believer from the love of God. God reaches toward His people with kindness motivated by deep and everlasting love. He is eager to do the best for them, if they will only let Him. After many words of warning about sin, this reminder of God's magnificent love is a breath of fresh air. Rather than thinking of God with dread, look carefully and see Him lovingly drawing toward Himself.

Romans 8:35, NKJV: "Who shall separate us from the love of Christ? Shall tribulations, or distress, or persecution, or famine, or nakedness, or peril, or sword."

Romans 8:36, NKJV: "For Your sake we are killed all day long. We are accounted as sheep for the slaughter."

Romans 8:37, NKJV: "Yet in all these things we are more than conquerors through Him who loved us.

Romans 8:38, NKJV: "For I am persuaded that neither death nor life, nor angels, nor principalities, nor powers, nor things present, nor things to come."

---

[148] 2 Corinthians 5:17
[149] Life Application Study Bible, New King James Version, 1 Corinthians 15.
[150] Life Application Study Bible, New King James Version; John 10:28-29.
[151] 1 Peter 5:8

Romans 8:39, NKJV: "Nor height, nor depth, nor any other created things, shall be able to separate us from the love of God which is in Christ Jesus our Lord."

These verses contain one of the most comforting promises. Believers have always had to face hardships in many forms: persecution, illness, imprisonment, even death. These could cause them to fear that Christ has abandoned them. However, Paul exclaims that it is impossible to be separated from Christ. His death for us is proof of His unconquerable love. Nothing can stop Christ's constant presence with us. God tells us how great His love is so that we will feel secure in Him. If we believe these overwhelming assurances, we will not be afraid.[152]

There is another example of Samson committing the act of suicide.[153] The questions most of us ask, will Samson go to heaven after committing such an act? We too can experience victory through faith in Christ. Our victory over oppressors may be like those of the Old Testament saints, but more likely, our victories will be directly related to the role God wants us to play. Even though our bodies die and deteriorate, we will live forever because of Christ. In the promised resurrection, even death will be defeated, and Christ's victory will be made complete.

Samson received his eyesight after having faith in the Lord again. In his mind, he probably wanted to destroy those cruel rulers and idol worshippers, not serving the one and only God. After analyzing the scenario, is it suicide when you are trying to destroy the evildoers and not allowing the Lord to take care of this? We tend to want to help God out when the Lord tells us that, "Vengeance is the Lord," and sometimes we want to take matters into our own hands. Earlier on, Samson lost his eyesight, because of being blinded by lust and desires of the heart and flesh, and not obeying God's will for his life. Therefore, his disobedience, he had to face consequences. Unfortunately, it was his eyesight and extraordinary strength. Finally, when his eyesight returned, he knew and received insight on how to destroy these people, including him.

God will allow things to happen in our lives for many reasons. Usually things of the world and/or flesh blind us, and until we seek Him for guidance, we shall receive the light and able to see His purpose. Open your eyes. Seek the Lord Jesus, our Savior, so we can let our light shine under our feet.

Hebrews 11:32-40, summarizes the lives of other great men and women of faith. Some experienced outstanding victories, even over the threat of death. Nevertheless, others were severely mistreated, tortured, and even killed. Having a steadfast faith in God does not guarantee a happy, carefree life. On the contrary, our faith almost guarantees us some form of abuse from the world. While we are on earth, we may never see the purpose of our suffering. However, we know that God will keep His promises to us. Do you believe that God will keep His promises to you?

---

[152] Life Application Study Bible, New King James Version, 1996.
[153] Hebrews 11:32

Many think that pain is the exception in the Christian life. When suffering occurs, they say, "Why me?" They feel as though God deserted them, or perhaps they accuse Him of not being as dependable as they thought. In reality, however, we live in an evil world filled with suffering, even for believers. Think of Elijah, he wanted death to come on him, suicidal thoughts, when Jezebel and her worshippers were after him for a death sentence. However, God is still in control. God will allow some followers of Christ to become martyrs for the faith, and He allows others to survive persecution. Our faith, the values of the world, is on a collision course. If we expect pain and suffering to come, we will not be shocked when it hits. However, we can also take comfort in knowing that Jesus also suffered. God understands our fears, our weaknesses, and our disappointments. God promised never to leave us,[154] and He intercedes on our behalf. In the times of pain, persecution, or suffering, we should trust confidently in Christ.

Examples Of Killing That Is Not Murder And Not Prohibited By The Sixth Commandment

Capital punishment for murder, under the old covenant, there were twenty-six crimes punishable by death. Eleven are mentioned below:[155]

1. Murderers were executed [156]
2. Child who struck his father or mother [157]
3. Rebellious son [158]
4. Kidnappers [159]
5. Loss of a child in a fight [160]
6. Negligence resulting in the death of a person [161]
7. Adulterers and adulteresses [162]
8. A child who cursed his father or mother [163]
9. Fornication before marriage, resulting in the loss of ones' virginity [164]
10. Rape [165]
11. Homosexuality [166]

Capital punishment in the New Testament:[167] [168]

---

[154] Matthew 28:18-20

[155] Malone, Julius. *Introduction to the Ten Commandments*. Sermon at New Testament Church (Milwaukee, WI) notes taken by author, 2004.

[156] Genesis 9:6; Exodus 21:12-14; Leviticus 24:17, 21; Numbers 35:16-21, 30-33

[157] Exodus 21:15

[158] Deuteronomy 21:18-21

[159] Exodus 21:16

[160] Exodus 21:22-23

[161] Exodus 21:28-29

[162] Leviticus 20:10; Deuteronomy 22:22

[163] Exodus 21:17

[164] Deuteronomy 22:16-17

[165] Deuteronomy 22:23-24

[166] Leviticus 18:22; 20:13; Romans 1:24-28; 1 Corinthians 6:9-11

1. Accidental killing is not murder [169]
2. Killing in self-defense is not murder [170]
3. Killing plants and animals for food and shelter is not prohibited by the Sixth Commandment [171]
4. Killing of insects
5. Killing in a war is not murder. What is a just war? [172]

Deeper Look At War: The Sixth Commandment

Killing in a just war is not murder. In the fourth century, St. Augustine developed the just war theory and the seven principles are:[173] *Proper authority* is a war that must be declared by a legitimate government, and not by private individuals and groups.[174] *Proper cause* is a war for defense, protection, etc., and would be a just cause. *Right intention* is goals for peace, safety, freedom, not revenge, plunder, and conquest. *Comparative justice* is the evil that is fought and must be sufficient to justify killing. *Murder* is the deliberate taking of an innocent human life that is forbidden, even in wartime. *Proportionality* is where the government waging war must be sure that the destruction caused by their responses to aggression does not exceed the destruction caused by the aggression itself. Annihilation of a country that is under attack on a city would be *disproportion*. *Probability of success* must be a confident expectation that will achieve its objectives. *Last resort* is when war should not be waged, unless all negotiation possibilities have been exhausted.

There are wars defending against evil aggression.[175] There are Scriptures elaborating further on deliverance from evil aggression,[176] and to deter the spread of evil when in battle.[177] President George W. Bush had our soldiers in Iraq under digress by seeking counsel from government officials and leaders that can either start and/or end a war.[178] Is there a reasonable sense of hope of the success in war? Is there a confident expectation that going to war will end more evil than it will cause? Should we serve in the military? The New Testament does not condemn soldiers for serving in the military. Some examples are listed below.

---

[167] Romans 13:1-5; 1 Peter 2:13-14
[168] Malone, Julius. *Introduction to the Ten Commandments*. Sermon at New Testament Church. Milwaukee, 2004.
[169] Numbers 35:9-15; Deuteronomy 19:4-15; Joshua 20:1-6
[170] Exodus 22:2
[171] Genesis 3:21; 9:3: 1 Timothy 4:3-5
[172] Exodus 17:8-16; 1 Samuel 15:1-3
[173] Malone, Julius. *Introduction to the Ten Commandments*. Sermon at New Testament Church. Milwaukee, 2004.
[174] Romans 13:1
[175] 2 Chronicles 20:1-30; Romans 13:1-7
[176] Genesis 14:1-24; 1 Samuel 30:1-19; and Judges 6:11-16; 13:5
[177] Numbers 33:55-56; Deuteronomy 20:16-18; Deuteronomy 20:10-12; Ecclesiastes 3:8; Romans 12:18
[178] Proverbs 20:18; 24:6

1. John the Baptist responds to the soldiers that came to him[179]
2. Jesus to the centurion who came to Him[180]
3. Peter to Cornelius[181]
4. Picture of the soldier is used in the letters of Paul to describe the Christian life[182]

Believers are to pray for our leaders in office and for our soldiers in war.

1 Timothy 2:1-8, NIV: "I urge, then, first of all, that requests, prayers, intercession and thanksgiving be made for everyone—for kings (president, officials, government) and all those in authority, that we may live peaceful and quiet lives in all godliness and holiness. This is good, and pleases God, our Savior, who wants all men to be saved and to come to knowledge of the truth. For there is one God and one mediator, the man Christ Jesus, who gave Himself as a ransom for all men and His testimony was given in its proper time. And for this purpose I was appointed a herald and an apostle—I am telling the truth, I am not lying—and a teacher of the true faith to the Gentiles (everyone that is not a Jew). I want men everywhere to life up holy hands in prayer, without anger or disputing."

Believers of Christ whom participate in the government process by voting and voicing their opinion in a respectful manner.[183] We rest in His sovereignty.[184] Security of a nation is not in its wealth, wisdom, weapons, warriors, but in God.[185] We are to witness to the lost and to those that are anxious.

The wars will not cease until Jesus returns in *Matthew 24:6-8, NKJV: "And you will hear of wars and rumors of wars. See that you are not troubled; for all these things must happen, but the end is not yet. For nation will rise against nation, and kingdom against kingdom. Moreover, there will be famines, pestilences, and earthquakes in various places. And these are the beginning of sorrows."*

When the Prince of Peace returns, there will be peace in the valley, and nations will study war no more.[186] Internal peace can be experienced now.[187]

Reasons For The Sixth Commandment

Human life is sacred because we are made in the image of God.[188] God is the source of all life. He also has the right to end life when He chooses, and no one has the

---

[179] Luke 3:14
[180] Luke 7:1-10
[181] Acts 10:1-48
[182] Ephesians 6:13-17; 2 Timothy 2:3-4
[183] Romans 13:1-7; 1 Peter 2:13-14
[184] Psalm 37:7; Isaiah 26:3-4; Daniel 4:35
[185] Psalm 20:7; 33:12, 16-17; 90:1-16; 121:1-8; 127:1
[186] Isaiah 2:1-4; 11:6-9; Micah 4:1-3
[187] John 16:33; Romans 5:1; Philippians 4:6-7; Ephesians 2:14; Isaiah 26:3
[188] Genesis 1:26-27; 9:6

right to take a life, unless God grants it to him or her.[189] To protect life from being cut short by another human being since we are created to bring glory to God.[190] A life that is taken cannot be restored. However, there are murderers who were forgiven by God. Some murderers who were forgiven are Moses;[191] David;[192] and Paul.[193]

The *Sixth Commandment* is a prohibition against murder. The New Testament prohibits the emotions of anger and hatred of which are attributes that leads to murder.[194] The Bible teaches that the source of evil is from the heart. Therefore, God looks at the heart. We are commanded to guard the heart. The act of murder with the hands starts with the attitude of murder in the heart. The form of murder in the heart is unrighteous or unjustified anger.[195] The anger that is prohibited by Jesus is the anger that is nurtured, that is not allowed to die, that holds grudges, that refuses to forgive, that does not desire reconciliation, that holds on to resentment, and that results in a 'root of bitterness.'[196] Some examples of unrighteousness anger:

1. The anger of Cain because of jealousy [197]
2. The anger of King Saul because of jealousy [198]
3. The anger of Jonah because of the grace, mercy and kindness of God to save Nineveh [199]
4. The anger of the brother of the Prodigal Son because of how his brother was treated on his return home [200]

Not all anger is a sin.[201] Three things that caused Jesus to become angry is the hardness of hearts of the Pharisees;[202] the hindering of children from coming to Jesus;[203] and the hindering of worship in the house of God.[204] However, unrighteous anger is dangerous to us and to others. Studies show that men who have an anger problem are four times more likely to die young than the average person. Unresolved and uncontrolled anger can cause ulcers, heart attacks, high blood pressure, and many other diseases. To deal with unrighteous anger, one has to confess it,[205] to control it,[206]

---

[189] Romans 13:1-5
[190] Isaiah 43:7, 21; 1 Corinthians 10:31
[191] Exodus 2:11-12
[192] 2 Samuel 12:9-12
[193] Acts 8:1-3; 1 Timothy 1:12-17; Proverbs 28:13; 1 John 1:9
[194] Matthew 5:21-22; 1 John 3:15
[195] Matthew 22
[196] Hebrews 12:15
[197] Genesis 4:1-8; 1 John 3:11-15
[198] 1 Samuel 18:6-9
[199] Jonah 4:1-11
[200] Luke 15:25-32
[201] Psalm 4:4; 7:11; Ephesians 4:26
[202] Mark 3:1-6
[203] Mark 10:13-16
[204] Matthew 21:12-13; John 2:13-17
[205] 1 John 1:9
[206] Galatians 5:23

and channel their anger. *Channeling anger* is by walking away, refusing to argue, or be involved in anything that would make you upset, and to find something constructive to do.

Slander is a form of murder.[207] *Raca* is rendered 'empty headed,' 'you good for nothing,' 'brainless idiot,' 'worthless,' and other crucial words that can kill a person's spirit, reputation, and relationships with others, including self-esteem. Another form of *slander* is gossip. How many people have been murdered with words said by someone else?[208] In addition, words spoken in unrighteous anger can be destructive.[209] Additionally, condemning the character of a person is a form of murder.[210] One way to condemn someone's character is by calling him or her a 'fool.' *Fool* meaning stupid. It is from the Greek word *Moros*, where we get the English word *moron*. According to Webster, *moron* is a mentally retarded person, who has a potentially mental age of between eight through twelve years old. Jesus prohibits calling a person a fool out of anger and hatred. *Hatred* is another form of murder.[211] Unrighteous hatred is a sin because we are commanded to love, and hatred usually results from unrighteous anger.[212]

Solutions to the sin of murder are: the new birth;[213] to forgive;[214] seek reconciliation quickly;[215] experiencing the presence of the Holy Spirit;[216] and the fruits of the Holy Spirit.[217] First, we have to love, and love is the antidote to hate.[218] [219]

---

[207] Matthew 5:22
[208] Matthew 12:36-37
[209] Proverbs 12:18; 18:8, 21
[210] Matthew 5:22
[211] 1 John 3:15
[212] Matthew 5:43-44; John 13:34-35; 15:12
[213] 2 Corinthians 5:17; John 1:12-13; 1 John 3:9
[214] Matthew 6:14-15; Mark 11:25-26; Ephesians 4:31-32
[215] Matthew 5:24-26
[216] Ephesians 5:18; Galatians 5:16
[217] Galatians 5:22-23
[218] Galatians 5:22; 1 John 3:14-15
[219] Malone, Julius. *Introduction to the Ten Commandments*. Sermon at New Testament Church (Milwaukee, WI) notes taken by author, 2004.

~Let Your Day Begin With Christ, Day 7~

Let your Day Begin Activity: God does not want us to kill or murder, or commit suicide. Have you ever thought of ending your life, felt worthless and believed the best thing to do was to end it. We forgot that God is the one who gives us life. Yahweh breathes in us. Take time to pray to God. Share your feelings with Him, be honest with God, He knows your heart and inner thoughts. Why do you truly value your life? Put all your feelings on the table by letting Him know all your concerns and why you choose life rather than death.

Today's Questions:

If you are having suicidal thoughts, what is the first thing you will do?

What are your views on if someone dies from suicide; will they go to heaven? Write down your thoughts. Think of Samson, many argue that he committed suicide. Do you believe he will be in heaven with God? Why or why not?

What are your thoughts on war? When is it okay to kill someone, relating to war? Do you pray for your leaders, government officials, President, and soldiers that are in war or in battle?

Review to Begin your Day with Christ:

Sixth Commandment: Jonah (Jonah 4:1-3) and Elijah (1 Kings 19:1-4) that wanted to commit suicide, but God interceded and allowed them to accomplish their missions regardless of their circumstances.

Day Begins 8: Seventh Commandment

The *Sixth Commandment* protects the sacredness of life, and the *Seventh Commandment* protects the sacredness of marriage. *Adultery* was punishable by death in the Old Testament.[220] Definition of *adultery* is a voluntary sinful sexual act, involving at least one married person other than one's husband or wife. *Fornication* is another form of adultery. *Fornication* involves voluntary sex between unmarried people. *Fornication* is a sin that is to be avoided.[221] The Greek word *neia*, means two people who are not married. Incest and homosexuality are sinful sexual acts for people who are not married.

There are different forms of adultery:
1. Physical
2. Mental
3. Divorce
4. Spiritual

Physical adultery involves two physical bodies that engage in sexual activities such as oral, anal and vaginal.[223] Some people do not want to consider oral sex as sexual contact with their partner, but it is a form of sex to satisfy or fulfill lustful thoughts and feelings. The Bible speaks against anal sexual activities too.

> *Genesis 19:4-5, NKJV: "Now before they lay down, the men of the city, the men of Sodom, both old and young, all the people from every quarter, surrounded the house. In addition, they called to Lot and said to him, "Where are the men who came to you tonight? Bring them out to us so that we can have sex with them carnally."*

The phase, *that we may know them carnally,* means the men wanted sexual relations with Lot's male guests. Or dressed up as a transsexual, according to *Deuteronomy 22:5: "A woman shall not wear anything that pertains to a man, nor shall a man put on a woman's garment, for all who do so are an abomination to the Lord you God."*

Scripture commands men and women not to reverse their sexual roles.[224] Today, role rejections are common. Ideally, there are men who want to become women and women who want to become men. It is not the clothing style that offends God, but acting out a different sex role. For example, a man dressing in women's clothing, wearing makeup, and/or transforming their body parts to emerge as a woman. God had a purpose in making us uniquely male and female. Moreover, these desires are sins of sexual immorality and sorcery, including less obvious sins such as hatred, selfish

---

[220] Leviticus 20:10; Deuteronomy 22:23-24
[221] Acts 15:20; 1 Corinthians 6:13, 15-18; 10:8; Galatians 5:19; Ephesians 5:3; Colossians 3:5; 1 Thessalonians 4:3-7; Hebrews 13:4
[223] Genesis 19:4-5; Judges 19:22
[224] Life Application Study Bible, NKJV, 1996.

ambition, and envy. Those who ignore or refuse such sins will have to deal with them, and they have not received the gift of the Spirit that leads to a transformed life.[225]

God views lesbians and homosexuals to have a depraved mind, according to *Romans 1:26-28, NIV*:

"Because of this, God gave them over to shameful lusts. Even their women exchanged natural relations for unnatural ones. In the same way the men also abandoned natural relations with women and were inflamed with lust for one another. Men committed indecent acts with other men, and received in themselves the due penalty for their perversion. Furthermore, since they did not think it worthwhile to retain the knowledge of God, he gave them over to a depraved mind; to do what ought not to be done."

God's plan for natural sexual relationships is His idea for His creation. Unfortunately, sin distorts the natural use of God gifts. Sin often means, not only denying God, but also denying the way we are. When people say that any sex act is acceptable if nobody gets hurt, they are fooling themselves. In the end, sin hurts people such as individuals, families, and whole societies.[226]

Homosexuality was as widespread in Paul's day as it is in ours. Many heathen practices encouraged it. Yet, homosexuality is strictly forbidden in the Scripture.[227] There are many who consider homosexuality as an acceptable practice today, even in some churches. However, society does not set the standard for God's law. Many homosexuals believe that their desires are normal, and that they have a right to express them. Nevertheless, God does not obligate nor encourage us to fulfill all our desires. Our lustful desires violate His laws. We must seek the Holy Spirit for it to be controlled. If you have these desires, flee from fornication and resist. Consciously avoid places or activities you know will kindle these temptations. Do not underestimate the power of Satan to tempt you, nor the potential for serious harm if you yield to temptation.

God is willing to receive anyone who comes to Him in faith, and believers are to love and accept others regardless of their background. God can and will forgive our sexual sins, just as He forgives other sins. Surrender yourself to the grace and mercy of God, asking Him to show you the way out of sin, and into the light of His freedom and His love. You can count on God to hear your prayer. Strong support in a Christian church can help you to gain strength to resist these powerful temptations. If you are already deeply involved in homosexual behavior, seek help from a trustworthy professional pastoral counselor.

---

[225] Malone, Julius. *Introduction to the Ten Commandments*. Sermon at New Testament Church (Milwaukee, WI) notes taken by author, 2004.
[226] Life Application Study Bible, NKJV.
[227] Leviticus 18:22

Mental adultery can be found in *Matthew 5:27-28, NJKV: "You have heard that it was said to those of old. You shall not commit adultery. But I say to you that whoever looks at a woman to lust for her has already committed adultery with her in his heart."*

The Old Testament law said that it was wrong for a person to have sex with someone other than his or her spouse. Jesus explained that the desire to have sex with someone other than your spouse is *mental adultery*. Jesus emphasized that if the act is wrong, then so is the intention. To be faithful to your spouse with your body, but not your mind, is to break the trust is so vital to a strong marriage. Jesus is not condemning natural interest in the opposite sex, or even a healthy sexual desire, but the deliberate and repeated filling of one's mind with fantasies that would be evil if acted out. Some think that if lustful thoughts are a sin, a person can go ahead and fulfill the lustful actions too.[228] Acting out sinful desires is harmful in several ways:

1. It causes people to excuse sin rather than to stop sinning
2. Destroys marriages
3. It is deliberate rebellion against God's Word
4. It always hurts someone else besides to the sinner

Sinful action is more dangerous than a sinful desire and that is why desires cannot be acted out. Nevertheless, sinful desire is just as damaging to righteousness. Left unchecked, wrong desires will result in wrong actions, and turn people away from God.

Look is a translation of the Greek verb *blepo*, which is referring to the continuous action of looking. *New Strong Concise Concordance* and *Vine's Concise Dictionary of the Bible* states that *blepo* means primarily 'to have sight, to see,' then 'observe, discern, and perceive.' Overall, Jesus is prohibiting, not a momentary glance, but a continuous glaze. Jesus is prohibiting intentional looking for those lusting or fantasizing about having sex with someone. Adultery starts in the mind or the heart.[229]

> *Matthew 15:18-20, NJKV: "But those things which proceed out of the mouth come from the heart, and they defile a man. For out of the heart proceed evil thoughts, murders, adulteries, fornications, thefts, false witness, (and) blasphemies. These are the things which defile a man, but to eat with unwashed hands does not defile a man."*
>
> *Mark 7:20-23, NKJV: "And He said, 'What comes out of a man, that defiles a man. For from within, out of the heart of men, proceed evil thoughts, adulteries, fornication, murders, thefts, covetousness, wickedness, deceit, lewdness, and evil eye, blasphemy, pride, foolishness. All these evil things come from within and defile a man.'"*

These two Scriptures are saying an evil action begins with a single thought by allowing our minds to dwell on lust, envy, hatred, or revenge, which will lead to sin. Do not defile yourself by focusing on evil instead follow Paul's advice in *Philippians 4:8*.

---

[228] Life Application Study Bible, NKJV, 1996.
[229] Matthew 15:18-20 and Mark 7:20-23

Lust, the Greek term *epithumia*, denotes 'strong desire' of any kind.[230] The word *lust* is used in reference to a *good desire* in *Luke 22:15*; *Philippians 1:23*; and *1 Thessalonians 2:17* only. Everywhere else, the word *lust* is used in a bad sense. In *Romans 6:12*, there is the injunction against letting sin reign in our mortal body to obey the 'lust' thereof, refers to those evil desires, which are ready to express themselves in bodily activity. They are equally the *lusts* of the flesh. Moreover, the term *lust* describes the emotions of the soul, the natural tendency towards things evil.[231] Such *lusts* are not necessarily base and immortal, they may be refined in character, but are evil if inconsistent with the will of God.

Divorce adultery can be found in *Matthew 5:31-32; 19:8-9.*

Spiritual adultery is idolatry by loving someone, or someone more than God, or unfaithfulness to God. In the Old Testament, the nation of Israel is called the wife of Jehovah. In the New Testament, the Church is called the Bride of Christ.[232]

Defenses against adultery, drastically deals with the things that tempt you to sin.[233] Second, guard your heart and mind.[234] Be careful about the things that you look at.[235] Avoid books, movies, videos, web sites, television programs, or anything that arouse or stimulate lust in you. Be careful what you listen to.[236] Places that you linger.[237] We can fill our minds with good thoughts.[238] Avoid idleness.[239] Someone has said, 'an idle mind is the devil's workshop.' Keep armor of God.[240] Watch and pray.[241] Pray without ceasing. We are to walk in the Spirit.[242] Remember that your body is the temple of the Holy Spirit.[243] Stay away from the edge.[244] Avoid being alone with the opposite sex who is not a relative.[245] Avoid flirting with those attractive to you.[246] Do not play with fire, you might be burned. Run if necessary.[247] Be aware that God knows all that we think, and He sees all that we do. All sins are committed in the sight of God.[248]

---

[230] New Strong Concise Concordance and Vine's Concise Dictionary of the Bible.

[231] Romans 13:4; Galatians 5:16, 24; Ephesians 2:3; 2 Peter 2:18; 1 John 2:16

[232] Scriptures in reference to spiritual adultery: Exodus 20:3-4; 34:14; Isaiah 54:5; Jeremiah 3:1-2, 6-10, 20-21; Hosea 4:9-19; Matthew 22:36-40; 2 Corinthians 11:2; Ephesians 5:22-33; James 4:4; Revelation 2:4-5; 19:7-9.

[233] Matthew 5:29-30; 1 Corinthians 6:12; 9:27

[234] Proverbs 4:23; Matthew 15:18-20; Mark 7:21-23; Luke 6:45

[235] Job 31:1; Psalm 119: 37; Daniel 1:8

[236] Psalm 1:1

[237] Psalm 1:1-2; 1 Corinthians 15:33

[238] 2 Corinthians 10:5; Philippians 4:8; Psalm 119:9, 11

[239] 2 Samuel 11:1-5

[240] Ephesians 6:10-17

[241] Ephesians 6:18; Colossians 4:2; 1 Thessalonians 5:17

[242] Galatians 5:16-23

[243] 1 Corinthians 6:18-20

[244] 1 Corinthians 10:12

[245] Genesis 39:10

[246] Proverbs 6:27-29

[247] Genesis 39:12; 1 Corinthians 6:18; 2 Timothy 2:22

[248] Psalm 51:4; 139:1-4, 7-12; Proverbs 15:3; Jeremiah 23:24; Hebrews 4:13

Remember that God can expose your cover-up sin whenever He is ready: You will eventually be caught.[249] For instance, those who were caught in the Bible and in our society today is David, Adam and Eve, Joseph's brothers, Achan, Jonah, Anianas and Sapphira, and Bill Clinton, to name a few. Be aware of the consequences of adultery. Remember that forgiveness does not erase all the consequences of adultery.[250] [251]

David's consequences for committing adultery with Bathsheba are demonstrated through his family troubles. God said that murder would be a constant threat in his family, his family would rebel, and someone else would sleep with his wives. All this happened as prophet Nathan had predicted. The consequences of sin affect not only us, but also those we know and love. Remember that the next time you are tempted to sin. David's wife, Michal, Saul's daughter, was childless. David gave her five nephews to the Gibeonites to be killed because of Saul's sins.

David's second wife, Ahinoam, from Jezreel, gave David his firstborn son, Amnion. David's other wife, Maacah, which is the daughter of King Talmai of Gusher, gave birth to Absalom, in which is David's third son and daughter, Tamar. Amnion raped Tamar (half-sister). Amnion was later murdered by Absalom in revenge. Absalom killed Amnion for raping his sister, Tamar, and then fled to Gusher. Later Absalom returned, only to rebel against David. Absalom set up a tent on his roof, and slept with ten of his father's concubines. Shortly later, Absalom's pride led to his death.

Next, his wife, Haggith, had David's fourth son, Adonijah. He was very handsome, but was never properly disciplined. He set himself up as king before David's death. Adonijah's plot was exposed. David spared his son's life, but his half-brother, Solomon, later had him executed. Bathsheba's unnamed son died in fulfillment of God's punishment for David and Bathsheba adultery. Later, Bathsheba had a son called Solomon, who became the next king of Israel. However, Solomon had many wives who caused his downfall. This defined sin can be labeled 'short term gain with long term pain.'

Adultery is the cause of 65% of divorces. Adultery causes pain that some say is greater than the pain caused by the loss of a spouse in death. Adultery causes the loss of trust. Adultery causes the loss of respect of children and other family members. God will judge adulterers in *Hebrews 13:4*. There can be other defenses against adultery. Ironically, there is deliverance from the sin of adultery.[252]

To keep romance alive in your marriage, read *Proverbs 5:15-19; 1 Corinthians 7:3-5.*

---

[249] Numbers 32:23

[250] 2 Samuel 12:1-20

[251] Malone, Julius. *Introduction to the Ten Commandments*. Sermon at New Testament Church (Milwaukee, WI) notes taken by author, 2004.

[252] John 8:1-11 and 1 Corinthians 6:9-11. Other Scriptures: 2 Thessalonians 3:5, 16-22; 1:2, 5

53

~Let Your Day Begin With Christ, Day 8~

Let your Day Begin Activity: Adultery. Review the terms of adultery and fornication. Take the time today to get rid of any lustful thoughts. Live the way God wants you to live. The purpose was to point out sin (or potential sin) and show the proper way to deal with that sin. I know that we all have at least one person in our lives that we lust for. Pray for God to remove that person out of your life, if they are not the one God has for you and to cast all imaginations and lustful thoughts out of your mind. Moreover, pray to God for the strength to walk in His path. This is a day-to-day struggle, so it needs to be a continuing progress and trusting God through the process.

Today's Questions:

There are different forms of adultery, which you have committed? Once you write them down, define, and evaluate God's views on this sin, what are some steps you will take to remove it out of your life?

What are your views on gay relationships and/or marriages? Some states have allowed gay wedding or marriages. There are remaining twenty states that are still in the process of passing the law to allow same-sex marriages to be legalized.

Review to Begin your Day with Christ:

Seventh Commandment: Adultery in the Old Testament was a punishable death (casting stones until you died). What are your thoughts on handling the sin, adultery?

Fornication is a sin that is to be avoided (Acts 15:20; 1 Corinthians 6:13, 15-18; 10:8; Galatians 5:19; Ephesians 5:1-3; Colossians 3:5; 1 Thessalonians 4:3-7; Hebrews 13:4).

There are different forms of adultery: *Physical* (Judges 19:22; Genesis 19:4-5; Deuteronomy 22:5; Romans 1:26-28; Leviticus 18:22); *Mental* (Matthew 5:27-28; 15:18-20; Philippians 4:8); *Divorce* (Matthew 5:31-32; 19:8-9); and *Spiritual* (Exodus 20:3-4; 34:14; Isaiah 54:5; Jeremiah 3:1-2, 6-10, 20-21; Hosea 4:9-19; Matthew 22:36-40; 2 Corinthians 11:2; Ephesians 5:22-33; James 4:4; Revelation 2:4-5; 19:7-9).

Day Begins 9: Eighth Commandment

The *Eighth Commandment* is a prohibition against stealing. How many of you have been victims of identity theft? We all have had something stolen from us. We all have had stolen something from others. Many stores have security systems, detectors at the exit doors, and security guards because of the problem of stealing. *Stealing* is taking what belongs to others. *Robbery* is taking from others openly and by force.[253] The *manifestations of stealing* are a failure to render to others what is due;[254] failure of employers to give employees their proper wages;[255] and failure of employees to give employers the proper amount of work.[256] Other *manifestations of stealing* are failure to pay the proper amount of taxes;[257] failure to give honor and respect to those to whom it is due;[258] failure to give glory to God;[259] and failure to give tithes and offering to God through a local church.[260] [261] God determines tithe. We determine what our offering will be. Grace goes beyond the law, more than 10%.

Other examples of stealing is the failure to return what is borrowed;[262] failure to return the correct amount of change; taking of someone's good name through slander or gossip; taking the virginity of someone who is not one's spouse; receiving goods that you know are stolen. Other examples are plagiarism and violation of copyright laws. The copying of tapes, CD's, DVD's, and software for profit, or to sell illegal merchandise is stealing.

Some motives for stealing is the lack of patience or failure to delay gratification; lack of understanding of the difference between need and greed;[263] *covetousness* is an intense desire to possess the possessions of another person;[264] the belief that what is stolen is desired; and the belief that stealing is okay because everyone else is doing it.

Some methods of breaking the habit of stealing are to practice the principle of replacement. Bad habits are to be replaced with good habits.[265] Note that when we are commanded to 'put off,' we are also commanded to 'put on' something else.[266]

---

[253] Luke 10:30
[254] Romans 13:7
[255] Leviticus 19:13; Deuteronomy 24:14-15; Jeremiah 22:13; Colossians 4:1; James 5:4
[256] Colossians 3:22-24
[257] Romans 13:6-7; Matthew 22:21
[258] Romans 13:7; 1 Peter 2:17
[259] Isaiah 42:8; 43:7; 1 Corinthians 10:31
[260] Malachi 3:7-12; Matthew 23:23; 5:20; Mark 12:41-44; Luke 19:8
[261] Malone, Julius. *Introduction to the Ten Commandments*. Sermon at New Testament Church (Milwaukee, WI) notes taken by author, 2004.
[262] Psalm 37:21
[263] Philippians 4:19
[264] Joshua 7:19-21
[265] Ephesians 4:28
[266] Ephesians 4:17-32; Colossians 3:5-17

Learn to be content.[267] Obtain possessions God's way by working (labor) to pay for possessions.[268] Save your money for possessions.[269] Learn to make some of the things you need.[270] Receive possessions such as gifts or an inheritance.[271] Receive possessions from investments.[272]

---

[267] Philippians 4:11; 1 Timothy 6:6-8; Hebrews 13:5
[268] Ephesians 4:28
[269] Proverbs 6:6-8
[270] Proverbs 31:13, 18-24
[271] 1 Kings 10:10; Proverbs 13:22
[272] Matthew 25:20-21

~Let Your Day Begin With Christ, Day 9~

Let your Day Begin Activity: Stealing. Our focus of today is stealing from the Lord. How many times have you not paid your tithes in church? Most people are selfish with their money even concerning the Lord and wonder why they do not always get the blessings bestowed on them. Starting today, with whatever money you have, take 10% out for God. See how your life is fulfilled with our Father's blessings. View other ways to tithe (offerings) your monies besides gross income, write them down. Hint: Tax Refund.

Today's Questions:

How can you change your habits of spending? Practice giving your first fruits (10% tithe to God first, 80% for bills and 10% for self). Make a budget.

Do you buy stolen goods e.g., CDs, DVDs, and so forth? You may want items on discounted or on sale instead of copying music files from online. Are you seeking things on sale or stealing goods? Should we continue to buy illegal items or pay full price for the items we desire?

Review to Begin your Day with Christ:

Eighth Commandment: Have you robbed God? Have you faced identity theft? Have you failed to pay someone money back that you borrowed? Have you violated copyright laws, plagiarism, and copying (burning) software? These are some of the ways we commit the sin, "thou shall not steal." We can break these dreadful habits. Review some methods of breaking the habit in the *Eight Commandment.*

Day Begins 10: Ninth Commandment

The *Ninth Commandment* is a prohibition against perjury. *Perjury* is lying under oath in a court of law. In the ancient times, the courts depended on witnesses to arrive at the truth so that justice could be rendered. There were no lawyers. There was no evidence such as fingerprints and DNA. False witnesses could cause the innocent to be punished and the guilty to go free. At least two witnesses were required to establish a verdict.[273] In capital punishment cases, the witnesses were to cast the first stone.[274]

The *Ninth Commandment* is a prohibition against lying. *Lying* is stating what one knows is not true. A nationwide telephone survey revealed that 91% of Americans survey confessed to regularly lying about their income, weight, age, and true hair color. Some of the reasons people lie is d*epravity;*[275] d*emonic influence;*[276] and *deception*. Satan deceived Eve with lies;[277] Jacob lied to deceive his father, Isaac, to steal his brother's birthright;[278] Gibeonites lied to deceive Joshua;[279] and the enemies of Daniel lied to deceive the King of Babylon.[280]

Other examples are to destroy someone by lying. For example, Jezebel destroyed Naboth with false witnesses,[281] and Mrs. Potiphar sought to destroy Joseph with lies.[282] Consequently, some will lie or tell a 'white lie' to protect one's self. Abraham and Isaac lied about their wives to protect themselves.[283] Peter denied Jesus to protect himself.[284] Lies were told during World War II to protect the Jews from death by German soldiers. The Hebrews midwives, Shiphrah and Puah, lied to Pharaoh to protect Hebrew boy babies.[285] Rahab lied to protect the spies from death by the King of Jericho.[286]

Some of the results of lying: those who lie imitate the devil, the father of lies;[287] those who lie lose the manifest presence of God;[288] those who lie lose the trust of others, and those who lie are condemned in the Bible.[289]

---

[273] Numbers 35:30; Deuteronomy 17:6; Matthew 18:16; 2 Corinthians 13:1; 1 Timothy 5:19; Hebrews 10:28

[274] Deuteronomy 17:6-7

[275] Psalm 58:3; 51:5; Matthew 15:19

[276] Acts 5:1-11

[277] Genesis 3:1-7; 1 Timothy 2:14

[278] Genesis 27:1-46

[279] Joshua 9:3-27

[280] Daniel 6:1-28

[281] 1 Kings 21:1-29

[282] Genesis 39:1-23

[283] Genesis 12:9-20; 26:6-11

[284] Matthew 26:69-75

[285] Exodus 1:15-21

[286] Joshua 2:1-24; Hebrews 11:31; James 2:25

[287] John 8:44; John 1:12

[288] Psalm 15:1-3; 101:7; Revelation 21:8; 22:15

[289] Proverbs 6:16-19; 12:17; 14:5; 19:28; 25:18; 24:28

One of the remedies for lying is to have a personal relationship with Jesus Christ.[290] As disciples of Jesus Christ, we imitate God, who cannot lie.[291] We will not lie if we are filled with the Holy Spirit.[292] Practice the principle of replacement.[293] In addition, we can meditate on what is true,[294] pray for God's help,[295] and love your neighbor.[296]

The *Ninth Commandment* is a prohibition against gossip. *Gossip* involves rumor or idle talk about the affairs of others. We shall not engage in gossip, nor listen to gossip.[297]

The *Ninth Commandment* is a prohibition against slander. *Slander* is speaking evil of others.[298] *Slander* is making statements that damage the character or good name of another person. We do the work of the devil when we slander. *Diabolos,* the Greek word, means to accuse falsely and slanderously.[299] *Slander* is translated 'devil' thirty-five times, 'false accuser' twice,[300] and 'slanderers' once.[301].

The most dangerous lie ever told is that there are many ways to God.[302] Jesus states, "I am the way, the truth; no men can come except by Him." Evidently, Jesus is the only way to God.

---

[290] John 1:14; 14:6; 2 Corinthians 5:17; 1 Corinthians 6:9-11
[291] Ephesians 5:1; Titus 1:2; Numbers 23:19
[292] John 16:13; Ephesians 5:18; Galatians 5:16
[293] Ephesians 4:22-29; Colossians 3:5-16
[294] Philippians 4:8; Proverbs 4:23
[295] Psalm 19:14; 141:3
[296] 1 Corinthians 13:5-6
[297] Matthew 12:34-37
[298] Ephesians 4:31; 1 Peter 2:1-2; James 4:11
[299] New Strong's Concise Concordance and Vine's Concise Dictionary of the Bible.
[300] 2 Timothy 3:3; Titus 2:3
[301] 1 Timothy 3:11
[302] John 14:6; Acts 4:12

~Let Your Day Begin With Christ, Day 10~

Let your Day Begin Activity: Lying. Today may be easy for some and hard for others. Today the activity is to tell the truth no matter the cost. I know that we all tell even baby lies. Today that will all change. Tell the truth, even if it hurts someone, they deserve to know the truth. At the end of the day, take out piece of paper and write down any lies that you could not avoid telling and repent to God for those lies you told. However, remember, we want to walk with Christ and to be more like Him in every way.

Today's Questions:

Have you asked for forgiveness from those you have lied to? If not, please find the words to say to them to tell them the truth and why you lied? You want to get right with God.

Have you ever bear false witness against your neighbor, friend, or family member. Are you willing to apologize to them? Make right with them soon, not later.

Review to Begin your Day with Christ:

Ninth Commandment: Lying against a person through gossip, slander, and defaming one's character. Please ask God for forgiveness and to renew your mind, not to repeat this sin. In addition, we have to control our mouths from engaging in gossip or slander. We are to find other ways to gratify God.

Day Begins 11: Tenth Commandment

The *Tenth Commandment* differs from the other nine since it involves the inner attitude rather than the outer actions. *Covetousness* is an unrighteous desire to possess something or someone that lacks the authority to possess.

Some causes of *covetousness* are a corrupted heart;[303] comparison of your possessions with the possessions of others; and how billions of dollars are spent each year on advertisement that causes people to covet.

The consequences of *covetousness* are discontentment, of which a covetous person is never satisfied.[304] *Covetousness* is a sin that leads to many other sins such as David's sin of covetousness led to adultery, lying, deception, stealing, and murder.[305] Achan's sin of covetousness resulted in the stealing of forbidden materials, the death of thirty-six soldiers, and the death of Achan and his family.[306] Ahab's sin of covetousness led to false witnesses and murder.[307] Micah points out that covetousness led to the taking of the property of others by violence.[308] Paul also points out that *covetousness* is a form of idolatry.[309] Moreover, covetousness causes the Word of God to become unfruitful after it is sown.[310] Covetousness leads to conflicts.[311] Covetousness cause financial difficulties. Someone has said, "Some people buy what they do not need with money they do not have, to impress people they do no like."

Some cures for covetousness is a clean heart.[312] Delight in the Lord.[313] Replace evil desires with good desires, or redirect your desires.[314] Set your mind on things above.[315] Lay up treasures in heaven, not earthly treasures.[316] Seek first the Kingdom of God.[317] Learn to be content with what you have.[318] We can practice being thankful for what you have.[319] Stay on guard against covetousness.[320] Pray for deliverance from covetousness.[321] Love your neighbor.[322] [323]

---

[303] Jeremiah 17:9; Mark 7:20-23
[304] Ecclesiastes 5:10
[305] 2 Samuel 11 & 12
[306] Joshua 7:1-26
[307] 1 Kings 21:1-29
[308] Micah 2:2
[309] Ephesians 5:5; Colossians 3:5
[310] Mark 4:18-19
[311] James 4:1-2
[312] 1 Corinthians 6:9-11; Psalm 51:10; 1 Samuel 16:7
[313] Psalm 37:4
[314] Psalm 27:4; 73:25-26
[315] Colossians 3:1-2; Ephesians 2:6; Philippians 3:20
[316] Matthew 6:19-21; 1 John 2:15-17
[317] Matthew 6:33
[318] Philippians 4:11-13; 1Timothy 6:6-10; Hebrews 13:5
[319] Philippians 4:6-7; Colossians 3:15-17; 4:2; 1 Thessalonians. 5:18; Daniel 6:10; Psalm 100:4
[320] Luke 12:15-21; Mark 8:36-37; Proverbs 4:23
[321] Psalm 119:36

Keeping God's Commandments: Reasons To Follow The Laws Of The Lord

1 John 3:22, NKJV: "And whatever we ask we receive from Him, because we keep His commandments and do those things that are pleasing in His sight."

This Scripture is simply saying that we come to God without fear, confident that our requests will be heard. Our desires will be fulfilled once we seek God first.[324] It does not mean that you will get everything that you want, but if you are seeking God's will, there are some requests that you will not even make.

God did not touch or literally place his fingers on the tablets of the stone, when creating the *Ten Commandments*. The *Ten Commandments* were created out of good intentions for His people, and now formulated in the 'Holy Word,' 'God's Word,' or the 'Bible,' which was written by men or prophets of God that were inspired by the Holy Spirit. The reasons that we obey God's law are found in *Galatians 2:16-21*. Moreover, Paul recognized that 'the law is holy.' [325] In other words, Paul is saying that the law can never make us acceptable to God. The law still has an important role to play in the life of a Christian. The law guards us from sin by giving us standards for behavior. The law convicts us of sin, leaving us the opportunity to ask for God's forgiveness. In addition, it drives us to trust in the sufficiency of Christ because we can never keep the *Ten Commandments* perfectly.

Some of the reasons for the law are given for protection. Obedience to the law protects others and us. The law reveals the will of God.[326] The law reveals sin.[327] The law reveals our need for Christ.[328] However, the law cannot possibly save us. The law was given to people who were already saved.[329] The law was not given for salvation.[330] [331]

Nevertheless, once we become new creatures in Christ, God's laws can guide us on how to live according to what God requires. What is a Christian? *Christian is* a person professing belief in Jesus as the Christ or the teachings of Jesus.[332] *Christian is* a decent, respectable person of Jesus Christ or His teaching; or professing the religion

---

[322] Matthew 22:36-40; Romans 13:8-10; 1 Corinthians 13:1-13

[323] Malone, Julius. *Introduction to the Ten Commandments*. Sermon at New Testament Church (Milwaukee, WI) notes taken by author, 2004.

[324] Matthew 7:7; 21:22; John 9:31; 15:7 and Psalm 37:4

[325] Romans 7:12

[326] Psalm 119:97-100

[327] Romans 7:7

[328] Galatians 3:24-25

[329] Exodus 19:4; 20:2; Colossians 1:11-14

[330] Romans 3:20; 10:1-4; Galatians 2:16; Ephesians 2:8-9; Philippians 3:7-9; Titus 3:5

[331] Life Application Study Bible, NKJV, 1996.

[332] Webster's New World College Dictionary.

with these teachings; having the qualities demonstrated and taught by Jesus Christ, which are love, kindness, and humility.[333]

On a further note, Paul realized that he could not be saved by obeying God's laws.[334] The prophets knew that God's plan of salvation did not rest on keeping the law. Because we are infected with sin, we cannot keep God's law flawlessly. Fortunately, God has provided a way of salvation that depends on Jesus Christ, not on our own efforts. Although we know the truth, we must guard our heart and minds against the temptation of using service, good deeds, charitable giving, or any other effort as a substitute for faith.[335]

How have we been crucified with Christ? Ideally, God looks at us as if we had died with Christ. Because our sins died with Him, we are no longer condemned.[336] Relationally, we have become one with Christ, and His experiences are ours. Our Christian life began when, in unity with Him, we died to our old life.[337] In our daily life, we must regularly crucify sinful desires that keep us from following Christ.[338]

Another law mentioned in the Bible that seems to carry out today in various countries,[339] refers to the poor and debtors, who were allowed to pay their debts by selling themselves or their children as slaves. God ordered rich people and creditors not to take advantage of these people during their time of extreme need.[340] Evidently, the woman's creditor was not acting in the spirit of God's law. Elisha's kind deed demonstrates that God wants us to go beyond simply keeping the law.[341] We must also show compassion, just like Jesus showed His compassion for us.

Lastly, religion can compel people to include synthetic laws, believing that God has favor over those that obey these additional laws created.[342] However, these laws usually are doctrine of religion and not scriptural. Yet, they are not trusting in Jesus Christ completely. It takes God to change man or woman through sanctification, resting in God's power to save man or woman through justification. If those believe that if we are good people, then Jesus Christ did not have to die for us. The cross was the only way to our salvation.

---

[333] Webster's New World College Dictionary.
[334] Galatians 2:17-21
[335] Life Application Study Bible, NKJV, 1996.
[336] Colossians 2:13-15
[337] Romans 6:5-11
[338] Life Application Study Bible, NKJV, 1996.
[339] 2 Kings 4:1
[340] Deuteronomy 15:1-8
[341] Life Application Study Bible, NKJV, 1996.
[342] Galatians 2:21

~Let Your Day Begin With Christ, Day 11~

Let your Day Begin Activity: Covetousness. Start your morning by praying to God to have a clean heart and not to want anyone else's possessions. Then, as you go on with your day, write down any possessions that you are lusting over, write them down, and ask God to change your heart.

Today's Questions:

Are you taking God's Laws in vain today? What can you do to get right with God?

Do we still follow His commandments today? Why?

What are the reasons for God's Law (protection, obedience, etc)?

Review to Begin your Day with Christ:

Tenth Commandment: What is covetousness? *Covetousness* is an unrighteous desire to possess something or someone that someone else has. Have you looked at your neighbor's home, car, and other items in which you prayed that God would bless you with the same things? Have you found yourself engaging in networking groups to obtain more financial gain and secrets for a better life? If so, seek God and He will answer your prayers. He knows what you need (John 14:14-15) and give you the desires of your heart (Psalm 37:4). Review the cures of covetousness.

For example, the Israelites did not know their potential sins after being enslaved to the Egyptians. Once Moses led them out, God wanted to give His people guidelines and rules to abide by. Why do you think it was difficult for them to follow the *Ten Commandments*? Why do you think they complained and nagged instead of remembering what God had done for them?

Day Begins 12: Three Laws Given By God To The Prophets

The Fulfillment Of The Law

The three types of laws given by God are *civil laws*, *ceremonial laws,* and *moral laws.*[343]

> 17: *"Do not think that I came to destroy the Law or the Prophets. I did not come to destroy but to fulfill."*

> 18: *"For assuredly, I say to you, till heaven and earth pass away, one jot or one title will by no means pass from the law till all is fulfilled."*

> 19: *"Whoever therefore breaks one of the least of these commandments, and teaches men so, shall be called great in the kingdom of heaven."*

> 20: *"For I say to you, that unless your righteousness exceeds the righteousness of the scribes and Pharisees, you will by no means enter the kingdom of heaven."*

In *Matthew 5:17*, we are able to see that Jesus did not come to destroy the law, but to fulfill it. In the Old Testament, there were three categories of law. *Civil laws* are dealing with the legal and social life of the Israel nation. These laws contained a temporal punishment because there were no prisons among the Israelites. These laws have disappeared, yet, they were used as an example. *Ceremonial laws* are dealing with the priesthood, sacrifices and rituals. All foreshadowed by Jesus Christ, who fulfilled the laws. These laws are no longer necessary since the death and resurrection of Jesus Christ has been fulfilled and set us free from following these laws. Although we are not bound to ceremonial laws, we are still bound to worship and love God.[344] *Moral laws* are a direct command of God and require strict obedience. Yet, it reveals the nature and will of God, still applies today. Jesus obeyed this law entirely. *Moral laws* are also dealing with God's rules for holy living.[345]

---

[343] Matthew 5:17-20
[344] Colossians 2: 16-17; Hebrews 5-10
[345] Exodus 20:1-17

Contrast Of Moral And Ceremonial Laws

Moral Law	Ritual or Ceremonial Law
Royal Law of Liberty—James 2:8-12	Law…contained in ordinances—Ephesians 2:15
Spoken by God—Deuteronomy 4:12	Spoken by Moses—Leviticus 1:1-3
Written by God on stone—Exodus 24:12; 31:18	Written by Moses in book—2 Chronicles 35:12
Placed in the Ark—Hebrews 9:4; Exodus 40:20	Placed in the side of the Ark—Deuteronomy 31:24-26
To stand forever—Psalm 111:7,8	Ended at the cross—Colossians 2:14-17
Gives the knowledge of sin—Romans 3:20; 7:7	Was given because of sin—Galatians 3:19
Not grievous—I John 5:3	Contrary to us—Colossians 2:14-17
Judges all men—James 2:10-12	Judges no man—Colossians 2:14-17
Spiritual—Romans 7:14	Carnal—Hebrews 9:10

What these laws are used for?

These laws are not only focusing on telling people to take orders and to follow them, but that to obey God's laws are more important. Today, it is easier to quote the *Ten Commandments*, or even the *Two Greatest Commandments*, but we are unable to put it into practice on a regular basis. We are not to focus on the fellow man or fellow woman for the answers. Additionally, we will not focus on other members in the church, or even your pastor for the answer. You are accountable for your own actions and words. God is counting on you to follow His commandments and laws, which will show how much you truly love your Heavenly Father. Jesus made the sacrifice for our sins in order for us to have eternal life, and to spend a lifetime with Him. He wants to see your face, and wants to see you happy, remember God loves you. Nevertheless, He deserves our love for Him, others, and to be obedient servants.

Think of how your parents feel about you. They want you to be able to listen and obey their rules. Our parents or guardians want to protect you from harm or past mistakes because they love you. You are a part of them, just like we are God's creation. We are all His children and God wants the best for us. He created these laws to protect us, and to show how much He truly loves us. Remember that He did it out of love.

Why is love for others so important to God? We are children of God, and are reminded how Jesus Christ lavished His love on the Cross for us, poured out His spirit and flesh for us. How can we repay Him? In return, we are to show love to our neighbor and our enemies. First, let us ask ourselves, what is a neighbor and an enemy, or are these words interchangeable? The word *neighbor* is a person who lives near another; a fellow human being; any person; to have friendly relations.[346] *Enemy*, on the other hand,

---

[346] Webster's New World College Dictionary.

means a person who hates and wishes, or tries to injure him; military or wartime adversary; and a hostile nation.[347] Of course, the two words have differences, however, the similarity of the word *neighbor* and *enemy* is 'any person.' In other words, we are to learn to accept and to love everyone, whether they are your neighbor or enemy.[348]

Matthew 5:43-48 reads:

43: *"You have heard that it was said, 'You shall love your neighbor and hate your enemy.'"*

44: *"But I say you, love your enemies, bless those who curse you, do good to those who ate you, and pray for those who spitefully use you and persecute you,"*

45: *"that you may be sons of your Father in heaven; for He makes His sun rise on the evil and on the good, and sends rain on the just and on the unjust."*

46: *"For if you love those who love you, what rewards have you? Do not even the tax collectors do the same?"*

47: *"And if you greet your brethren only, what do you do more than others? Do not even the tax collectors do so?"*

48: *"Therefore, you shall be perfect, just as your Father in heaven is perfect."*

Webster's New World College Dictionary for *just* and *unjust*: *Just:* lawful, proper, rightful, fair, impartial, righteous, and upright. *Unjust:* not just or right, unfair, contrary to justice, dishonest or unfaithful.

Jesus keeps us from taking the law into our own hands. By loving and praying for our enemies, we can overcome evil with good. Once you are able to love your enemies, it shows that Jesus Christ is the Lord in your life. This shows that people are unselfish, and able to trust the Lord to show us how to love those we dislike, even if we do not think we can show love towards them. We will grow in character, in holiness, and able to spiritually mature in love. In character, we are showing characteristics more like Christ by loving all, including our enemies or people we strongly dislike. Those that persecuted Jesus Christ, He remained humble and loving throughout his sufferings.

Our enemies can cause us to suffer emotionally, mentally, spiritually, and even physically. With Jesus Christ in our lives, we will be able to overcome what they dish out. If you show love in replace of hate, how would that make them feel? I hope that it will break that man's hardness, and recognize his cruel and evil deeds to be able to repent for his sins. Then, able to ask you for forgiveness and show love or gratitude in return. A smile in place of a frown or hateful words, despite what your enemy is throwing

---

[347] Webster's New World College Dictionary.
[348] Matthew 5:43-48 and Luke 6:27-36

at you. In time, God will make a way, especially if you show love towards them. Let go, and let God. Over time, your character will be Christ-like.

Next, it will lead to holiness, once we are able to separate ourselves from worldly sins and values. As followers of Christ, we are to be devoted to God's will and desires for our lives, rather than what we want for ourselves. Then, we are able to carry out God's will, and then we are able to show love and mercy in this cruel world. By becoming more like Christ and living holy and righteous, we are able to mature spiritually. However, we may have a hard time being holy and achieve a godly character right away. However, in time, we will grow maturely and in complete wholeness. God will mold us. It will build our character by going through trials, temptations, and tribulations to strengthen us, and to be able to love one another unconditionally as Jesus loves us. That is why we seek to love others as much as Jesus loves us. We can act perfect on the outside or around others, but from time to time, we tend to sin again.

Even though Christ calls us to excel, to rise above all temptations, trials and tribulations, we will mature in every area, to become more like Him. Jesus was tempted. Jesus turned to the Word, for it is written, and He loved His Heavenly Father so much, that He would not fall into sin. Let us meditate on how much we truly love our Father when we are tempted.

After watching the movie, *The Passion of Christ*, does it make you want to change your lifestyle and represent Jesus Christ to the fullest? Every time that we go through a trial or tribulation, think of Job, how he overcame his trials through faith and truly loving his Heavenly Father. In addition, Daniel still praised the Lord three times a day, even though King Nebuchadnezzar wanted everyone to worship and praise him. King Nebuchadnezzar thought of himself as a god, to worship an image made of gold that all were required to worship. There are other examples throughout the Bible that preserver over temptations, trials, and/or tribulations with the grace of God.

Nine of the *Ten Commandments* are repeated in the New Testament under grace:[349]

> 8: *Let no debt remain outstanding, except the continuing debt to love one another, for he who loves his fellowman has fulfilled the law.*
>
> 9: *The commandments, "Do not commit adultery," "Do not murder," "Do not steal," "Do not covet," and whatever other commandment there may be, are summed up in this one rule: "Love your neighbor as yourself."*
>
> 10: *Love does no harm to its neighbor. Therefore love is the fulfillment of the law.*

Loving others simply means actively seeing that their needs are met. However, people who worry about others more, suffer from low self-esteem.[350] Furthermore,

---

[349] Romans 13:8-10, NIV
[350] Life Application Study Bible, NKJV, 1996.

believers of Christ are to obey the law of love that supersedes both religion and civil laws.[351] We are to go beyond human law regulations and imitate on the laws of God. In the Old Testament, civil laws are filled with deep spiritual meanings that are written for our benefit today.[352] When we step out of God's law, we step into Satan's territory. We are not only to obey God's laws, but also to love one another. However, 95% of us do not practice neighborly love towards one another. We are known for the battles and wars between one another, sibling rivalries and gang related wars.

In *2 Peter 3:1-2*, we know the commandments, but do not remember it because we allow something or someone else to take first place in our minds. If we are mindful of our Lord and Savior, we will follow His commandments, and in everything we do, will abide in love.

---

[351] Life Application Study Bible, NKJV, 1996.
[352] 1 Corinthians 9:8-9

~Let Your Day Begin With Christ, Day 12~

Let your Day Begin Activity: Fulfillment of the Laws. Take time to review the *Ten Commandments* and the *Two Commandments* (Jesus spoke about in New Testament). See how these commandments are active in your daily walk with God. What are some things you can improve?

Today's Questions:

What is a Christian or a Disciple of Jesus Christ?

What is religion and how do believers differ?

Review to Begin your Day with Christ:

Fulfillment of the Law: Name three types of these laws. Which one do we still follow or apply in our lives?

Day Begins 13: Bodies Are A Temple Of The Lord

Our health is a vital part of our lives. The Bible speaks about our health further in *3 John 1:2: "Beloved, I pray you may prosper in all things and be in health, just as your soul prospers."* Health principles are important to God since man's body, mind, and spiritual well-being are all interrelated and interdependent. If our bodies are misused, our minds and spiritual natures cannot become what God ordained they should be.

John was concerned for Gaius' physical and spiritual well-being. Today, many people still fall into that way of thinking that there is a separation of spirit and matter, despite the physical side of life. Non-Christian attitude logically leads to one of the two responses: neglect the body and physical health, or indulgence of the body's sinful desires. God is concerned for both your body and soul. As a responsible Christian, you should neither neglect nor indulge yourself, but care for your physical needs, and discipline your body so that you are at your best for God's service.

God knows what is best for the human body. Following God's rules results in saving health,[353] and a more abundant life.[354] The diet God gave people in the beginning was fruit, grain, and nuts (Eden's diet). Vegetables were added a little later.[355] In addition, the Bible has ample evidence that there were clean and unclean animals from the very dawn of Creation. During Noah's day, he took into the ark the clean animals by 'sevens' and unclean by 'twos.' *Revelation 18:2* refers to some birds as unclean before the second coming of Christ. The death of Christ had not an altering effect on all who break, but they will be destroyed when Jesus returns.[356] Alternatively, these health laws are for all people for all time.

Discipline has derived from *sophronismos. Sophronismos* came from the word *sophron,* meaning saving the mind, primarily an admonishing or calling to soundness of mind, or to self-control, which is also used in *2 Timothy 1:7,* 'a sound mind.'

"For God has not given us a spirit of fear, but of power and of love and of a sound mind."

When we allow people to intimidate us, we neutralize our effectiveness for God. The power of the Holy Spirit can help us overcome our fear, so that we can continue to do God's work. Furthermore, in *2 Timothy 1:7*, Paul mentions three characteristics of the effective Christian leader: power, love, and a sound mind (wisdom). These three characteristics are available to us because of the Holy Spirit that dwells in us. Do we acknowledge that our bodies are the temple of the Lord?

---

[353] Psalm 67:2
[354] John 10:10
[355] Genesis 3:18
[356] Isaiah 66:15-17

1 Corinthians 6:19-20, NKJV: "Or do you know that your body is the temple of the Holy Spirit who is in you, whom you have from God, and you are not your own? For you were bought at a price; therefore glorify God in your body and in your spirit, which are God's."

What did Paul mean when he said that our bodies belong to God? Many people say that they have the right to do whatever they want with their own bodies. Although they think that this is freedom, they are really enslaved to their own desires. When we become followers of Christ, the Holy Spirit fills and lives in us. Therefore, we no longer own our bodies. For instance, 'bought at a price,' refers to slaves purchased at auction. With His death, Jesus Christ paid the cost to redeem us from our slavery of sin. Christ's death freed us from sin, but also obligated us to His service. Because your body belongs to God, you must not violate His standards of living.[357]

Temple also was referred as *palace temple*. This is a construction often very beautiful and ornate, as the dwelling place of a king or a god for the true God. The word *palace* in English versions is a residence for a king.[358] Paul told believers that each one of their bodies was a *naos*, a sanctuary for God.[359] Paul also said that the church, as Christ's body, is a spiritual temple for God.[360] What a special privilege it is to be God's spiritual dwelling place, both individually and corporately. The glory of God filled the tabernacle and the temple. Now the glory of God is when the Holy Spirit dwells within every believer,[361] and thus inhabits the entire church. In the New Jerusalem, there will be no need for a physical temple because God and the Lamb will be the eternal temple.[362]

Exodus 15:26, NKJV: "...If you diligently heed the voice of the Lord, your God, and do what is right in His sight, give ear to His commandments and keep all His statutes, I will put none of the diseases on your which I have brought on the Egyptians. For I am the Lord who heals you."

God promised that if the people obeyed Him, they would be free from the disease that plagued the Egyptians. Little did they know that many of the moral laws, which He later gave them, were intended to keep them free from sickness? For example, following God's law against prostitution would keep them free of venereal diseases. God's laws for us are often designed to keep us from harm. Men and women are complex beings. Our physical, emotional, and spiritual lives are intertwined. Modern medicine now is acknowledging what these laws assumed. If we want God to care for us, we need to submit to his directions for living.[363] What do we do?

---

[357] Life Application Study Bible, NKJV on 1 Corinthians 6:19, 20.

[358] 2 Kings 20:18; Nahum 2:6

[359] 1 Corinthians 6:19

[360] 1 Corinthians 3:16, 17; 2 Corinthians 6:16; Ephesians 2:21

[361] John 14:16, 17

[362] Revelation 21:22

[363] Life Application Study Bible, NKJV, 1996.

Romans 12:1, 2, NKJV: "I beseech you therefore, brethren, by the mercies of God, that you present your bodies a living sacrifice, holy, acceptable to God, which is your reasonable service. And do not be conformed to this world, but be transformed by the renewing of your mind, that you may prove what is that good and acceptable and perfect will of God."

When sacrificing an animal according to God's law, a priest would kill the animal, cut it in pieces, and place it on the altar. Sacrifice was important, but even in the Old Testament, God made it clear that obedience from the heart was much more important.[364] God wants us to offer ourselves, not animals, as living sacrifices by daily laying aside our own desires to follow Him, putting all our energy and resources at His disposal and trusting Him to guide us. We do this out of gratitude that our sins have been forgiven. God has good, acceptable, and perfect plans for His children. He wants us to be transformed people with renewed minds, living to honor and obey Him. God wants only what is best for us and because He gave His Son to make our new lives possible. We joyfully give ourselves as living sacrifices for His service.[365]

1 Corinthians 10:31: "Therefore, whether you eat or drink, or whatever you do, do all to the glory of God."

God's love must permeate our motives that all we do will be for His glory. Keep this as a guiding principle, by asking, "Is this action glorifying God?" Alternatively, "How can I honor God through this action?"[366]

---

[364] 1 Samuel 15:22; Psalm 40:6; Amos 5:21-24
[365],[347] Life Application Study Bible, NKJV, 1996.

~Let Your Day Begin With Christ, Day 13~

Let your Day Begin Activity: Ponder on how you can value your body. You can talk to your doctor or nutrient specialist on how to get your health better (e.g., exercise, diet, and medications). Think about how God views your health and taking care of your body. He wants you to live long on the earth to do His purpose. Practice eating smaller meals at designated times, snack before 8:30 p.m. or two hours before retiring to bed, and do not glutton on anything you desire to eat. Detoxify your body to get it back into functioning properly. Try it for 2-3 days (maximum is two weeks), read books such as *The New Detox Diet* by Elson Haas, *Get Healthy Through Detox and Fasting* or *Toxic Relief* by Dr. Don Colbert and/or Raw Diet books.

Today's Questions:

What are some steps you are willing to take to improve your health?

Do you view your body as a temple of the Lord's?

Do we glorify the Lord with our bodies? If so, how do we glorify the Lord with our bodies? If not, what changes are you willing to make?

Review to Begin your Day with Christ:

Paul told believers our bodies was a *naos,* a sanctuary for God
(1 Corinthians 6:19).

The church, part of Christ's body, a spiritual temple for God
(1 Corinthians 3:16, 17; 2 Corinthians 6:16; and Ephesians 2:21).

Day Begins 14: Eating Well-Balanced Meals

Food High In Fiber And Low In Fat: Original Diet

Dietary fiber is the part of the plant foods such as vegetables and grains that are not broken down by digestive juices in the intestine, as are other food elements. It is important for normal functioning of the digestive tract. The digestive tract holds water in the intestine, adds bulk to, and softens stools, and regulates the time it takes for food wastes (toxic) to move through the body. There are two major types of dietary fiber: insoluble fiber and soluble fiber. Insoluble fiber helps prevent constipation and hemorrhoids. It also helps satisfy the appetite by creating a feeling of fullness. Soluble fiber may play a role in reducing blood cholesterol and blood glucose (sugar level).

Sugar, unbelievably, will not make you gain weight. In fact, studies show that overweight people eat less sugar than lean people do. Although obesity has increased, sugar consumption has remained constant. Yet, this does not mean you can stuff yourself with sugary candies, which are made of refined and/or processed sugar, and have no nutritional value, plus it is also terrible for your teeth.

Sugar alone makes your blood glucose level go up very fast, and drop just as fast, leaving you as hungry as you were before. Instead, enjoy the natural simple sugars in apples, grapes, pineapples, and other fruit, which provides vitamins and minerals with fiber to satisfy your hunger. Eat as much of them as you like. However, the odd sugary treat will not hurt your weight loss, if the sugars are not accompanied by fat. Cakes, cookies, brownies, and chocolate bars, all are high in fat that will make you gain weight. The occasional vanilla wafer or sugar in your tea will not slow down your weight loss.

Your needs are 20-35 grams of dietary fiber a day. Good sources of fiber include whole grain cereals, breads and pasta, bran, fruits and vegetables, legumes, nuts and seeds. Bran cereal is a concentrated source of fiber. You can get about 20 grams of dietary fiber if you choose at least three servings a day of vegetables, plus two servings a day of fruit, plus three servings a day of whole grain products. In addition, drink eight to twelve glasses of water or other fluids such as 100% juices, herbal or non-caffeine teas. Milk or soy protein products such as Rice Dream, Soy Dream, and other soy brand names are also recommended daily. It is important to drink plenty of fluids when increasing fiber intake. If fluids are not taken, severe constipation will result.

Dietary Fiber In Food

Breads & Crackers	Amount	Fiber (grams)
Graham Crackers	2 squares	1.5
Pumpernickel	¾ slice	1.5
Rye Bread	1 slice	1.0
Whole-Wheat Bread	1 slice	0
Whole-Wheat cracker	6 crackers	2.0
Whole-Wheat roll	¾ roll	1.0

For other bread/crackers products, check the Dietary Fiber intake.

Cereal	Amount	Fiber (grams)
All Bran 100%	1/3 cup	8.5
Bran Chex	½ cup	4.0
Corn Bran	½ cup	4.5
Corn Flakes	¾ cup	2.5
Grape Nuts Flakes	2/3 cup	2.5
Grape Nuts	3 tbsp	2.5
Oatmeal	¾ pkg	2.5
Shredded Wheat	1 biscuit	3.0
Wheaties	¾ cup	2.5

For other Cereals, check the Dietary Fiber intake.

Fruit	Amount	Fiber (grams)
Apple	½ large	2.0
Apricot	2	1.5
Banana	½ medium	1.5
Blackberries	¾ cup	6.5
Cantaloupe	1 cup	1.5
Cherries	10 large	1.0
Dates (dried)	2	1.5
Figs (dried)	1 medium	3.5
Grapes (white)	10	.5
Grapefruit	½	1.0
Honeydew Melon	1 cup	1.5
Orange	Small	1.5
Peach	1 medium	2.5
Pear	½ medium	2.0
Pineapple	½	1.0
Plum	3 small	2.0
Prunes (dried)	2	2.5
Raisins	1 ½ Tbsp	1.0
Strawberries	1 cup	3.0
Tangerine	1 large	2.0
Watermelon	1 cup	1.5

Meat, Milk, Eggs	Amount	Fiber
Beef, Pork	1 ounce	0
Chicken, Turkey	1 ounce	0
Cheese	¾ ounce	0
Cold cuts, Franks	1 ounce	0
Egg	1 large	0
Fish	2 ounces	0
Ice cream	1 cup	0
Milk	1 cup	0
Yogurt	5 ounces	0

Rice	Amount	Fiber (grams)
Brown Rice (cooked)	1/3 cup	1.5
White Rice (cooked)	1/3 cup	0.5
Leaf Vegetables	Amount	Fiber (grams)
Broccoli	½ cup	3.5
Brussel Spouts	½ cup	2.5
Cabbage	½ cup	2.0
Cauliflower	½ cup	1.5
Celery	½ cup	1.0
Lettuce	1 cup	1.0
Spinach (raw)	1 cup	.5
Turnip Greens	½ cup	3.5

Root Vegetables	Amount	Fiber (grams)
Beets	½ cup	2.0
Carrots	½ cup	2.5
Potatoes (baked)	½ medium	2.0
Radishes	½ cup	1.5
Sweet Potatoes (baked)	½ medium	2.0

Other Vegetables	Amount	Fiber (grams)
Green Beans	½ cup	2.0
String Beans	½ cup	2.0
Cucumber	½ cup	1.0
Eggplant	½ cup	2.5
Lentils (cooked)	½ cup	4.0
Mushrooms	½ cup	1.0
Onions	½ cup	1.0
Tomato	1 small	1.5
Winter Squash	½ cup	3.5
Zucchini Squash	½ cup	2.0

This is a general guide provided by the Nutrition Therapy Department at Milwaukee Medical Clinic. If you have more questions or concerns, please contact your dietitian or doctor.

30 Fat Burning Foods

Apples	Jam (sugar free, low cal only)
Bananas	Leeks
Beans	Lettuce
Bread (plain, preferably wheat)	Melons
Broccoflower	Pasta (low-fat, whole grain)
Broccoli	Pears
Cabbage	Peas (all types)
Cauliflower	Peppers
Celery	Pineapple
Citrus Fruits (lemons, oranges, grapefruit)	Root Vegetables
Corn (also air popped popcorn)	Cranberries
Grains and Grain products	Tomatoes (salt-free, sugar-free sauce and salsa)
Grapes	Waffles and Pancakes (low-fat and frozen)
Zucchini	Spinach

~Let Your Day Begin With Christ, Day 14~

Let your Day Begin Activity: Take the time today to go through the list of Dietary Fibers (in foods) and Fat Burning Foods, and write down all the foods that you can eat. Then, make an effort to go to the grocery store and purchase as many of those items as your budget will allow. We have to eat right and be healthy.

Today's Questions:

Are we eating according to God's will for our lives? What are we willing to do to take care of our bodies?

How many grams of dietary fiber a day is required?

How can you improve your body's image? What are your short-term and long-term goals to improve your body image?

Review to Begin your Day with Christ:

Read other books that are health related (diabetics, thyroids, or general health) for weight loss, eating habits, and exercise.

Dietary fiber= vegetables and grains. Broken into two parts: insoluble fiber (prevent constipation and hemorrhoids) and soluble fiber (reduces blood cholesterol and blood glucose).

Be more conscious of your sugar intake and caffeine and other deadly foods like cakes, cookies, processed foods high in fat and calories.

Eat at least three servings of grain, two servings of fruit, and three servings of vegetables.

Day Begins 15: Eden Diet (Vegetarian)

Eden Diet And Eat Foods That Are Good For Us

Eden diet started in the Garden of Eden, when Adam and Eve roamed the earth in such a paradise created by God for man originally, and a diet that He had fit for them. This diet consisted of nuts and seeds. *Genesis 1:29*, God is speaking to Adam in the Garden of Eden, the first human life: *"And God said, 'See I have given you every herb that yields seed which is on the face of all the earth, and every tree whose fruit yields seed; to you it shall be for food."*

Isaiah 55:2, NKJV: "Why do you spend money for what is not bread, and your wages for what does not satisfy? Listen carefully to Me, and eat what is good, and let your soul delight itself in abundance."

Food costs money, which only lasts for a short period, yet it only meets our physical needs. Nevertheless, God offers us free nourishment that feeds our soul. We come,[367] listen,[368] seek, and call on God.[369] God's salvation is freely offered, but to nourish our souls, we must eagerly receive it. We will starve spiritually without this food as surely as we will starve physically without our daily bread.[370] Not only does God's salvation supply what is necessary for life, but it also provides what brings joy. Salvation cannot be bought, but can receive when desired.[371] [372]

Daniel 1:12: "Please test your servants for ten days and let them give us vegetables to eat and water to drink."

The Babylonians were trying to change the thinking of the Jews by giving them a Babylonian education, their loyalty by changing their names, and their lifestyle by changing their diet. Without compromising, Daniel found a way to live God's standards in a culture that did not honor God. Wisely choosing to negotiate rather than to rebel, Daniel suggested an experimental ten-day diet of vegetables and water, instead of the royal foods and wine the king offered. Without compromising, Daniel quickly thought of a practical, creative solution that saved his life, and the lives of his companions. As God's people, we may adjust to our culture, so we do not compromise God's laws.[373]

[367] Isaiah 55:1
[368] Isaiah 55:2
[369] Isaiah 55:6
[370] Life Application Study Bible, NKJV, 1996.
[371] Isaiah 52:3; Deuteronomy 8:3; Romans 6:23
[372] Nelson Study Bible, NKJV and emphasis added by the author.
[373] Life Application Study Bible, NKJV, 1996.

~Let Your Day Begin With Christ, Day 15~

Let your Day Begin Activity: We need to look at our personal spending and to be more responsible. When buying groceries, write a list first, and do not buy items that are not included on the list unless, it is a healthy choice and fits in your budget.

Today's Questions:

What is the Eden diet? Some people would call it today, a Raw Diet. Elaborate on what it is and what foods you would include in your diet from the Raw/Eden Diet.

Are you eating better for weight loss, healthier body, and/or to follow God's standards for your life?

Review to Begin your Day with Christ:

Isaiah 55:2: asks these questions 'Why do you spend money for what is not bread, and your wages does not satisfy.' We are to focus on eating what is good for our health. We are to look at our budget. We are to focus on spending the money we have, not to overspend (leads to debt and gluttony). We will live prosperous (in good health). We cannot compromise with eating unhealthy foods that choke our pocketbooks. We can look at foods that we used to eat, by using substitute foods that are light in calories, cholesterol and fat. We are making better choices. For example, instead of buying lard or shortening, we can purchase Extra Virgin Olive Oil. Replace white sugar with brown sugar, Stevia, agave nectar, or honey.

Day Begins 16: Meat-Eaters Diet

Forbidden Foods And Pleasing Food To God

Genesis 9:3-5: Three new realities mark the post-Flood world: meat may be eaten with plants; blood is not to be eaten with meat; and taking of a person's life is not punishable by death.

9:3: argues that men and women ate only vegetables.

9:4: blood – is a prohibition against God. Blood represents animal's life was used for rituals or sacrifice, for all life belongs to the Lord (Old Testament).

9:5: lifeblood is more sacred than the life of an animal because it is the life of a person. Animals may be slain for food, but not wanton slaying of human is allowed.[374]

A *reckoning* means that God will require each person to account for his or her actions.[375] We cannot harm or kill another human being without answering to the Creator. A penalty must be paid. Justice will be served. In addition, God explains why murder is wrong: to kill a person is to kill one made in God's image. Human beings are made in God's image, which all people possess the qualities that distinguish them from animals: mortality, reason, creativity, and self-worth. When we interact with others, we are interacting with beings made by God, beings to whom God offers eternal life. God wants us to recognize His image in all people.

> *Leviticus 3:17: "This shall be a perpetual statue throughout your generations in all your dwellings: you shall eat neither fat nor blood."*

Perpetual dwellings: some regulations in the Law of Moses were observed only in the land that God was giving the Israelites. However, the prohibition of eating fat or blood applied wherever an Israelite might live. There were no exceptions. These sacrificial regulations consistently emphasize the theme of only the best for God. As it was in ancient Israel, so it is today, only our best is good enough to give to God.[376]

On the other hand, *Leviticus 11:2-43,* shows what is forbidden and what we are able to eat according to God.

11:2: On the earth: as distinct from the sea and the air. A similar grouping of animal life is found in *Genesis 1:20-31.*

11:3: Chewing the cud (regurgitating it back and chews it a second time): that is the ruminants, like cows, sheep, goats, deer, and antelope. The ruminants eat only plants,

---

[374] Nelson Study Bible, NKJV.
[375] Life Application Bible, NKJV, 1996.
[376] Nelson Study Bible, NKJV.

mainly grasses and grains. No meat-eating animal chews cud. The animals allowed for food are not mentioned by name as they are in the book of Deuteronomy.

11:4, 5. Cattle, sheep, and goats provided most of the meat for the ancient Israelites. They ate meat much less often than we do, usually only on special occasions such as the sacrificial feasts or to honor guests in their home.

11:4: The camel was eaten by some of Israel neighbors, who considered it a delicacy. However, the camel would not have been an important source of meat for Israel even if it had been permitted, for it never was a numerous in Israel or as important to Israel's economy as it was to their neighbors. The camel does have a split hoof, but its sole or pad is so thick its imprint is like a single pad.

11:5: The rock hyrax lives in colonies among the rocks.[377] Though it is sometimes called a rock badger, it is not a badger. The rock hyrax is about the same size as a rabbit. Hyraxes appear to chew constantly while sitting outside their dens sunning themselves.

11:6: The hare is not a ruminant, although it does appear to chew constantly. It lacks a hoof.

11:7: The swine is the best known of the unclean animals and continues to be avoided by both Jews and Muslims. Israel's neighbors in both the Old and the New Testament periods most commonly ate the swine. All the reasons for labeling an animal as unclean fit the swine:

1   Inadequately cooked pork could transmit disease to humans
2. Pigs were sacrificed to pagan deities
3. Because pork tasted so good, refusing it would be a suitable test of faithfulness and obedience

11:8: In case of these unclean animals, eating their meat or touching their dead carcasses caused an Israelite to be unclean or ritually impure. However, touching a live animal did not make a person unclean, and an Israelite could raise and use a donkey or camel as a beast without becoming unclean.

11:9: A water creature had to possess both fins and scales to be eaten. Only true fish -- and not all of them -- fit this description. Oysters, clams, crabs, lobsters, and eels were unclean. Whether in the seas or in the rivers, this applied to God's command to both saltwater and freshwater species.

11:10-12: Abomination is a stronger word than unclean. It implies that not just avoidance, but active, fierce repulsion. Fins and scales are 'appropriate' water creatures. Fish that have them are clean. Water creatures that appear to mix categories -- suggesting disorder -- are not merely unclean. They are an abomination. There are good health reasons for being cautious in eating some of these creatures, but this was not the main reason for classifying them as unclean.

---

[377] Proverbs 30:26

11:19: The hoopoe is a migratory bird. It spends its winters in tropical Africa and its summers in Israel and father north. The bat is not a bird. However, in the pre-scientific age, it was grouped with birds because it has wings and flies.

11:20: Creep on all fours is an idiom for crawling on the ground, as insects do on their six legs. Many insects move about in filth and eat droppings. Their association with death, impurity, and disorder made them unclean.

11:21: Insects with jointed legs, those that leap, were permitted to be eaten. The joints are the enlarged third legs of locusts and grasshoppers that enable them to leap. Locusts and grasshoppers do not live in filth or eat dung. They eat only plants.

11:24: This refers to the flying insects of the previous paragraph or to all the unclean animals discussed so far. Merely to touch an unclean carcass caused a person to be unclean until evening, when the new day began for the Israelites.

11:25: If a person carried or picked up a carcass or part of a carcass, that person's uncleanness was greater. Therefore, the remedy had to be more thorough.

11:26: The word, carcass is not in the Hebrews text, but clearly, that is what is meant here. A live unclean animal, such as a donkey or camel, could not make a person unclean simply by touching it. Otherwise, many people would have been unclean all the time.

11:27-28: Whatever goes on its paws is unclean because it lacks a cloven hood. As with the previous group, to touch a carcass was to be unclean and to carry a carcass was to be even more unclean, requiring thorough cleansing.

11:29-30: Another group of animals is introduced here. Many of these animals could be found in or around human dwellings. Since these animals were unclean, it was important to know how to deal with them and with objects and utensils they touched. These are small creatures crept the earth. This refers not only to their great numbers, but also to their quickness of movement. The group includes small rodents such as mice, voles, shrews, and hamsters, also some kinds of lizards.

11:31: When they are dead: literally 'in their death' or 'in their dying.' The Israelites farmer was more likely to kill a small rodent in the course of the day than any other creature named in this chapter. It was important to remember as they killed these pests that they themselves would be unclean until evening if they touched them.

11:32: Expensive vessels of wood, fabric, leather, or fiber were to be put in the water. Whether they were only to be washed or soaked until evening is unclean. However, at evening, the start of the new Jewish day, they would be clean.

11:33: Any earthen vessel…you shall break: Pottery was plentiful, cheap, and easily replaced. Vessels made of pottery were also used for food preparation and eating. Again, hygiene is an important result of avoiding the unclean. We are to wash dishes and food when preparing to avoid bacteria and salmonella or other diseases.

11:34: The contents of any vessel made unclean in this way became unclean as well.

11:35: These ovens were made of clay and so had to be broken also.

11:36: A spring or a cistern could hardly be emptied. Only the person removing the carcass became unclean -- until evening.

11:37-38: Dry planting seed did not become unclean.

11:39-40: If animal dies: This refers to animals that died of natural causes, and not those killed for food. The carcass caused the person who touched it to be unclean because its blood had not been drained. Eating or carrying the carcass involved more than merely touching it and required a greater remedy --washing one's clothes by waiting until evening. Eating meat without draining its blood apparently was not as serious an offense as eating and drinking blood by itself.[378] Carrying the carcass would have been unavoidable in many situations such as removing the animal for burial. Uncleanness often was not a moral issue at least in the way a person became unclean.

11:41-43: Crawls on its belly and has many feet are new descriptions. They were not mentioned in the previous ban on eating creeping things.
   —Scriptures above were a breakdown from the Nelson Study Bible

---

[378] Leviticus 7:26-27

Unclean (forbidden foods)	Clean foods
Eagle	Chicken
Vulture	Duck
Buzzard	Goose
Red Kite (all kinds)	Grouse
Falcon	Partridge
Raven (all kinds)	Pheasant
Ostrich	Quail
Owls	Turkey
Sea Gull	Song Birds
Hawk	Fish: Anchovy, Barracuda, Bass, Bowfin, Buffalo
Jackdaw	Deer: Roe deer (male deer)
Stork	Antelope
Hoopoe	Gazelle
Bat	Hart (male red deer), Fallow
Flying Insects: creep on all fours and leap on the earth	Carp, Tarpon, Trout, Tuna, Whitefish, Sole, Snapper
Camel or Donkey	Cod (fish)
Rock Hyrax	Darter (fish)
Swine or Pig	Sardine (fish)
Humans (flesh)	Salmon (fish)
Carcass: food with outer shell such as oysters, clams, crabs, lobsters	Haddock (fish)
Creep on the earth: mole, mouse, lizard, gecko, sand reptile, chameleon, snake, hamsters	Other fish: Grayling, Flounder, Halibut, Herring, Jack, Mackerel, Minnow, Mullet, Perch, Pike, Shad, Sunfish
Hare (Rabbit)	Lamb or Sheep
Fish: Catfish, Eels, Swordfish, Sturgeons, Shellfish, Shrimp	Beef (Cow or Oxen)
Eel	Goat

Not only the Jews had to follow these practices of preparation and foods under God's standards that were allowed, but also Noah knew how to distinguish the clean from the unclean.[379] The pairs of every animal that joined Noah in the ark; seven pairs were taken of those animals to be used for sacrifice -- the 'clean' animals. Scholars estimated that almost forty-five thousand animals could fit in the ark.[380] You may be asking or thinking to yourself, why do I have to follow the diet that God has required?

In *Genesis 5:5*, it shows that Adam lived to be 930 years old. This appears that one will live longer if we follow God's standards concerning our diet, whether it is Eden diet, which are seeds, but today can also consist of vegetables and fruits, or meat-

---

[379] Genesis 7:2-3
[380] Life Application Study Bible, NKJV, 1996.

eaters diet, including fruits, grains, nuts and vegetables. However, Adam only ate seeds until he was removed from the Garden of Eden, and then ate whatever seeds grew such as fruits and vegetables. Animals were used as sacrifices (sheep's or lambs) later.

In *Exodus 15:26*, stating that if we obey God standards on what we eat, we will be free of diseases and sickness. In *Daniel 1:15*, better and fatter, shows that Daniel and his friends were healthier than the young men who ate of the king's delicacies. Some of us do not want to change our eating habits because we grew up as meat eaters or vegetarians. Once we become adults, we are able to conclude on our own, or remain stubborn to old habits. God is concerned about our eating and our bodies to become healthier. Yet, Paul knew the danger of criticism on this issue in *Romans 14*.

1) Accept believers who are weak in faith, and do not argue with them about what they think is right and wrong.
2) For instance, one person believes it is all right to eat anything. However, another believer who has sensitive conscience will eat only vegetables.
3) Those who think it is all right to eat anything must not look down on those who will not. Additionally, those who will not eat certain foods must not condemn those who do, for God have accepted them.
4) Who are you to condemn God's servants? They are responsible to the Lord, so let him tell them whether they are right and wrong. The Lord's power will help them do as they should.
5) Those who have a special day for worshipping the Lord are trying to honor him. Those who eat all kinds of food do so to honor the Lord, since they give thanks to God before eating. Those who will not eat everything also want to please the Lord and give thanks to God (like Daniel).
6) For we are not our own masters when we live or when we die.
7) While we live, we live to please the Lord. In addition, when we die, we go to be with the Lord. Therefore, in life and death, we belong to the Lord.
8) Christ died and rose again for this very purpose, so that he might be Lord of those who are alive and of those who have died.
9) So why do you condemn another Christian? Why do you look down on another Christian? Remember, each of us will stand before the Judgment Seat of God.
10) For the Scriptures read, "As surely as I live, say the Lord, every knee will bow to me and every tongue will confess allegiance to God."
11) Yes, each of us will have to give a personal account to God.
12) So, do not condemn each other anymore. Decide to live in such a way that you will not put an obstacle in another Christian's path.
13) I know and am perfectly sure on the authority of the Lord Jesus that no food, in and of itself, is wrong to eat. But, if someone believes it is wrong, then for that person, it is wrong.
14) If another Christian is distressed by what you eat, you are not acting in love, if you eat it. Do not let your eating ruin someone, for whom Christ died.
15) Then you will not be condemned for doing something you know is right.

16) For the Kingdom of God is not a matter of what we eat or drink, but of living a life of goodness and peace and joy in the Holy Spirit.

17) If you serve Christ with an obedient attitude, you will please God. Additionally, other people will approve of you, too.

18) So then, let us aim for harmony in the church and try to build each other up.

19) Do not tear apart the work of God over what you eat. Remember, there is nothing wrong with these things in themselves. However, it is wrong to eat anything if it makes another person stumble.

20) Do not eat meat, drink wine, or do anything else if it might cause another Christian to stumble.

21) You may have the faith to believe that there is nothing wrong with what you are doing, but keep it between yourself and God. Blessed are those who do not condemn themselves by doing something they know is right.

22) If people have doubts about whether they should eat something, they should not eat it. They would be condemned, for not acting in faith before God. If you do anything you believe is not right, you are sinning.[381]

Some would ask why God created the hog or pig, if we are not able to eat it. He made it for the same purpose that He made the buzzard as a scavenger to clean up garbage, and the hog serves this purpose admirably. In *Romans 14*, Verse 3 and 6 are a discussion of those who eat certain things versus those who do not. The passage does not say it is right, but rather counsels not to pass judgment on the other. Instead, let God be the judge.[382] Alternatively, foods were first offered to idols and were ceremonially unclean.[383] The point of the discussion is that food is 'unclean' or 'impure' because it was first offered to the gods, which is 'part of worldly ways.'[384] If a person's conscience bothers him or her for eating such a food, he or she needs to leave it alone. Or even if it merely offends a brother, God requires us to abstain from it.

> *1 Timothy 4:3-5, NKJV: "…and commanding to abstain from foods which God created to be received with thanksgiving by those who believe and know the truth. For every creature of God is good, and nothing is to be refused if it is received with thanksgiving; for it is sanctified by the Word of God and prayer."*

In review, *1 Timothy 4:3-5*, we are to abstain from processed foods and other foods that were not created by God, if we want to remain healthy, look and feel great. Additionally, a superb book to read is *The Seven Pillars of Health* by Dr. Don Colbert.

---

[381] New Living Translation (NLT) found on BibleGateway.com.

[382] Romans 14: 4, 10, 12

[383] 1 Corinthians 8:1, 4, 10, 13; Romans 14:14, 20

[384] 1 Corinthians 8:4

~Let Your Day Begin With Christ, Day 16~

Let your Day Begin Activity: Look in your cabinets, refrigerators, or where you store your food. Make a list of forbidden foods you have and pleasing foods you have. For all the forbidden foods that you eat, substitute them for foods that are pleasing to God. Give in to your indulgences and live and eat like God wants us to. Or will you keep subduing to what your flesh desires and wants, and watch your body's health go down faster with more medical expenses. Preventive health is cost-effective for any future doctor bill's and emergency calls. Do not give in. Make healthier choices.

Today's Questions:

What are some reasons God does not want us to eat the unclean meats?

When did God allow people to eat meat? Can we eat any type of meat we like? If not, why?

What does God mean by unclean foods and the purpose of these animals that roam the earth?

Review to Begin your Day with Christ:

Compare and contrast: *Romans 12:2* and *1 Corinthians 10:31*.

Agree or disagree with *Leviticus 11:2-43* to apply with your daily diet? In contrast, some refer to *Romans 14* to eat what they wish. What do you think? Look at your health and medical records, review your past eating or current eating habits.

Day Begins 17: Health Overview

Health Laws Overview

1. Eat your meals at regular intervals and do not use animal fat or blood.[385] "Eat in due season."[386]
2. Do not overeat.[387] Jesus Christ warns against *surfeiting*, which means overeating in the last days. Overeating or gluttony is responsible for many degenerative diseases.
3. Do not harbor envy or hold grudges.[388] Jesus Christ even commands us to clear up grudges that others may hold against us.[389]
4. Maintain a cheerful, happy disposition.[390] Many diseases, from which people suffer, are a result of mental depression. A cheerful, happy disposition imparts health and prolongs life.
5. Put full trust in the Lord. Trust in the Lord strengthens health and life.[391] Therefore, health comes from obedience to God's commands, and from putting full trust in Him.
6. Balance work and exercise with sleep and rest.[392] "The sleep of a laboring man is sweet."[393]
7. Keep your body clean.[394]
8. Be temperate in all things.[395] "Let your moderation be known to all men."[396] A believer of Christ will completely avoid all things that are harmful and eat or drink in moderation. Some foods or things such as alcohol, tobacco, and drugs that are bad for our bodies are like committing suicide on an installment plan.
9. Avoid all harmful stimulants. Medical science confirms that tea, coffee and soft drinks, contain the addictive drug caffeine and other harmful ingredients that are positively harmful to our bodies. Stimulants give a dangerous, artificial boost to the body. Many Americans are sickly because of their addiction to coffee, tea, and caffeinated soft drinks. However, the real tragedy is that men and women seek peace and strength through drinks such as caffeine tea and coffee, as cheap substitutes. This delights the devil and wrecks the human life.
10. Make mealtime a happy time.[397] Unhappy scenes at mealtime hinder digestive system, so try to avoid them.

---

[385] Leviticus 3:17
[386] Ecclesiastes 10:17
[387] Proverbs 23:2; Luke 21:34
[388] Proverbs 14:30
[389] Matthew 5:23-24
[390] Proverbs 17:22; 23:7
[391] Proverbs 19:23, Proverbs 4:20-22
[392] Exodus 20:9, 10
[393] Ecclesiastes 2:22-23; 5:12; Psalm 127:2
[394] Isaiah 52:11
[395] 1 Corinthians 9:25
[396] Philippians 4:5
[397] Ecclesiastes 3:13

11. Help those who are in need. *Isaiah 58:6-8*. We help the poor and needy, but we need to improve our own health. It would be good to join a club, gym or a health partner, to get advice on healthy eating tips and exercise, and ways to lose weight or restore your health.

If you choose your 'own ways' in which God 'delighted not,' will cost people their eternal salvation.[398] The people of God's new kingdom will obey His health laws, and there will be no sickness or disease. They will be blessed with eternal vigor and youth, and will live with God in supreme joy and happiness throughout all eternity.

1 Timothy 4:4: *"Every creature of God is good, and nothing to be refused..."*

This Scripture refers to meats that God created to be received with thanksgiving. God accepted these animals, sanctified by God's Word to say they are 'clean,' and by a 'prayer' of blessing when offered before the meal.[399] This will eliminate any poisons or defiling the body in anyway, once it has been blessed and prepared, with no blood or fat. God will destroy people who try to 'sanctify themselves' while eating unclean food.[400]

Matthew 15:11, NIV: "What goes into a man's mouth does not make him 'unclean,' but what comes out of his mouth, that is what makes him 'unclean.'"

Matthew 15:2-3, 10, 16-20, refers to those eating without washing their hands first. The focus is not so much on eating, but washing. The Scribes taught that eating any food without a special ceremonial washing defiled the eater. Yet, Jesus pointed out to the Scribes (religious leaders), it is not literally washing your hands defiles a person, but what is in your own heart defiles a person. In Verse 2, it speaks about the tradition of the elders, not the Law of Moses.[401] It was the oral tradition with the interpretations of the law. Additionally, both of these charges were an outgrowth of the accusations of the Scribes and Pharisees. Some religions tend to interpret the Bible to their own understanding, and follow certain traditions today.

Here, they washed their hands ceremonially to remove defilement, not for hygienic purposes.[402] Jesus answered the accusations of the Scribes and Pharisees with a question, "Why do you also transgress the commandment of God because of your tradition?"[403] Do we find ourselves caught up in tradition or following God's commandments? Pharisees challenged Jesus for His disciples' violation of the teachings of former rabbis. Jesus challenged them back with their traditions, instead of abiding to the commandments of the Lord. Moreover, the Scribes and Pharisees placed

---

[398] Isaiah 66:3, 4, 17
[399] Leviticus 11; Deuteronomy 14
[400] Isaiah 66:17
[401] Mark 7:3
[402] See Mark 7:2-4
[403] Matthew 15:3

their own views above the revelation of God, and yet claimed to be following Him. Jesus rebuked the Scribes and Pharisees for being so obsessed with traditions that they failed to observe basic commandments.[404] Jesus chided them for being so concerned with external ceremonial washings and dietary regulations that they failed to deal with character. It is what you say and think that makes you unclean. This statement offended the Pharisees, who were very concerned about what people ate and drank. Does this statement offend you too coming from the mouth of Jesus Christ? Please take heed to God's Word.

In *Matthew 15, Verse 19*, it lists certain evils such as murders, thefts and adulteries. However, Jesus determined in *Matthew 15, Verse 20: "These are the things, which defile a man, but to eat with unwashed hands does not defile a man."* We work hard to keep our outward appearance attractive, but what is in our hearts is even more important.[405] The way we are deep down, our souls, our spirits, where others cannot see, what truly matters to God. What are you like inside? When people become believers of Jesus Christ, God makes them different on the inside. He will continue the process of change inside them if they only ask. God wants us to seek healthy thoughts and motives, not just healthy food and exercise.

---

[404] Mark 7:11-13
[405] Mark 7:16-20

~Let Your Day Begin With Christ, Day 17~

Let your Day Begin Activity: Make a list of ten things that you can add to your everyday activity. Take the activity, one day at a time, for a total of ten days. When you start the first day, do number one, on the second day, do number one and two, on the third day, do number one, two, and three. For you to live a healthy life, it has to be a lifestyle change.

Today's Questions:

If we follow God's law on diet and exercise, will we be free from diseases and sickness? True or False.

What are some ideas not to overeat or glutton?

Review to Begin your Day with Christ:

1 Timothy 4:3-5: what does this passage mean? Some would view this Scripture as abstaining from unnatural foods or processed foods.

What are some harmful substances God wants us to avoid putting in our bodies? Why does Satan want you to put these harmful substances in your body?

Day Begins 18: Exercise

Get Plenty Of Exercise

First, we will look at ways to improve your body image:

1. *Exercise*: can do wonders for body image. 87% of women say exercise improves the way they feel about their bodies. Try dancing, yoga, walking, biking, etc. The average woman should get 30-60 minutes of exercise a day and at least three times a week.
2. *Accentuate the positive*: even the toughest self-critics can take pride in their eyes, hair, hands, or some other body part. Zero in on what you like rather than what you hate.
3. *Pamper yourself*: enjoy your body by indulging in small, sensual pleasures such as soaking in a scented bath, lather on lotion, get a massage, and wear sexy attire.
4. *Use Visualization*: recall times with parents, lovers, or friends have used uncomplimentary (terrible) names to your body such as fat-so, big, double-chin, etc. and imagine yourself stripping off those labels one by one. Visualization is a key to becoming comfortable and at peace with your body and yourself.
5. *Give yourself time*: transforming the way you feel about your body is a slow process.

Second, answer these questions below. Are you hung up about your weight?

1. My life would be better if only I could lose some weight. True or False
2. I often eat when I am upset, depressed, anxious, or angry, to feel better. True or False
3. I tend to overeat in social situations. True or False
4. I avoid mirrors. True or False
5. I keep eating even when I am full. True or False
6. If I ate whenever I wanted to, I would get very fat. True or False
7. I choose clothes that hide the size of my body. True or False
8. I often feel guilty after I eat. True or False
9. I am afraid to have a taste of dessert because I might lose control and eat too much. True or False
10. I have tried many diets. True or False
11. I prefer to make love in the dark because I am too embarrassed about my body. True or False
12. I eat even when I don't feel hungry. True or False
13. I compare my body unfavorably with those of others. True or False
14. I eat normally when I am with friends, but when I am by myself, I tend to pig out. True or False
15. I think about food nearly all the time. True or False
16. I am embarrassed about the fact that I like to eat. True or False

If you answered **five or fewer True**: Congratulations. You are in tune with your hunger and you have resisted the pressures at a social or cultural gathering that causes women to be dissatisfied with their bodies. If you answered **six or more True**: You probably realize that your relationship with food and your view of your body are slightly troubled. Try to ease up on yourself, and take steps to relearn a more natural way of eating.

The Bible talks about avoiding overeating. To be careful when eating with an important or influential person (or social gathering) since it causes you to eat more.[406] No good will come from the meal. Why exercise? It takes more than physical components to look good. Moreover, exercising and eating healthy can prevent high blood pressure, heart disease, high cholesterol levels, strokes and some cancers. Many people wait until their physician to inform them of the at-risk conditions before engaging in any physical activities. Then, one wants to find the nearest gym, or sign up for some physical activity program, expecting physical trainers to provide them with results.

It could all be avoided by practicing self-discipline and self-control. Exercising on a consistent basis, at least 3-5 days a week, will lower blood pressure, increase energy level, build muscle mass, reduce risk factors for stroke and heart disease, and much more. Anyone who lives a sedentary lifestyle needs to incorporate some form of exercise into his or her daily lives. Do it for your loved ones. You will be amazed at the way you will feel after a day of exercising. There are benefits of exercise: a prescription for prevention. If your doctor gave you a prescription for medication, would you take it? Obesity is the fastest growing health threat.

Below are the benefits of taking your prescription of exercise:

- ❖ Improves working memory, reaction time and working IQ
- ❖ Feels sick 30% less often
- ❖ Relieves stress
- ❖ Eight (8) times less likely to die from cardiovascular disease
- ❖ Four (4) times less likely to die from cancer
- ❖ Decreases blood pressure
- ❖ Improves lipid profile
- ❖ Improves body composition, increases muscle mass and decreases fat
- ❖ Increases metabolic rate
- ❖ Improves tolerance of arthritis
- ❖ Helps prevent bone loss and osteoporosis
- ❖ Slows down muscle atrophy which occurs with age
- ❖ Decreases the need for insulin if diabetic
- ❖ Helps relaxation in response to stress
- ❖ Helps smokers in kicking the habit
- ❖ Moderates depression and increase a sense of optimism

---

[406] Proverbs 23:1-3

- ❖ Improves sex life
- ❖ Fifty (50%) less likely to get breast cancer
- ❖ Less likely to develop varicose veins
- ❖ Improves skin
- ❖ Improves sleep and helps prevent insomnia

--SB (Spiritually Beautiful) Fitness Inc.

Body Fat And Its Relationship To Your Health

Get a scale that measures, not only your weight, but also body fat.

Body fat: 18.5-24.9 -- normal
25.0-29.9 -- overweight
30.0—34.9 -- obese

Too much body fat can cause serious health problems, diabetes, cancer, heart disease, etc.

1) *Apple shaped*: stores fat around abs increases risk of developing heart disease and diabetes
2) *Pear shaped*: stored fat around hips and thighs have lesser risk
3) *Overweight*: increased body weight relative to height
4) *Obesity*: high amount of fat relative to lean muscle

How to reduce body fat?

1) Cardiovascular exercises or strength training
2) Diet
3) Eat throughout the day (small portions)
4) Consistency -- very important

--SB (Spiritually Beautiful) Fitness Inc.

Four	Body	Types	Exercise	Other
Endomorph	High percentage of body fat and gains weight easily	Gains mainly in the lower body	Aerobics, power walking, jump rope, biking at low intensity (60 % of maximum heart rate) for 40-60 minutes, 4 days a week. Strength training for 15 minutes, 2 to 3 days as week. Lower abdominal	Aerobics to reduce body fat and maintain optimum weight. To lose weight, increase your aerobic activity to 5 days a week. Avoid step aerobics, ankle weights, and stair climbing. Focus on

			exercises. Stretch for 5 min before and after every workout.	upper body to draw away from heavier body
Mesomorph	Large chest and thick waist with narrow hips and slender legs. Usually have tight joints, prone to exercise-related injuries.	Tends to be muscular with a lower body-fat % and a lean physique.	Aerobics include running, step classes, and stair climbing at high intensity (70% to 85% for maximum heart rate for 30 minutes, 3 to 4 days a week. Strength training for 15 minutes, 3 days a week, focusing on your lower body to balance your physique.	To lose weight, add an extra day of aerobics since your upper body is naturally muscular, avoid rowing machines and swimming. Develop flexibility by doing yoga or Tai Chi or stretch-oriented classes, at least 15 minutes, 5 days a week.
Ectomorph	Hips and chest are in proportion, but inflexible and lack strength.	Quick metabolism and an athletic wiry physique.	All types of aerobics including running, swimming, rowing machine, and step aerobics at medium intensity (60 % maximum heart rate) for 20 minutes, 3 to 4 days a week.	For weight loss, add an extra day of aerobics. Emphasize strength training using heavier weights for upper and lower body for 30-40 minutes, 3-4 days a week. Focus on abdominal strengthening exercises at least 15 minutes before

				and after ever workout. More prone for back injuries.
Meso-endomorph	Hips and chest are in proportion.	Lean muscles with body fat and good flexibility.	All types of aerobics including swimming, power walking and biking at low intensity (60% of your maximum heart rate) for 40-60 minutes, 4 days a week. Use light weights with multiple repetitions for 15 minutes, 3 days a week. Focus on lower abdominal exercise. Stretch for at least 5 minutes before and after every workout.	Increase to 5 days for weight loss.

Genetics play a key role in determining your physical potential. If you exercise according to your particular body type to reduce body fat, improve your cardiovascular fitness level, and increase lean muscles mass—you will look and feel great no mater what size you are.

Three Step Guide To Losing Weight And Feeling Great

Step 1: Eating Smart
- ❖ Eat a variety of foods.
- ❖ Balance the food you eat with physical activity to maintain or improve your weight.
- ❖ Choose a diet with plenty of vegetables, fruits, and grain products.
- ❖ Choose a diet moderate in sugar.
- ❖ Choose a diet moderate in salt and sodium.
- ❖ If you drink alcoholic beverages, do it in moderation.
- ❖ Choose a diet low in fat, saturated fat, and cholesterol.

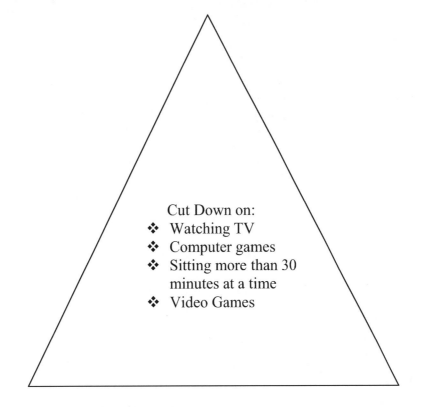

Cut Down on:
- ❖ Watching TV
- ❖ Computer games
- ❖ Sitting more than 30 minutes at a time
- ❖ Video Games

Step 2: Energize with Exercise
❖ The Activity Chart

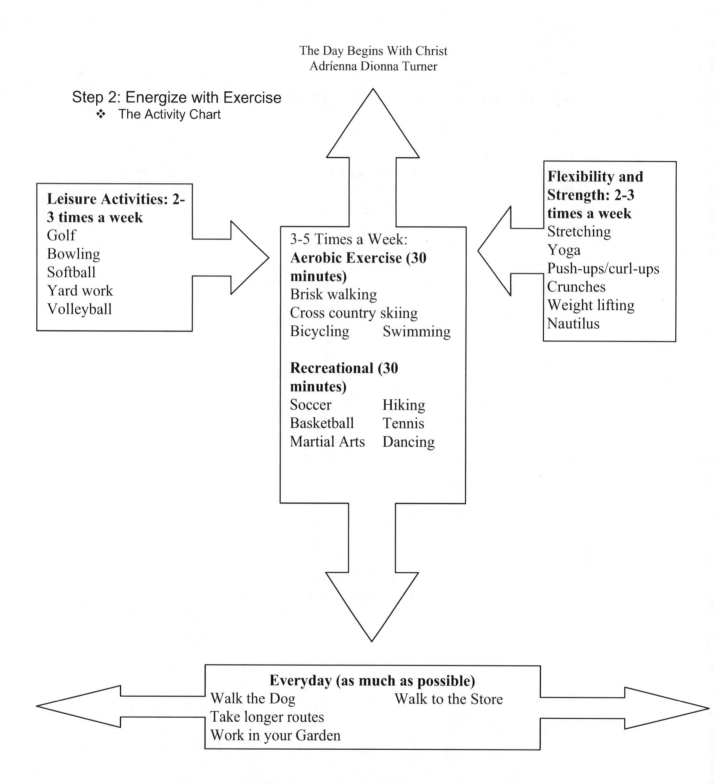

Leisure Activities: 2-3 times a week
Golf
Bowling
Softball
Yard work
Volleyball

3-5 Times a Week:
Aerobic Exercise (30 minutes)
Brisk walking
Cross country skiing
Bicycling   Swimming

Recreational (30 minutes)
Soccer   Hiking
Basketball   Tennis
Martial Arts Dancing

Flexibility and Strength: 2-3 times a week
Stretching
Yoga
Push-ups/curl-ups
Crunches
Weight lifting
Nautilus

Everyday (as much as possible)
Walk the Dog   Walk to the Store
Take longer routes
Work in your Garden

❖ *Keep a daily tracker:* Exercise 3-5 times per week for 20 to 30 minutes is recommended for overall health and fitness. Weight loss will occur more quickly if exercise is increased to 5 times per week for 40 to 60 minutes. Keep track of your daily exercise: calories burned in various activities.

Date	Activity	Time (in minutes)	Calories burned

❖ *Target your heart rate:* during your exercise session, pause, and take your pulse to check your exercise intensity or training heart rate -- check your carotid artery (on either side of the center of your neck), or your radial artery (wrist). You can find your rate by subtracting your age from 220.

Target Heart Rate Chart: 10-Second Count, Allowable Maximum %

Age	60%	70%	75%	80%	85%
Under 20	21	25	26	28	30
25	20	23	25	27	28
30	19	22	24	25	27
35	19	22	23	25	26
40	18	21	23	24	26
45	18	21	22	23	25
50	17	20	21	23	24
55	17	19	21	22	23
60	16	19	20	21	22
65	16	18	19	20	21
70	15	18	19	20	21
75	15	17	18	19	21

Source: Stretching, Inc. PO BOX 768, Palmer Lake, CO 80133

Step 3: Go for the Goals
❖ Short term goals:
  o Eating a piece of fruit instead of a doughnut
  o Walking during your lunch break instead of sitting in the cafeteria
  o Using jelly or jam on your bagel instead of peanut butter or cream cheese
❖ Long term goals:
  o Maintaining a healthy weight
  o Establishing a regular exercise routine
  o Maintaining a healthy eating pattern

Setbacks: Do not put yourself down for setbacks; we all have them. If you ate six chocolate chip cookies yesterday, just forget about it and move on. A common mistake made after overeating is that people fast or skip meals, which causes hunger and frustration. Follow your healthy eating plan with your next meal.

Rewards: You can reward yourself each time you reach a goal; just make sure it is not food. Take a long, luxurious bubble bath or get a professional massage.

Dubious Diets: Beware Of The Pitfalls Of Some Of The Most Popular Diets

The Diet	The Concerns
Low-Calorie Diets: (Under 1200 calories per day) Limited amounts of food: protein, complex carbohydrates, and fat.	⬥ RDA guidelines for daily nutrients often are not met ⬥ Although weight loss is often two to three pounds a week, it is usually water weight, and gaining it back more likely than with slower loss diets
High Carbohydrate and High Fiber Diets: Whole grains, cereals, raw fruits, and vegetables, some protein, and dairy products. Highly processed foods are discouraged.	⬥ High amounts of fiber may reduce the absorption of minerals
Liquid Diets: Powers and liquids are consumed as a meal replacement.	⬥ Most people quit due to lack of variety ⬥ Healthful eating habits are not established ⬥ Can cause constipation ⬥ May cause menstrual problems if calorie level is too low ⬥ Due to large amounts of water lost with very low calorie liquid diets, when normal eating is resumed, the body compensates by retaining massive amounts of fluid, which can dilute the body's potassium, causing abnormal heart rhythms ⬥ Use of these products is safer, if used daily for one meal only, with two meals of regular foods
High Protein Diets: High protein foods, such as chicken and cottage cheese are emphasized.	⬥ Can increase levels of blood fat and cholesterol ⬥ May cause menstrual problems ⬥ Dehydration ⬥ Osteoporosis ⬥ Aggravation of gout ⬥ Kidney stones or kidney failure
Single Food Diets: Only one type of food such as grapefruit or rice is allowed.	⬥ RDA guidelines for daily nutrients often are not met or are excessive in some areas ⬥ Most people quit due to lack of variety ⬥ Healthful eating habits are not established

Fasting: Water and any beverages without calories are allowed.	⬇ RDA guidelines for daily nutrients often are not met ⬇ Low blood pressure ⬇ Emotional disturbances ⬇ Death if prolonged ⬇ Healthful eating habits are not established
Do not fall for the diet gimmicks: it does not melt away extra weight and they can be costly. The safety of many gimmicks could be an issue. If losing weight were that easy, we would be a nation of very slender people.	⬇ A daily program of healthy, well-balanced diet and regular exercise is what works -- there are no overnight, instant or magic cures for weight loss

--Betty Crocker's New Eat and Lose Weight, 1996

Before turning to medical professionals for help to lose weight, try some of these simple solutions:

- ❖ Support from family, peers, and friends by encouraging one another to lose weight, or find someone that is in your shoes that is on the way to losing weight too. You are able to share secrets, methods that work, stories about how one feels about being overweight, struggles, and strategies to want to lose the weight.
- ❖ Simply limit food choices by not having any chocolate, candy, or ice cream in the house. Read food labels, check the sugar level, partially hydrogenated fats or MSG (check for other hidden names used in the place of MSG). Read the ingredients or chemicals that are listed on the labels of the food your purchase. For instance, 'partially hydrogenated' in potato chips will cause you to remain overweight. Find other snacks that are healthy and good for your body, remember our bodies are God's temple we have to take care of.
- ❖ Ban nighttime eating; try not to snack after 8:30 p.m. At first, it may seem difficult to break bad habits, but take a step at a time, and have faith that you will reach your goal once you take that first step to stopping. You will be able to see the weight results once you decide to stop eating snacks late.
- ❖ Stop dieting and start eating. Restricting calories by more than 500 a day, (conversant mode), slowing down metabolism by 20%, equals starvation. Eating regularly and exercising moderately burns more calories than someone who skips a meal and exercises.
- ❖ Aerobic exercise: 30-45 minutes can burn 400-500 calories per session.
- ❖ Weight training increases lean body mass and boost metabolic rate (best results after aerobic, bicycling, or pumping your heart rate).
- ❖ Metabolic rate=calories
  - o Formula: 665+(4.36*weight (lbs))+(4.32*height (in.))-(4.7*age (yrs))
- ❖ Plenty of sleep stimulates the body to burn more fat.

Stay Slim Tips:
- ❖ Try making a change for three weeks.
- ❖ 3-5 oz. of meat (size of your palm), half cup of potatoes, rice or pasta, medium piece of fruit (size of a fist).
- ❖ Spicy foods to speed up your metabolism; satisfy with small portions.
- ❖ Eat fruits and vegetables: receive your vitamins, minerals, fiber, fewer calories, and no fat. Five servings a day.
- ❖ Quench your hunger (hungry between meals, drink glass of water, wait for 15 minutes, 10 minutes before a meal, cuts appetite).
- ❖ Switch to light bread, sugar-free gelatin, read pasta sauce labels.
- ❖ Fry in cooking spray: sprit of canola or olive oil.
- ❖ Sauté stir-fry in bouillon, omit butter or margarine in rice, pasta, dried potatoes (baked).
- ❖ Low-fat or fat-free products.
- ❖ Snooze to loose (sleep more).

48 Steps To Losing Weight
(http://thriveonline.oxyGenesisesiscom/weight/52_small_steps/weight_loss/foods_to_eat/)
1. Double veggies (3-5 servings daily), which will appease hunger and shrink your waistline.
2. Skinless chicken can be marinade in BBQ sauce, basting sauce such as Teriyaki, and eat no more than 3 oz. of lean meat.
3. Drink less juice and eat more fruit. For example, orange juice has more calories than cola. Eat bananas, oranges, apples, watermelon, and other types of fruits.
4. Eat whole grains: whole wheat bread, pasta, or multigrain at least once a week.
5. Add veggies to lunch.
6. Dump the donut; replace it with English Muffins. You can add all-natural peanut butter or light cream cheese instead of butter or margarine.
7. Easy on the cheese: Low-fat, feta, parmesan.
8. More veggies in your sandwich (salad/tomatoes)
9. Lean ground turkey or chicken.
10. Skip soda and try flavored water.
11. Match grains with veggies (cup of rice or pasta is about 200 calories).
12. Switch to low fat milk, soy milk, almond milk, or Rice Dream.
13. Munch on pre-dinner veggies: carrots, celery, etc.
14. Veggie Pie: veggie pizza or more veggies than meat.
15. Scream for less ice cream: Cut back on the scoops (try 2).
16. Dress down salad (2-3 tablespoons of dressing).
17. Do not desert dessert.
18. Smaller bags of chips.
19. Snack smartly.

Exercises to Try: Fitness Planner, Weightlifting, Tae-Bo, Tai Chi, Yoga, etc.
20. Lap around the mall.
21. Get off bus early (extra block to walk or so).

22. Music and dance around the house.
23. Buy exercise gear: athletic shoes lose their cushion after 6 months of regular use, and can cause knee and ankle injury.
24. Unload one bag at a time when grocery shopping.
25. Quick walks (5 minutes a day, at least 35 minutes a week).
26. Outdoor activities: mow lawn, rake, or shovel.
    a. Raking burns 111 calories in a ½ hour.
    b. Mowing burns 225 calories in a ½ hour.
    c. Shoveling burns 557 calories in an hour.
27. Wash car weekly at least up to 30 minutes, which will burn 120 calories or 4 calories a minute.
28. Walk while you talk.
29. Deliver message by hand.
30. Take a long walk or long way.
31. Active outings such as softball, volleyball, etc.
32. Exercise with family and friends.
33. Stop sitting at the TV.

Habits to Change:
34. Eat breakfast.
35. Shop smartly.
36. Hide serving bowls (not to eat extra).
37. Walk off anxiety.
38. Put your fork down (enjoy your food).
39. Measure your portions once a week. For example, eat 3 oz. of meat for lunch and dinner (women's palm), and a cup of rice, pasta, veggies (women's fist).
40. Snacks: crackers, popcorn, pretzels, and corn chips (avoid vending machine snacks).
41. Sleep (at least 7-8 hours a day).
42. Stop munching, find things to do instead.
43. Eat before you drink alcohol.
44. Stop before getting stuffed.
45. Keep out of the kitchen.
46. Chart your success (food log).
47. Celebrate without food.
48. 3 meals, 2 snacks a day.

Stop Postpartum Weight Gain

Many women find they have become obese after pregnancy. They think that they ate too much, or did not exercise hard enough. However, studies show that women who gain weight after delivery, typically moms who are 60-70 pounds overweight, may have inherited the tendency toward post-pregnancy heaviness. Women can outsmart her Genesis's. Here are some tips below.

During pregnancy:
- ❖ Watch your calories: Pregnant women need only 300 extra calories daily, which comes from healthy meals. Take 400 mcg of folic acid.

After pregnancy:
- ❖ Breast-feed your baby: Women who nurse return to their pre-pregnancy weight faster than those who do not. Breast-feeding burns 500 calories a day.
- ❖ Do not eat too much: Women who gained weight were eating more after their pregnancy than before – a more stressful lifestyle could be the reason.
- ❖ Keep active: Many first time mothers say they cannot find the time to exercise. However, doing everyday activities may require you to roll up your sleeves by mopping the floor, gardening, walking the dog, and cleaning the house, this will make a significant difference.

Where does the weight go? What expectant mothers can expect on the scale: The weight gain that occurs during pregnancy may be easier to accept if you understand where it is coming from. During the first trimester, most women gain 3-4 pounds. During the second and third, it is normal to put on a pound a week, resulting in a gain of 20-30 pounds.

- ❖ Blood volume: 3-4 lbs (usually in the breasts)
- ❖ Body fluid: 1-3 lbs (usually in the breasts)
- ❖ Uterus expansion: 1-3 lbs
- ❖ Amniotic fluid: 1-2 lbs (stomach)
- ❖ Baby: 7-8 lbs
- ❖ Placenta: 1-2 lbs (in womb)
- ❖ Fat and protein: 6-8 lbs (usually in the hips)

One should get plenty of exercise and fresh air:

Genesis 2:15: *"Then the Lord God took the man and put him in the Garden of Eden to tend and keep it."*

The Garden was perfectly prepared. It was man's home, and he had to tend to it and keep it. Even paradise required work.[407] Therefore, we are to tend to the bodies that God has blessed us with and to be healthy.

Personal Hygiene

Isaiah 52:11: *"Depart! Depart! Go out from there, touch no unclean thing; Go out from the midst of her. Be clean, you who bear the vessels of the Lord."*

---

[407] Genesis 1:28

~Let Your Day Begin With Christ, Day 18~

Let your Day Begin Activity: At the beginning of your day, answer the 16 questions. Review to Begin your Day with Christ list under each goal (get a notebook or join a Free Online Diet Journal). Free Online Diet Journal: http://www.my-calorie-counter.com (sign up today).

Today's Questions:

What steps will work for you today and can add throughout the week?

Will you follow how to stay slim once you get to your ideal weight? If so, buy an exercise/food journal to keep track of your progress.

What time of the day will you exercise? How many days a week? How long?

Review to Begin your Day with Christ:
Body fat and its relationship to your health
- Do you have too much body fat? Review on how to reduce body fat and jot it down. Write at least four ways to reduce body fat in your diet. This is the beginning stage.

Eating smart
- Today, review the eating list. In the cutting down smart triangle diagram, there are four items listed. Think of an active substitute in the place of it.

Energize with exercise
- Choose one activity on each of the following list. Start with the hardest thing from each list for you. Starting today, keep a daily tracker and write down how much exercise completed in each category.

Go for the goals
- Today's activity is not only to write down everything that you are eating, but also to make a conscious effort follow the list in the book and eat everything healthy. Make an effort to start daily since it is a lifestyle change, at least for today to see how it makes you feel.

Day Begins 19: Harmful Substances For Your Body

Clean From Drugs, Alcohol, Tobacco, And Other Harmful Substances

The soothing comfort of alcohol is temporary. Real relief comes from dealing with the cause of the anguish and sorrow and turning to God for peace.[408] Do not lose yourself in alcohol. For instance, Israel was a wine-producing country. In the Old Testament, winepresses bursting with new wine were considered a sign of blessing. Wisdom is even said to have set her table with wine.[409] Nonetheless, the Old Testament writers were alert to the dangers of wine. It dulls the senses, it limits clear judgment,[410] it lowers the capacity for control,[411] it destroys a persons' efficiency.[412] To make wine, usually was a means of self-indulgence, or an escape from life, is to misuse it and invite the consequences of the drunkard.[413]

> Proverbs 20:1: *"Wine is a mocker, strong drink is a brawler, and whoever is led astray by it is not wise."*

This is a warning against the abuse of wine, or excessive drinking. A wise person takes the danger seriously. There is no wisdom in drunkenness, only brawling and confusion.[414] Please take heed that God loves you, and does not want you to misuse your bodies with liquor, drugs, or other harmful substances. It leads to confusion and more depression, and temporary relief is not the answer, Jesus is the answer. Do you want eternal happiness or temporary enjoyment that will not last once the liquor or drugs wear off? Harmful substances are slowly destroying your body, death, when you can be filled with the Holy Spirit forever. You can read more information about these substances that are harmful to your body in *Day Begins 44: Does Your Social Life Seem Empty?*

---

[408] Proverbs 23:29-35
[409] Proverbs 9:2, 5
[410] Proverbs 31:1-9
[411] Proverbs 4:17
[412] Proverbs 21:17
[413] Life Application Study Bible, NKJV, 1996.
[414] Nelson Study Bible, NKJV.

~Let Your Day Begin With Christ, Day 19~

Let your Day Begin Activity: Take time to evaluate all the harmful substances you are putting in your body. Try to find alternative things to do or find something else to replace your cigarette smoking, drinking alcohol, or any other harmful substances today. Pray to God to remove these addictions from your body and mind.

Today's Questions:

Do you want to be healthier? What are some steps you are willing to take to stop your bad habits such as smoking, drinking, etc?

Do you trust God in helping taking away these addictions?

Review to Begin your Day with Christ:

God loves you. Acknowledge what you are doing to your body. Take it slow. Change your thinking process, replace your bad habits with something good and after 30 days, you should be able to kick the habit.

Find Scriptures in the Bible on alcohol, smoking, and other harmful substances—moderation is not suitable since it is a slow death. We want to please God, not us.

Day Begins 20: Is God Involved In Your Home?

Job prayed that God would bless his home.[415] Through our daily prayers, we can ask God to bless our homes while we are away, raising our children, and taking care of our significant other, and to keep a peaceful environment within the boundaries of our home. Homes can be a place of worship. We can lift our praise and have a secret place for our prayers. Additionally, our homes can be a place for business, home schooling, and church services, and/or conducting Bible studies.

According to *John 14:22-23*, the disciples were still expecting Jesus to establish an earthly kingdom and overthrow Rome. Yet, the disciples found it difficult to articulate why Jesus did not tell the world that He was the Messiah. Judas, one of the disciples, had high expectations that the Messiah would free them from the horrifying earthly realm and make paradise on the earthly home. For instance, the paradise Adam and Eve experienced in the Garden of Eden, were later driven out because of their disobedience. However, Jesus was referring to our heavenly home, not here on earth.

Not everyone could understand Jesus' message since He spoke in parables. From the time at the Pentecost, the gospel of the kingdom has been proclaimed in the whole world, but not everyone is receptive to it. Jesus saves the deepest Revelation of Himself for those who love and obey Him.[416] Make our home with Him. If a believer loves and obeys the Lord, he or she will experience the true fellowship with God.[417]

Fellowship in Revelation 3:20, NLT: "Look! I stand at the door and knock. If you hear my voice and open the door, I will come in, and we will share a meal together as friends."

Jesus is knocking on the door of our hearts. Every time that we sense His presence, we can rely on Him. Jesus wants fellowship with us and He wants us to open up to Him. He is patient, not persistent, in trying to get through to us to come to Him. He is knocking at the door, small tabs at our hearts, and only waiting for us to open up to receive Him. He is not breaking and entering, but knocking. He allows us to decide to come to Him. Do you intentionally keep His life-changing presence and power on the other side of the door?[418] This fellowship with the Lord can start in your home. There is open fellowship. *Open fellowship* can also be viewed as hospitality.

In *Philemon 1:2*, the early churches often would meet in people's homes. Because of sporadic persecutions and great expense involved, church buildings were typically not constructed then.[419] Paul reflected on Philemon's love and faith. Philemon had opened his heart and his home to the church. We should do likewise, opening

---

[415] Job 29:4
[416] Life Application Study Bible, NKJV and emphasis added by the author.
[417] Nelson Study Bible, NKJV and emphasis added by the author.
[418] Life Application Study Bible, NKJV, 1996.
[419] Life Application Study Bible, NKJV, 1996.

ourselves and our homes to others, offering Christian fellowship to refresh people's hearts.[420]

> *Hebrews 13:2, NLT: "Don't forget to show hospitality to strangers, for some who have done this have entertained angels without realizing it!"*

There were three Old Testament people known as "unwittingly entertained angels."[421] They appeared to Abraham,[422] Gideon,[423] and Manoah.[424]

Some people say that they cannot be hospitable because their homes are not large enough or adequate. If you have a table and two chairs in a rented room, there are people who would be grateful to spend time in your home. Are there visitors to your church with whom you could share a meal? Do you know single people who would enjoy an evening of conversation? Is there any way your home could meet the needs of traveling missionaries. *Hospitality* simply means making other people feel comfortable and at home.[425] We can also conduct small group sessions in our homes even conduct choir practices and social outlets with believers.

> *Acts 5:42: "And daily in the temple, and in every house, they did not cease teaching and preaching Jesus as the Christ."*

Home bible studies are not new. As babes in Christ, we are to grow in our new faith. Therefore, home bible study met these needs. *Serving* also is introducing new believers to the Christian faith. During times of persecution, meeting in homes is the primary method of acquiring biblical knowledge. Followers of Jesus Christ throughout the world still use this approach when under persecution as a tool to upsurge believers.[426]

Jesus said that those who minister are to be cared for. The disciples could expect food and shelter in return for spiritual service they provided. Who ministers to you? Make sure you take care of the pastors, missionaries, and teachers who serve God by serving you.[427]

Moreover, the disciples' mission was short-term. In essence, they were to do a national survey to determine the people's response to Jesus as the Messiah. Each of the twelve disciples covered an area of about 75-125 miles radius. They did not need

---

[420] Philemon 4-7, Life Application Study Bible, NKJV, 1996.

[421] Life Application Study Bible, NKJV, 1996.

[422] Genesis 18:1, Genesis 19:1-4

[423] Judges 6:11

[424] Judges 13:2

[425] Genesis 12:14-16; 24:12-33; Ruth 2:14; Judges 19:1-10; 1 Kings 10:11-13; 2 Kings 6:18-23; Job 31:32; Psalm 101:7; 1 Corinthians 16:10-11; 1 Peter 4:9

[426] Life Application Study Bible, NKJV, emphasis added by author.

[427] See 1 Corinthians 9:9-10; 1 Timothy 5:17; also derived from Life Application Study Bible, NKJV, 1996: Matthew 10:10.

extensive provisions since people would provide meals or food on their journey and open their homes to meet their needs.[428]

In *Luke 10:7-10*, Jesus' direction to stay in one house avoided certain problems. [429] Shifting from house to house could offend the families who first took them in. Some families might begin to compete for disciples' presence. Some might think they were not good enough to hear their message. If the disciples appeared not to appreciate the hospitality offered them, the town might not accept Jesus, when he followed them there. In addition, by staying in one place, the disciples did not have to worry continually about getting good accommodations. They could settle down and do their appointed task.

Jesus told his disciples to accept hospitality graciously because their work entitled them to it. Ministers spreading the gospel of Jesus Christ deserve to be supported and it is our responsibility to make sure they have what they need. While serving in the ministry, several methods to remain encouraged. First, they make a decent salary. Second, there is a support system, or an event planner. Third, lift their spirits with special surprises occasionally. Our ministers deserve to know that we are giving to them cheerfully and generously. Jesus gave two rules for the disciples to follow as they traveled. They were to eat what was set before them by accepting hospitality without being picky and they were commanded to heal the sick. Because of the healing, people are willing to listen to the gospel.[430]

Church leadership (hospitality) in *Titus 1:5: "The things that are lacking,"* is the unfinished work of establishing correct teaching and appointing elders in every town. Paul had appointed elders in various churches during his journeys.[431] Furthermore, Paul was unable to stay at each church that was built, but he knew these new churches needed strong spiritual leadership. The men chosen were to lead the congregation by teaching sound doctrine, helping believers mature spiritually, and equipping them to live a life for Jesus Christ, despite opposition.[432] Additionally, Paul briefly described some qualifications that the elders or church leaders should have. For example, Paul had given Timothy a similar set of instructions for the church in Ephesus.[433] Most of the qualifications involve character, not knowledge or talent.

A person's lifestyle and relationship provides a window into his or her character. Consider these qualifications as you evaluate a person for a position of leadership in your church. It is important to have leaders who can effectively preach God's Word, but even more important to have those who can live out God's Word to be examples for

---

[428] Nelson Study Bible, NKJV and emphasis added by the author.

[429] See also Hospitality, Jesus is speaking to his disciples: Matthew 10: 9-10, 40-42; Luke 10:5-8

[430] Life Application Study Bible, NKJV, and emphasis added by the author.

[431] Acts 14:23

[432] Life Application Study Bible, NKJV, and emphasis added by author.

[433] 1 Timothy 3:1-7; 5:22

others to follow.[434] Other examples of hospitality can be found in the book of *Judges 19:12-21*.

Woman's role in the church or church leadership, *1 Corinthians 14:34, 35*: *"Let your women keep silent in churches, for they are not permitted to speak: but they are to be submissive, as the law also says. And if they want to learn something, let them ask their own husbands at home: for it is shameful for women to speak in the church."*

Does this mean that women are not to speak in church services today? Women prayed and prophesied in public worship.[435] It is also clear that women are given spiritual gifts and is encouraged to exercise them in the body of Christ.[436] Women have much to contribute and can participate in worship service.

Nonetheless, Corinthian women were not allowed to confront men in public. Apparently, some of the women who had become followers of Jesus Christ gave them the right to question the men during public worship service. However, this was causing division in the church. Women of that day did not receive formal religious education as men did. Women may have been raising questions during worship service, which could have been answered at home without disrupting church service. Plainly, Paul was asking women not to flaunt their Christian freedom during worship.

The purpose of Paul's words was to promote unity within the body of Christ, not to teach women about their roles in the church.[437] Today, there are women pastors, evangelist, and other ministries that are led by women. If God calls on women to do His business, man cannot scrutinize a woman's role in the church or a ministry. The Bible speaks against judging one's role in the church. In addition, we are to edify and encourage believers, not excluding women pastors and women evangelists from participating in leadership roles in the church.

When to refuse hospitality, the Scriptures warn us not to envy the lifestyles of those who have become rich. We want to get stingy with our tithes and offering. Furthermore, we will gain their favor by fawning over them. Here, their friendship is fake, in which they will just use you for their own gain.[438] They only want to know how God is in you and how you were so blessed beyond humanly measure.

On the other hand, hospitality to those that cannot repay, Jesus advised people not to rush for the best places at a feast. People today are just as eager to raise their social status, whether by being with the right people, dress for success, or driving a luxury car. Whom do you try to impress? Rather than aiming for prestige, look for a

---

[434] Life Application Study Bible, NKJV, 1996.

[435] 1 Corinthians 11:5

[436] 1 Corinthians 11:12-14

[437] Life Application Study Bible, NKJV, and emphasis added by author.

[438] Life Application Study Bible, NKJV, and emphasis added by author.

place where you can serve. If God wants you to serve on a wider scale, He will invite you to take a higher place.

Jesus taught two lessons: He spoke to the guests, telling them not to seek places of honor. Service is more important in God's kingdom than status. Second, He told the host not to be exclusive about whom he invites. God opens His kingdom to everyone that wants to receive God's gifts, blessings, and to live with Him one day in the heavenly realm of true paradise.

~Let Your Day Begin With Christ, Day 20~

Let your Day Begin Activity: Today's activity is simple. For God to be involved in your home, He needs to be involved in the church. When is the last time you helped with any church activity? Today, take the time to contact your pastor or church official and ask them if you can help. We have a lot on our plates, but I do not think we are ever to busy to glorify God.

Today's Questions:

Do you pray daily to God to bless your home?

Jesus taught two lessons in hospitality, what are they?

Are you seeking joy and expecting the Messiah to establish an earthly kingdom or are you seeking an eternal home in the Heavenly Kingdom? Explain.

Are you willing to get involved in missionaries, church ministries, or open your home for small group functions?

Do you agree or disagree with women roles in the church?

Review to Begin your Day with Christ:

Refer to *Job 29:4* and *Leviticus 27:14* to bless our home.

Define Hospitality.

Church leadership uses your spiritual gifts and willingness to volunteer with your church activities.

Share your thoughts on women roles in the church.

Elaborate on church leadership versus women's roles in the church, any similarities or differences, or both.

Day Begins 21: Dedicating Your Home

Dedicate Your Home To The Lord And Responsibilities Within Your Living Quarters

Man and woman are to dedicate their homes to be holy to the Lord.[439] A man or father is the *head of the household*, which he can guide his family into the leadership under the Heavenly Father's covering. His family can follow his path or direction, and pray for spiritual wisdom, knowledge, and insight to continue to raise his family in the Lord, by following duties set aside for him. However, if you are a single female parent, this will make you the head of your household, and the one to make decisions in your home.

Joshua told his family that we would always glorify the Lord in his home. Will you follow Jesus' footsteps for you and your family? In taking a definite stand for the Lord, Joshua again displayed spiritual leadership. Regardless of what others thought, Joshua decided to stand on a commitment to God, and he was willing to set the example with those around him. The way we live, shows others our strength of our commitment to serving God. Is God living in your home?[440]

In *Genesis 28: 16, "Surely the Lord is in this place, and I did not know it."* Do you find yourself like Jacob, or wondering if God is in this place? God sets up a ladder for us to be in His presence. Yet, Satan wants us to be ignorant of God's promises for our lives and in our homes, to remain discouraged. See your ladder that God has set up for you by following two provisions. *Number one:* Faith in God's Word.[441] Sometimes, we are unable to see God's purpose. Are we seeking eternal life and operating in the perspective of God's Word? Alternatively, whoever contradicts the Word is living a lie, which is one of Satan's most powerful weapons used against unbelievers and believers. Only Jesus Christ can set you free. *Number two:* Believe in God's Word and that Jesus Christ is the one standing at the top of that ladder.[442] Through the authority and power of God's Word, we can overcome any principalities, demonic spirits, or anything that one is facing. God can release His angels for protection, direction, and come to the rescue.

During our spiritual walk, we are to rely on God to change our attitudes to have a godly character in our homes, in our lives, and for spiritual leadership. For example, Eli had spent his entire life in service to God. His responsibilities were to oversee all the worship in Israel. Consequently, in pursing this great mission, he neglected the responsibilities within his own home. Do not let your desire to do God's work cause you

---

[439] Leviticus 27:14

[440] Joshua 24:15, Nelson Study Bible, NKJV.

[441] Matthew 4:1-11

[442] John 1:51; Matthew 10:33

to neglect your own family. If you do, your mission may degenerate into a quest for personal importance, and your family will suffer the consequences of your neglect.[443]

On another note, no earthly city will ever give permanent peace to its inhabitants. Abraham realized that. Abraham left Ur, the great city of his day, and became a wanderer for God's sake. Although Abraham settled in Hebron, he realized that it could never be the fulfillment of his quest. He sought a holy city, which he is the Builder and the Maker is God. That city, the New Jerusalem, will be a place where all who love God can live together in lasting harmony. All physical death and sorrow will be done away with.

In the New Jerusalem, there will be neither church, nor mosque, nor temple, for God Himself will dwell there. The crystal river of life will flow from His throne, and the tree of life will feed and heal the nations. In that city, the family of God will be reunited for all eternity. Not just Jew, Gentile, and Arab, but people from 'every nation, tribe, people and language,' for we are all one family. Until then, neither the might of arms, nor the power of diplomacy, but only God's Spirit of lasting peace comes. Moreover, we all have a responsibility to bring about peace and reconciliation wherever we can. To that end, we can all pray for the peace of Jerusalem. We can pray that God's Spirit will soften hearts, and transform minds so that the killing will end, and even on this earth, Jerusalem can become the 'City of Peace.'[444]

In our household, we have to believe on the Lord Jesus Christ. When we recognize Jesus Christ as Lord, and trust in Him, our entire life and salvation is assured to us. If you have never trusted in Jesus to save you, whether it is in your household, church or public place, do it quickly. Your life can be filled with joy once you allow Jesus Christ in your home and life. The saying, 'Home Sweet Home,' will be sweet to have our Holy Savior living in your home or where you reside.

Eternal Home And Life

John 14:2: "In My Father's house are many mansions; if it were not so, I would have told you. I go to prepare a place for you."

Jesus' word illustrating the way to eternal life is secure, is to trust in Jesus Christ. However, you may unwilling to believe. This Scripture is describing *everlasting life,* see also *Matthew 19:29*, and rich in promises. Jesus is letting us know that He will prepare a place for us and will come again. We can look forward to eternal life because Jesus has promised it to all who believe in Him. Although the details of eternity are unknown, we need not fear since Jesus is preparing for us, and will spend eternity with us.[445] God responds: "And the posts of the door were shaken by the voice of Him, who cried out,

---

[443] 1 Samuel 3:13, Life Application Study Bible, NKJV, 1996.
[444] Ed Dickerson, "Signs of the Times," November 2004.
[445] John 14:1-3, Life Application Study Bible, NKJV, 1996.

and the house was filled with smoke."[446] If the doorposts of the heavenly temple shook in response to God's holiness, how much more will the whole earth shake when the Lord visits it?[447]

---

[446] Isaiah 6:4
[447] Isaiah 6:3; Matthew 24:29-30, Nelson Study Bible, NKJV

~Let Your Day Begin With Christ, Day 21~

Let your Day Begin Activity: Today take the time to do something for the Lord as a family. Even if it is praying, helping the church, volunteering, or participating in an activity to honor God.

Today's Questions:

Where is your eternal home? Do you allow God in your home?

How is your life spent here on earth?

Is there more you would like to contribute in building the Heavenly Kingdom? If so, what are some things and steps you will take to accomplish this goal as a Disciple for Jesus Christ?

Review to Begin your Day with Christ:

Just like Joshua, he made a statement that his family will honor God in his home.

Genesis 28:16, Message Bible: "God is in this place…this is God's house. This is the Gate of Heaven."

Review other Scriptures on eternal home and God in your home.

The ladder God set for you has two provisions: faith and belief in God's Word. Then, once we apply faith and belief in God's promises, He will release His angels for our protection, provision, direction, and rescue.

Day Begins 22: Singleness, Courtship, Marriage, And Children

Haplous means 'simple or single,'[448] 'singleness' purpose keeps us from the snare of having a double treasure and a divided heart. Another term for *singleness* is *aphelotes*, which denotes 'simplicity.' In *Acts 2:46*, the idea is an unalloyed benevolence expressed.[449] *Singleness* can refer to someone that is separated from his or her spouse through divorce or separation, and those that have never been married.

What is the major problem being single? Usually most single people think that they have to mingle and date someone. No one wants to be alone. Bodies are craving to be with that someone to hold, cherish, admire, and to love. Are these cravings natural or lust? However, what standards are we following: God's or the worlds? In a dating relationship with the opposite sex, we tend to confuse the feelings of infatuation, lust, and love.

Infatuation is derived from the word, *infatuate*, meaning to make a fool of, to make foolish, cause to lose sound judgment, to inspire with foolish or shallow love or affection, infatuated -- a person who is infatuated.[450] How many of us have been infatuated, or are willing to admit it?

For example, I was dating a young man at the age of fourteen, introduced through his close friend. His close friend was a couple of years older than I was. However, the young man I was dating was infatuated with me, making plans of marriage once he graduated from high school within a year or two. Consequently, we were only dating for a month when he announced the good news to me. At the age of fourteen, I knew in my heart and mind that I was not ready for marriage when asked this question. Instead of taking this question seriously, I laughed.

Later, I had feelings for his close friend. My heart fluttered, pounded, fingers became clammy and sweaty whenever he was around us. I was more interested in his best friend. Our dating relationship started to digress. When we were left alone, I lost self-control by kissing him. He shared his feelings right away too, but wanted to be with me regardless of his friend dating me. We said the words 'I love you,' 'I have never felt this way for anyone before,' 'you made my heart pound at your presence, when I first laid eyes on you.' Alternatively, these are the same words that my boyfriend felt, and told me when he announced his interest in marriage. However, I was foolish to think that I could truly know what love is.

Instead, I ended up crushing both of these men's feelings all together. Yes, my boyfriend caught his best friend and me in the act of kissing. Imagine the anger my boyfriend had towards me and/or his best friend, his feelings and heart were being crushed all in one. Alternatively, I was lost for words, felt ashamed, and did not know

---

[448] Vine's Concise Dictionary.
[449] See also Ephesians 6:5 and Colossians 3:22
[450] Webster's New World College Dictionary.

what to do. My boyfriend's best friend tried to apologize, but he could not hear him because of his emotional status. Additionally, he wanted to ask his permission to date me and how we supposedly felt about each other. Then, a fight broke out. Overall, it was not worth all this commotion since I was only infatuated with both of them.

At the time, I thought that I loved one guy more than I loved the other, and then I had to choose. I confessed how I viewed both of their characteristics and personalities. I had to conclude what I liked most about them. Additionally, how I thought I felt about both of them. What is an even funnier thought is, although years has passed, when I talk to either one of these guys, my heart still pounds heavily, or I get a case of the sweaty palms. However, deep down inside, I know that it is not love for either of them.

Jesus had agape love for us.[451] The example allows us to see how we confuse the two terms, 'infatuation' and 'love,' once we find ourselves attracted to the opposite sex, usually for the wrong reason. Some of the wrong reasons consist of the smell of his cologne or her perfume, physical appearance such as facial structure, physique, and how they dress. Other reasons are their hair styles; the vehicle they drive; materialism and wealth. Finally, we can be attracted to his or her voice such as the smoothness or deepness of it; their reactions around others, and how they treat a person; emotional status; and other characteristics that attract us such as their intellect and confidence. We may focus on their business management skills, educational background and or career outcomes. The list can go on endlessly, which can cause one to feel infatuated, to lust after, or even to love a person.

The best way to know the truth is from the man himself, Jesus Christ. Ask God for spiritual discernment and insight to know if this person is the one for you that He has planned. If not, to remove this person from your life. Eventually, I concluded, while living the single life that I want to be more intimate with God. In addition, we can mess up God's plan for our lives and/or mate, which will delay or miss our blessing.

Nonetheless, *spiritual vision* is our capacity to see clearly what God wants us to do, and to see the world from His point of view.[452] Consequently, spiritual insight can be easily clouded with self-serving desires, interests, and goals may block God's vision. Therefore, serving God is the best way to restore it. A *good eye* is one that is fixed on God. Furthermore, the *lamp* represents Christ, and the *eye* represents spiritual understanding and insight. Evil desires make the eye less sensitive and blots out the light of Christ's presence. If you have a hard time seeing God at work in your life, check your vision. Are there any sinful desires blinding you to Christ? [453]

I have dated men in the past that were not for me. After prayer, I am thankful that God sent the signs and warnings to no longer be with that person. Furthermore, God spoke to me about who He has planned for me. In addition, my blessings for a mate will

---

[451] 1 Corinthians 10:13
[452] Matthew 6:22, 23; Luke 11:34
[453] Life Application Study Bible, NKJV, 1996.

not be delayed any longer once I follow His will. I felt like I was stuck in a rut by allowing myself to be caught up in believing what the world believed that we have to be with someone, and not to be alone.

Therefore, I will wait on God's plan for me since I keep falling for the wrong men. If I am willing to wait on God, I will not be stuck with someone that God does not see fit for me, and then break the *Tenth Commandment* of desiring to be with someone else. Do not put all your energies on someone that is not in God's will. I will no longer view the world's reasons for being with someone, or pointing the finger at someone else by asking, 'why are you alone?' Yet, some people are meant to be single.[454]

First, we are to know our purpose for being with someone. God wants us to focus on His purpose for our lives first. Partner comes second. Purpose puts you in position to receive the right partner. Quit feeling sorry for yourself. God gives us the power to choose, so stop focusing on the loneliness and misery of not being with someone. For example, when I focused on being alone and longing to be with someone, it would lead to the feelings of lust. I would lust to be with someone, which lead to fantasizing about them on an intimate level, which are not the plans for singleness according to God's standards that are written in the Bible. Paul points out the instructions of singleness, which illustrates how Jesus was tempted.[455] Instructions on a Christian relationship and marriage --[456] will be further discussed in my upcoming book, *Unleashing the Spirit*.

The meaning of the word, *lust*: pleasure, delight, appetite, sexual senses, a desire to gratify the senses in a bodily appetite or sexual desire, as seeking unrestrained gratification, inclination, overmastering desire, lust of power, and 'lusts of the flesh' described in *1 John 2:16*.[457] *Lust* is not love. It is an abnormal desire, so do not confuse it with love such as love for self, family, wife-husband, it is the desire of possession. This is why lust is a sin, which is to have a desire to own something that belongs to someone else, and willing to do anything to possess it, whether it is to lie, steal, and even kill. Jesus said we could be content with what God has provided, and lust not for our neighbor's wife or his possessions. Although it seems harder to be single than someone already married, we are to remain righteous and holy. Men and women will never achieve such holiness, but can only continue to try to fight their human emotions caused by living in this world.

Furthermore, lust can lead to relationships that God views as an abomination: 'homosexuality,' 'bi-sexuality,' and 'bestiality.' Because of the feelings of sexual lust, your flesh will never be satisfied, and desires grow stronger as the cravings take control over your senses, and leads you to sin that could have been avoided with conviction of the Holy Spirit. If you would only take the time to listen to God's voice, any lustful

---

[454] Matthew 19:10-12
[455] 1 Corinthians 7:33-34 and Matthew 4:1
[456] 1 Corinthians 7
[457] Webster's New World College Dictionary.

emotions tugging at your heart or any sexual pressures will vanish, and you are able to resist sin with God's help. In conclusion, I want to please God and not self.

Another form of lust is self-gratification. You are gratifying to please self. Homosexuality or bi-sexuality can be interpreted in many ways, but in a biblical sense, this is a contradiction of God's command to be fruitful and multiply, of which is to increase the human population. Humans are the only species that practice this form of sexuality. Medically speaking, it could be said that because of abnormal hormones during gestation, when the sex organ of the fetus is formed, causes one to be receptive to the same sexes. Some people are born as a male, but with an increased amount of female hormones and surgery, they are becoming women, and some women prefer to be males. Would you say that you were born this way?

Bi-sexuality is an over-sexed desire for sex with the same sex. *Bestiality* is over-sexed desire for sex with animals.[458] In other words, God did not create homosexuals or bisexuals. Each of us chooses our reality, circumstances, and conditions of life before coming into the body of Christ. God granted us freewill, where people are able to create their own experiences by their choices. God blessed us with sacred gifts. These gifts are our sexual identities that are to be saved until marriage or union. However, we continue to misuse and abuse our bodies with our own sexual desires and lusts.

Moreover, God gave 'you' the authority and power to decide and declare for yourself, so why you are performing these sexual acts with self or others? These sexual acts can be masturbation, physical contact, oral, or anal sex. God expects us to practice 'celibacy' or 'preserve our virginity' until we are married. We may struggle with lustful desires by lusting with our eyes, minds, or even in our hearts -- 'need of a relationship' to avoid loneliness. In contrast, we can join a supportive group, or speak with a family member or friend to help you with the issues you are facing. Alternatively, you can join a single fellowship class, to hear other confessions and solutions to your problems. Moreover, once we are convinced that sin is disgusting and grow to hate sin, and then we are able to conquer and overcome our feelings of lust. God informs us to love Him first, others second and self last.

Alternatively, *love* has too many definitions in the *Webster's New World College Dictionary*. Here are a few meanings of *love*: a deep and tender feeling of affection for or attachment or devotion to a person or persons; an expression of one's love or affection; and a strong liking for or interest in something or someone. Other meanings are a strong, passionate, affection of one person for another, sexual attraction (sweetheart or lover); and sexual passion and/or sexual intercourse. *Love* can also refer to God's tender regard and concern for humanity. Human's devotion to, and desire for God as the supreme God, is another form of *love*. Some believe to *show love* is by embrace, fondle, kissing, or some physical form of affection towards another. Others

---

[458] Statement by Sonny J. Turner

argue that it is an emotion of love such as to be in love or to love someone. Delight in, or take pleasure in, is another meaning of *love*.

Old Testament

Ahab means to love; like, which is a strong emotional attachment to, and desire either to possess or to be in the presence of the object; familiar, romantic, or friendship.[459] In some references, it can signify sexual lust.[460] Making love usually is represented by *yada* -- to know, or by *shakab* – to lie with. Sometimes *ahab* depicts an overtone of family love; his master as a son loves his father.[461] [462]

Ahabah, which means love, has the same range of meanings as the term, *ahab*. It can refer to a family, friend, romantic, or sexual love, as a state of being or actions of strong affection and commitment.[463]

New Testament

Agape describes the attitude of God toward His Son,[464] those who believe on the Lord Jesus Christ,[465] to convey His will to His children concerning their attitude one toward another,[466] and toward all men,[467] who express the nature of God.[468] There are Scriptures on *agape love*, where God demonstrates His love for humanity by sending His Son, Jesus Christ to earth. Moreover, Christian love, whether exercised towards men and women, generally is not an impulse from the feelings. It does not always run with natural inclinations, nor does it spend itself only on those for whom some affinity is discovered. Love seeks the welfare of all, and works no ill to any;[469] love seeks opportunity to do well to all men, and especially toward them that are of the household of the faith.[470]

- *Phileo* represents tender affection. The words *agape* and *phileo* are used for the love of the Father for the Son.[471]
- *Philanthropia* denotes love for man, hence, kindness,[472] and His love towards man.[473]

---

[459] Genesis 22:2; 24:67; 34:3; Ruth 4:15

[460] 2 Samuel 13:1

[461] Deuteronomy 15:16; 1 Samuel 16:21; 18:16; Exodus 21:5

[462] Vine's Concise Dictionary.

[463] Genesis 29:20; Deuteronomy 7:8; 1 Samuel 18:3; Hosea 3:1

[464] John 17:26; 3:16; Romans 5:8

[465] John 14:21

[466] John 13:34

[467] 1 Thessalonians 3:12; 1 Corinthians 16:14; 2 Peter 1:7

[468] 1 John 4:8

[469] Romans 15:2

[470] Galatians 6:10; 1 Corinthians 13 and Colossians 3:12-14

[471] John 3:35; 5:20 for the believer; 16:27 both refer to Christ's love, and the love for his disciples John 13:23; 20:2

- *Philotheos* -- a lover of God
- *Philoxenos* -- loving strangers; lover of hospitality
- *Philagathos* -- loving that which is good, lover of good
- *Philarguros* -- loving oneself
- *Philedonos* -- loving pleasure, lovers of pleasure

In a relationship, we are seeking *agape* love. Generally, it starts with physical attraction that catches our attention, also known as *Eros*. *Eros* can refer to *erotic*, another term for lust and physical stimulation that causes our heart to pump fast and hard, sweaty hands, and want to get know their name and phone number. You want to see more of that person, and want to get to know them, hopefully not sexually. Then, it leads to *phileo*, which is having feelings or affection for that person. It can also refer to a close relationship or friendship.

Once we are engaged or married, hopefully this affection can grow to *agape*, unconditional love for the other person. However, delight in and take pleasure in, is a form of *lust*. Be careful not to confuse the two. We tend to look at the styles of dating because of a world's perspective, and God's standard on dating is known as *courtship*. *Courtship* means the act, process, or period of courting or wooing. In layman terms, someone that God has destined for your life, and you date them for a period that leads to holy matrimony.

Paul gave instructions to 'unmarried and widows,' and aspects on singleness and marriage.[474] For instance, Paul foresaw the impending persecution that the Roman government would soon bring on Christians. He gave this practical advice because being unmarried would mean less suffering and more freedom to throw one's life into the cause of Christ, even to the point of fearlessly dying for Him. Paul's advice reveals his single-minded devotion to spreading the good news.[475] Many people naively think that marriage will solve all their problems. Here are some problems marriage will not solve:[476] loneliness; sexual temptation; satisfaction of one's deepest emotional needs; and/or elimination of life's difficulties.

Marriage alone does not hold two people together, but commitment does because it is a commitment to Christ and then to each other, despite conflicts and problems. As wonderful as it is, marriage does not automatically solve every problem. Whether married or single, we must be content with our situation and focus on Christ, not on loved ones, to help address our problems.

On the other hand, Paul urges all believers to make the most of their time before Christ's return. Every person in every generation should have this sense of urgency

---

[472] Acts 28:2
[473] Titus 3:4
[474] 1 Corinthians 7:25-40
[475] 1 Corinthians 7:26, 29; Life Application Study Bible, NKJV, 1996.
[476] 1 Corinthians 7:28

about telling the Good News to others.[477] Life is short – there is not much time. Additionally, Paul urges believers not to regard marriage, home or financial security as the goal of life. As much as possible, we are to live unhindered by the cares of this world, not getting involved with burdensome mortgages, budgets, investments, or debts that might keep us from doing God's work. A married man or woman, Paul points out, must take care of earthly responsibilities, but to make every effort to keep them modest and manageable.[478]

Nonetheless, some single people feel tremendous pressure to be married. They think their lives can be complete only with a spouse. Nevertheless, Paul underlines one advantage of being single, in which is the potential of a greater focus on Christ and His work. If you are unmarried, use your special opportunity to serve Christ wholeheartedly.[479] When Paul says the unmarried person does even better, he is talking about the potential time available for the service to God. The single person lacks the responsibility of caring for a spouse and raising a family. Singleness, however, does not ensure service to God such as the involvement in service depends on the commitment of the individual.[480] Furthermore, Paul's advice comes from the Holy Spirit, who guides and equips both single and married people to fulfill their roles.[481]

I have no commandments from the Lord: Paul clearly distinguishes his words as an apostle from the words of Christ. *Virgins:* is the classification of the unmarried in the church, which included widows and those who had been married before. Though Paul is concerned with both celibate men and women, the attention here is on the women.[482]

On the contrary, Paul saw turbulent days ahead for married believers because in times of persecution, consideration for family can make it difficult to live out Christian convictions fully. A virgin would have lesser family responsibilities and would not be deterred by the possibility of repercussions affected by her husband or children.[483] Consequently, Paul does not want to be understood as prohibiting marriage altogether. Paul is not saying to get married is a ticket out of sin, but married couples are to dedicate themselves to God's work.[484]

The father of an unmarried virgin tries to marry his daughter off to the best man once she is past the flower of youth, showing that the virgin is approaching an age at which marriage would be unlikely. Under these circumstances, it would be perfectly acceptable for the father to give her away in marriage. A second interpretation suggests that the fiancé carry out celibacy until marriage since his mate is still a virgin. If a man has difficulty in controlling his sex drive or his will is weak, he ought to marry. On the

---

[477] 1 Corinthians 7:29, Life Application Study Bible, NKJV, 1996.

[478] 1 Corinthians 7:29-31; 33-34, Life Application Study Bible, NKJV, 1996.

[479] 1 Corinthians 7:32-34, Life Application Study Bible, NKJV, 1996.

[480] 1 Corinthians 7:38, Life Application Study Bible, NKJV, 1996.

[481] 1 Corinthians 7:40, Life Application Study Bible, NKJV, 1996.

[482] 1 Corinthians 7:25-40, Nelson Study Bible, NKJV.

[483] 1 Corinthians 7:26, 27, Nelson Study Bible, NKJV.

[484] 1 Corinthians 7:28-29, Nelson Study Bible, NKJV.

other hand, if the man can control himself and keep himself from immoral action, he can stay single.[485]

Moreover, Paul used marriage as a tool to illustrate our obligation to the law.[486] Paul also emphasizes that marriage is to be lifelong. Where a marriage partner has died, the only restriction concerning remarriage is for the person to marry a fellow Christian. Even though some people think that remarriage is permitted, Paul still believes that it is wiser to remain unmarried. The Holy Spirit enabled Paul, not only to speak with apostolic authority, but also with spiritual wisdom.

On another note, singles are breaking the *Seventh Commandment*. Some may label unmarried persons that are having sex as 'adulterers or adulteresses,' which is breaking God's law of adultery. Others refer to unmarried couples engaging in any sexual acts as 'fornicators.' After the moment of pleasure, it stinks. However, some argue that the 'clothes' one wears creates distraction and thoughts of lust. It can also be enticing to the weak woman or man eyes -- staring too long at what someone is wearing. According to biblical principles, *clothes* refer to the old man, before one was saved. Yet, sometimes, people are quick to make accusations about someone by outer appearance such as attire. It can be seductive to the man's eye and lure him to her with wrong intentions.[487]

Furthermore, some things that can have influence on a person in a lustful state of mind: a willingness to change their outer appearance and/or personality to fit in with the crowd; approval of acceptance from peer group; do not want to seem different or an outcast, among their peers; and not concerned about death and/or sexual orientation.

Several possible solutions are to ask God for a new heart and mind. Seek God's purpose for your life and God will turn you into a 'spiritual creature searching for the truth.' We are always looking beyond the obvious since God is a miracle worker and healer. Likewise, Sherlock Holmes had to narrow down the facts or evidence at hand to solve the mystery, and never was satisfied until he uncovered the truth. Additionally, the purpose for all of us will be revealed.

Consequently, you cannot find these answers by hanging out with the world, which will cause you to think and act like they do. Jesus tells us that we are to be holy, which means to be set apart from those things of the world. If you are caught in the web of the worldly ways, God cannot speak to your heart and mind. We are to open up to the Holy Spirit and dedicate your life to Jesus Christ to hear from our Heavenly Father. In the long haul, if you do not allow God in, you will find yourself unhappy, will not know your purpose, and there will be no substantial joy in your life. You will be left with despair and depression unless you allow God in -- greater is He that is in you.

---

[485] 1 Corinthians 7:8, 36-38; Life Application Study Bible, NKJV, 1996.
[486] 1 Corinthians 7:39, 40: bound by law: this passage is similar to Romans 7:2
[487] Harden, Michael. Sermon on 8.15.04 at New Testament Church (Milwaukee WI) and author emphasis.

~Let Your Day Begin With Christ, Day 22~

Let your Day Begin Activity: Before you can find the ideal mate, you need to work on yourself. Today take two pieces of paper and write down your strengths and weakness you could bring into a relationship. We all have shortcomings and faults, but we must be willing to acknowledge them and work on it. Write down three things you can do to improve them. Be honest with yourself because no one fully knows and understand you, but you. Daily, make an effort to change these things about you for the benefit of God and the mate He has for you.

Today's Questions:

Differences of infatuation, lust, and love. Have you ever experienced one or more of them? If so, explain or give scenarios.

What are some reasons why God wants us to be married instead of fornicating?

If we say we love God, ask yourself should we keep lying down with someone to please our fleshly desires.

What is the direction of your life? Are you headed toward God or away from Him to please your sexual desires? If you are a drifter, the choice for God may seem difficult, but puts everything in a different light.

Review to Begin your Day with Christ:

Name several problems for single people go through. The main reason for those that are *single* is to enjoy an intimate relationship with God, without the responsibilities and cares of a husband and/or children to attend to, which can cause one to miss their alone time with God.

Share your viewpoints on movies with sexual enticement, sex appeal, and/or unmarried couples having sex.

Day Begins 23: Boundaries For Singles

Singleness Boundaries Out On The Scene

Nathan Bailey views the dating scene as an outlet to hide one's true feelings and all their faults, giving a false impression to keep their partner liking them. For example, women are wearing fake eyelashes, falsies (silicon breasts), weave, bootie busters (extra padding), etc., to attract men. Then again, men are willing to lie about their financial income, status, and drive rent-a-cars, rent-a-suits, and whatever it takes to impress a woman. Some men believe a woman is only seeking a man with fame and/or wealth. Usually, men are willing to impress a woman to the extreme to have a one-night stand. Additionally, some women are willing to attract a man to satisfy her needs too.

After watching the movie *Jersey Girl* with Ben Affleck and Jennifer Lopez, it displays how a man marries the woman he loves. Jennifer Lopez, Ben Affleck's wife in the movie, dies after giving birth to a baby girl. Ben's character becomes single again. Later, we see a woman in a video store flaunting her sexual appetite on him. She is overly throwing herself on him, once she realizes that he is a single parent raising his child on his own. When the couple meets at a local restaurant, video store girl finds out that he has not had sex for several years, and feels that she can encourage him to make out. In her opinion, she feels a man should get laid and not to deprive their sexual desires after so many years. Here, Ben Affleck's character was not willing to have sex after his wife's death, but an outgoing and outspoken woman, who is flaunting her body, lures him to have sex. He allowed flattery and enticement to meet his sexual appetite.

There are believers of Jesus Christ hanging out in bars and other unchristian places to meet their mate, including online dating services. These are some things one would do to appeal to the opposite gender such as a willingness to please their date, dressed in sexy attire, and spray on cologne or perfume to arouse their senses. Other things to beguile his or her significant other is dressed in provocative wardrobe, engaging in phone sex, cyber sex (online interaction such as web cam on Instant Messenger (IM) by Yahoo, AOL, or MSN and/or web cam access in chat rooms), and participating in a virtual fantasy on online dating services to appear as a 'good catch.'[488]

> *Romans 5:3-5, NKJV: "And not only that, but we also glory in tribulations, knowing that tribulation produces perseverance; and perseverance, character; and character, hope. Now hope does not disappoint, because the love of God has been poured out in our hearts by the Holy Spirit who was given to us."*

Our actions reveal our strengths or weaknesses.[489] One has to beware of impulse decisions since most singles fight emotional storms within their souls, concerns, and wondering if God will keep His promises. God will restore our weary souls through

---

[488] Viden, Holly and Michelle McKinley Hammond. *If Singleness is a Gift What's the Return Policy?* (emphasis added by author).
[489] 2 Corinthians 10:3-4

His Word. His Word will nourish us, replenish us, and rejuvenate us again to believe in the invisible God through our 'faith.' Do not sink into repetition of sins and continue to pray for forgiveness to God repetitiously, only to find yourself returning to the same sin. This cycle can be broken once we turn away from our sins. Jesus said to Mary Magdalene, "Go sin no more," no longer giving in to our fleshly desires. For instance, Joseph fled from his master's house when Potiphar's wife wanted to lie down with him. Joseph fled from fornication.[490]

Flee means to run from.

Loneliness is the absence of intimacy.

Purpose comes first. Partner is second. Purpose puts you in position to receive the right partner. Quit feeling sorry for you. God will grant us the power to choose. Stop focusing on loneliness and misery.[491]

Singleness can destroy individual's lives.[492] The main reason that singles can destroy us is through temptation by giving in, or engaging in the sinful act, and/or putting those lustful thoughts in action. Devil's best weapon is tempting us.[493] If we overt to sin, it can tempt us in another direction, to distract us from Christ. Satan has people believing that they are good enough to enter the Kingdom of Heaven.[494]

---

[490]   Genesis 39 and 2 Timothy 2:22.
[491]   Viden Holly and Michelle McKinney Hammond. *If Singleness is a Gift What's the Return Policy?* p 200.
[492]   1 Peter 5:8
[493] 1 Thessalonians 2:17-18; James 3:13-16
[494] Evans, p. 217.

~Let Your Day Begin With Christ, Day 23~

Let your Day Begin Activity: Today take the time to create some boundaries in your life: what you will tolerate in a relationship. We have to remove the sinful acts to present ourselves to God. What are you doing to attract or appeal to your companion? If God is not pleased, change them today. Make a list of all the things that you feel are keeping you from finding a good spouse, or even if you have a spouse, what is keeping you from being closer with them and eliminate those things immediately.

Today's Questions:

What are some boundaries you have to set for yourself as a Christian?

How can you avoid sexual advances?

What are some godly practices you can do to avoid fornication?

Review to Begin your Day with Christ:

Some believers of Jesus Christ are in local bars, clubs, and other ungodly places hoping to find their soul mate. What are your thoughts on this behavior? Should you be humble and patient to wait on God's will for your mate. Why or why not?

See *Ephesians 5:21-6:9* for similar instructions.

As singles, we are to follow our purpose first and then seek our partner next. Just because we are lonely, we are to flee from fornication.

Day Begins 24: Woman's Perspective On Dating

If a man appears 'needy,' and sees you as a 'motherly image,' it is a turn off for most women. Additionally, a needy man seems insecure within himself, needing some reassurance from a woman. Women are usually attracted to a man who is confident, not arrogant. Most women are looking for a new type of relationship: intimacy, open to communication, and a good listener, intellectual, and romance.

Women are not only soft and assertive, but also feminine. Today, too many women are approaching men, and not waiting for them to approach them. Younger women do not know what they want in a relationship, only seeking for the now, and not worrying about the later, which are consequences. Women do not realize that men are viewing those flirtatious women. Men see these women through their lustful eyes with sexual images overcoming their thoughts. Furthermore, these sorts of women are worrying about getting a man, instead of keeping him.[495] Moreover, a woman pursuing a man, he will relax more and become more passive about the relationship. Overall, a woman who pursues a man will succeed usually in getting him, but not what she hoped for once he loses interest. However, when a woman decides to end the relationship, then a man is suddenly attracted to her and becomes more interested. He likes a challenge, something to fight for, and go after it. Once he loses it, he realizes that maybe she was the one for him after all, or trying to prove to his 'ego' that I can get her back.[496]

A woman is excited by the thought of being seen, heard and desired, and reassured by the possibility of getting what she needs and wants. When a man makes a woman feel feminine, her mind is stimulated and intrigued, of which is a feeling of warmness, tenderness, and vulnerable inside, which her heart begins to open as she remembers that she is special. What allows a woman to bring the best out in a man could be summarized as 'feminine radiance.' A woman expresses her feminine radiance, embodying the three basic characteristics of femininity: she is self-assured, receptive, and responsive. These three qualities in a woman make a man more attracted to her.[497]

Self-assurance will always get you what you need. *Webster's College Dictionary* defines *self-assurance* as someone confident in oneself, or in one's ability, talent, etc. When a woman shifts from feelings of self-assured to receiving a man's affection, she becomes less attractive. When a man pulls away, a woman tends to blame him, and does not realize how she can be part of the equation. Sometimes we should not put the

---

[495] Mars & Venus On A Date: A Guide For Navigating The 5 Stages Of Dating To Create A Loving & Lasting Relationships.
[496] Mars & Venus On A Date: A Guide For Navigating The 5 Stages Of Dating To Create A Loving & Lasting Relationships.
[497] Mars & Venus On A Date: A Guide For Navigating The 5 Stages Of Dating To Create A Loving & Lasting Relationships.

blame on the other party. Instead, do not point the finger at someone else; we need to check our own shortcomings.[498]

Examine the woman or man in the mirror, seeing yourself inside and out, notice what you are dishing out in relationships first, before jumping to conclusions such as assuming he is cheating. Alternatively, he has mental, emotional, or social issues can diffuse the dating relationship. Review your own behavior around him. What you say can be a part of the relationship ending in turmoil, or to the point of breaking up. A man will respect your decision, but a woman most likely assumes that he wants to hear what she has to say. Attitude of being self-assured draws a man's interest.

A woman needs to remember that she is the 'jewel,' and he is providing the setting for her to 'shine.' A woman has to not only be confident, but also have a high self-esteem about her first. Do not allow a man to bring you down in the gutter, but open your heart only if he is respecting and treating you like a woman should be treated first. If the relationship does not feel right, and you see the signs, don't allow this relationship to progress since in the end, you will end up hurt and torn apart.

A woman's desire to please a man is clearly a demonstration of love, but at the same time, a woman must know that if she denies herself to please him, it makes her less attractive. A *receptive woman* is able to receive what she gets, and not resent getting less. *Receptivity* is being able to receive whatever can be received in a circumstance and the ability to benefit something good in every situation. *Webster College Dictionary* defines *receptive* as receiving or tending to receive, take in, admit, or contain, able or ready to receive new ideas, inclined to the favorable reception of request, suggestion. Therefore, when a woman displays her sexual side before she is ready, she has stopped being receptive and becomes accommodating. Instead of allowing a man to please her, she tries to please him. A man may become frustrated. When a woman gives more in a relationship, she is no longer receptive to what a man has to offer, and begins to expect more from the man. Additionally, a woman loses her sense of receptivity when she expects more than a man has been giving, and her assumption that he will support her because he owes her. A woman being receptive to a man does not mean she agrees with him all the time.

A woman's responsiveness is most attractive when it is authentic and not exaggerated. It is not so much what a woman does for a man who makes him happy, but the way she responds. Each time a woman chooses to find and express her positive responses to a man's attempts to fulfill her, he feels encouraged to pursue her. As a woman responds to a man with each of these three attributes of femininity is being assured, receptive, and responsive. These three attributes of femininity is most attractive to men. When woman give more than they are getting, they become increasingly unfulfilled. The more successful a woman is, the less inviting to a man she may become.

---

[498] Matthew 7:3-5

Sadly, too many women are so desperate to have the perfect man where they do not ask questions, they do not do their homework, and they do not think about the fact that they are putting their lives in jeopardy by engaging in unprotected sex. Furthermore, society puts so much pressure on women to be in relationship. Even if women have furthered their education and have a Ph.D., own a home, and have mastered in success and/or wealth, however, she is viewed as a failure without a mate. People tend to question what is wrong with a woman who has so much going on in her life, but is not with a significant other.

Additionally, mothers and grandmothers pressure women and young girls to have a man, always saying things like, 'When are you going to bring a man home?' Alternatively, they will say, 'You're so pretty, why don't you have man?' In addition, many will focus on a woman's age because she is in her prime, and once she reaches over forty and still not married, addresses a woman as an 'old maid.' Many believe that if you want a man, you have to please him. It appears that you have to change everything about yourself to keep him. Evidently, society expectations are highly focused on women in a relationship.

Women have tremendous power inherent in the choices. For instance, some women start in a platonic relationship with men, meaning not to have any sexual relations with him. Others will accept a man as a homey, lover and friend, which sends mixed signals when she wants the relationship to become more serious. As a result, we learn to listen to him, watch his habits, and get to know his friends and family. Women get intuition, sensing something is wrong because of his secrecy. Instead of assuming he is cheating, she should confess her feelings to him. Too often women ignore the inner voice that tries to give them an early warning signal.

Women, do not fall for the Devil's deception, believing that you have finally found your soul mate, and discover that you have married the wrong person. Conversely, God expects us to honor the covenant He set for married couples. Although you married the wrong person, you have to withhold that marriage unless he dies, or infidelity is proven, and can file for a divorce under the Mosaic Law. There may be other reasons to divorce your mate, but not primarily because you married the wrong person. God does not want to see you miserable. Yet, He wants you to turn to Him before making this covenant with the person you plan to marry in the beginning.

How God views marriage. God will bless us with our soul mates. We are to flee from any covet activity, which is to desire what someone else has. We cannot only focus on desiring and wishing to be joined with a man you hope will become your husband someday, instead, we seek confirmation from the Lord. Do not settle for less than God's ideal person for you. God cannot bless a mess when your heart is based on covetousness, envy, and jealousy since these facets will always cause us to lose.[499]

---

[499] James 3:14-16

Women have forgotten who you are. What is love? How do we love someone? To love someone, it is unconditionally, from the depths of our heart and soul, not expecting any appreciation from our companion.[500] According to the book, *The Unspoken Love: What Women Don't Know and Men Don't Tell You*, while you wait for a godly man, we are to remain a well-kept woman. In other words, we are to keep our hair done up, dress eloquently, and hygiene.

As woman, we are to support our men spiritually and emotionally, we are feminine creatures created to help our mates. Yet, this does not mean that we have to go out on a limb and support him financially. We must not be involved with anyone that cannot improve the quality of his own life. Ideally, the man is the breadwinner, and to provide for his home. However, we can review all the finances and make sure the checkbook is in tact. Sometimes, we may have to work to help take care of the household and bills, but not doing it all. To maintain whom you are, and allow God to be meticulous for you. God knows your needs, and when the right person comes along, God will lead them to your door.

Men classify women in these categories: freak, friend, or forever. *Freak* is the attraction, sex appeal, and sexual gratification he gets from her. Some women believe that if they are having sex with a potential mate, he will marry her, except he is never thinking about a serious relationship that leads to engagement or marriage. He gets what he wants since she is giving it up. He likes her, and may feel love for her, continue to have sex over a period until he meets someone he values, and then he will drop the freak and marry the woman he values.

Friend is viewed as a platonic friendship with a man. Women may see things in a different light leading up to marriage since he is pleasant to you, says wonderful things about you, but he never has the intentions on marriage. Friendship seems to confuse women since normally you are sharing deep secrets and other feelings with him. This may cause a woman to think it is love since she has never shared this information with anyone else. Even though courtship starts as friends, then leads or ends in matrimony. Learn to listen to what the man says, however, sometimes men lie only to deceive you. Yet, women deceive themselves in believing he is the one. Men are usually committed to their words: friendly, caring and helpful, but it does not mean that he loves you or desires to marry you.

Overall, women must protect their hearts and take heed to what the man is conveying to you. Likewise, please try not to imagine yourself with this person. Do not underestimate the power of imagination. Where you see a future with your best friend by projecting lustful desires and play out the scene in your mind. Visualizing and fantasizing a lifelong relationship with them.

_____

Although people desire to be married, and meet someone she is attracted to, begin to think what life will be with that particular person. The relationship dies before it starts by losing hope, setting unrealistic goals for their future, which is only breaking their hearts and leaving them with a great disappointment. Therefore, it takes discipline to be with someone who is wonderful, and you enjoy being in their company, but resist from fantasizing about being with someone that is not promised in your life. In addition, God wants to protect our hearts from heartbreak and disappointments.[501] We are unable to change our past, but our past has an effect on the present. We are to move forward, and not dread on our past or past relationships. Not to repeat the same mistakes of our past, accept what the present has to offer us. God wants to give us a future. Protect our hearts, by not allowing a man to compromise our commitment with God.

Forever:

1. Pursuit of you
2. Does not leave anything to the imagination
3. Deeper relationship than a friendship
4. Dynamics of romance and prospect of marriage surface in conversations
5. Dream about future with him
6. Conversations filled with 'us' not 'I' or 'me'
7. Market himself as potential husband by painting a picture of what life would be like with him
8. Meet important people in his life
9. Purge activities or people from his life to make room for you
10. Relationship intensifies
11. Seek out presence either by phone or in person frequently and acknowledges when he misses you
12. Consistency to his interactions with you
13. Day-to-day details of your life integrate into a partnership
14. Backed up by actions confirming his intentions

If your man is not saying anything about commitment, then do not move in that direction. Listen to his words and watch for confirming actions. If a man wants sex, or seeking a good time briefly, subjectively, it shows that any woman will do. If a man wants you, please be aware that only you will do. Women possess the power of sexuality. We must hold the goodies (sex) until marriage. If he is willing to wait, usually, it will fully prove he is committed.[502] It is important when qualifying a man for potential marriage that we recognize the intentions of his heart. Then, articulate your standards, and if he opposes your values, then he does not value you and probably never will. Listen to what he is saying, how he views your value, which will give you a picture of an ideal relationship.

---

[501] Jeremiah 29:11-13

[502] The Unspoken Love: What Women Don't Know and Men Don't Tell You (emphasis added by author).

Men know when women are attracted to them. Women are willing to commit to a man who will not commit to her. Waiting on the man to commit does not make her feel the indication of true love. If he tells you that marriage is not his immediate plans, but later he asks you to marry him -- believe him. Men decide when it is time for them to get married, and then search for a mate. Women, on the other hand, fall in love with their feelings, in which they come to their decision to marry. No exclusive relationship with him assumes you are the one. Consider and enjoy other options.

If you are trying not to lust, do not entertain with pornographic activities, and be careful what dating sites you go to online when surfing the Internet, or pop-ups going to pornographic sites. In addition, chat lines are not the answer either. Most people are looking for fun and a quick way to meet someone to have sexual relations. Do not behave as if you are in a committed relationship when you are not. If so, this leads to disappointment, especially if he chooses not to be in a committed relationship. Just view him as a friend or remove him from your life. On the other hand, most men do not want a woman to say let's be friends, when she thinks about a serious long-term relationship, but it is best to be honest and not lead a man on.

Best of all, women think they can change a man after they are married. Men are highly motivated to win you, but change only occurs with the Holy Spirit. Except women tend to forget the broad range of abilities and talents that we possess. Women can take a vision, refine it, advance it, and complete it. Good women are a stabilizing and blazing force in the life of a man. To encourage a man, you must first hear him.[503] *Empathetic listening* is to comprehend where he is coming from, to be alert to his feelings, and to listen without talking, nagging, complaining, or giving advice.

---

[503] Proverbs 20:5

~Let Your Day Begin With Christ, Day 24~

Let your Day Begin Activity: Today women and men, take the time to write down what you look for in a mate. What qualities do you want? What qualities will you not accept? In order for you to look for a mate, you already have to know what you want. Keep this list for another activity in the future.

Today's Questions:

Men are seeking for a freak, friend, and lover. Which one have you been classified as and are you willing to improve on your behavior to be ready for your mate?

Women are seeking for a friend, long-time partner, and love. In your past relationships, write down what females or males you viewed as one of the three, list all three areas and ask yourself what type of woman or man you want to settle down with.

Review to Begin your Day with Christ:

We have to evaluate our relationships with the opposite sex. Review what is pleasing to God while we are single and seeking our future mate.

Change our views on dating. We forgot how to love ourselves. We need to build character, personality, and confidence in ourselves to attract the person for us.

Day Begins 25: Man's Prerogative On Dating

Men are attracted to success. He feels that he is a success in fulfilling a woman desires and wants; this is when he finds himself more attracted to her. What allows a man to bring the best out in a woman is his masculine presence, embodying the three basic characteristics of masculinity. He is confident, purposeful, and responsible, which makes a woman more attracted to him.

When a man makes a woman feel feminine, she is turned on by his unique talents, traits, interests, or characteristics. If a man does not turn a woman on, it does not matter how funny, rich or successful he is. A man tends to bring out the best in a woman through his masculine presence. The most attractive attribute of masculine presence is confidence. Confidence in a man makes a woman breathe deeper, relax, and open up to receive the support he has to offer. When a man has a can-do attitude, even if he doesn't have all the answers, a woman can relax.

A confident man contains his feelings until he has figured out what to do. A confident attitude reassures women who believe everything will be alright. When a man is confident, he is able to come up with a plan. Women love a man with a plan. Women do not like it when a man is too dependent in her for direction. A woman is happy to do some of the planning, but she wants the man to lead the way confidently.

On the other hand, if a woman is a sympathetic listener, a man can transform even a disappointing date into an intimate and rewarding experience for the woman. A man with a purpose is most likely to have a sense of direction or vision, provide his interests, and a sense of concern for his significant other. Does not matter how great the plan or purpose is, women find him to be attractive since he is passionate about achieving his purpose. Even more attractive is when he focuses his purposefulness on her by focusing on making her happy, and then he succeeds at sweeping her off her feet. However, a woman knows that she cannot fulfill all his needs. There seems to be too much pressure on her and their relationship. Sometimes, a woman does not want a man to give up his goals or dreams to make her happy.

Nothing affects a man as deeply as a woman who has womanly qualities. Three things that a man seeks, is to be loved, fed and appreciated. You will hear men say, 'a way to a man's heart is through his stomach.' Most men love a woman who knows how to cook and caters to her man. Second, man desires to be loved and wants a woman who meets his needs sexually, emotionally and mentally. She not only pleases him in the bedroom, but also is willing to listen to his problems at work, at school, or his diverse temperaments. Furthermore, they are seeking a best friend or motherly love, including someone that is a good girl with a freaky side. Lastly, a man wants to feel appreciated for all that he does.

Most men are expecting their mates to work, whether it is as a homemaker, or at a large corporation. Women sometimes take for granted that he pays the bills, buy all necessities, and financially takes care of the household. We can shower them with small gifts, cards, hot bathes, and other things that your mate would enjoy most. To say I love you and thank you for everything you do is a small token of showing your appreciation.

Another way to show how much you care is to take him out to dinner or a movie, or to wear sexy lingerie, play his favorite song, and dance for him in the privacy of your home. Whisper sweet love words in his ear, and kisses that are soft and delicate, as you give him a massage. Be willing to listen or to be silent, while he is speaking, and ignore how your day went unless he asks.

On the other hand, women can make life miserable for men too. Always complaining and nagging about how things could be, or wishing things were different. Our words can crush a man's self-esteem and lose their motivation and drive. In addition, a woman's attitude can eat up a man, and destroy him mentally, emotionally, and spiritually. A woman sets the tone in the household. A man is supposed to be your protection and provider, and a woman was created to protect his heart as his helper. Learn how to build your house now and perfect your gifts while being single.

However, a man does not feel a home is a home until it has that feminine touch. When a man is in love, he is in love. A man needs to be able to trust a woman not discussing his business with her friends, family, and his friends. His business becomes only your business. Then, you are able to make a place in his heart and in his home. Yet, men fail to realize that we are not their mothers, and to treat us with respect and love as their women.

A man needs to have a sense of direction first, and then he is ready to create a relationship to support him in making his dreams come true. When a man is passionate about his work, his interests, his goals, and his future, a woman's desire to be with him becomes greater. When he is self-directed and self-motivated, a woman feels very relaxed and comfortable with him. Rather than feeling she needs to take care of him, she feels he has the energy and motivation to take care of her. A man's sense of responsibility allows her to chill. However, a way to kill romance is for a man to tell a woman all his problems. Before sharing his vulnerable side, a man should clearly demonstrate that he could be responsible for himself and for her. Independent women are accustomed to taking care of themselves, to where she no longer requests a man to meet her needs.

Instead of needing a man primarily for survival and security, a woman needs a man for emotional comfort and nurturing. Then, she feels a natural chemistry on all levels: physical, emotional, mental, and spiritual. Moreover, a man's gift is to be responsible for a woman's fulfillment, while a woman's gift is to be responsive and receptive to his gift. Giving is an expression of love. The problem comes up when women cannot get back the support they need and deserve.

From a man's point of view, there is a world of disappearance between needy women and women who need him. When a woman is needy, she feels that she needs more than a man is offering. It is her lack of appreciation for what he is offering that makes her 'needy.' Instead of appreciating what a man offers, she can start the attitudes of self-assurance, receptiveness, and responsiveness. Alternatively, a woman can require more, however, she should appreciate what a man has to offer. This does not mean that a woman has to be helpless. From a man's perspective, a woman is most attractive when he understands her needs, and she feels self-assured that her needs will be fulfilled. When a woman denies fulfilling her needs for a man, it sabotages the dating process.[504] [505]

Ministers have an excellent opportunity to provide education, compassion, and understanding. The church must preach the truth and become a place where all men can come to hear the Word, without feeling they will be ostracized, regardless of their sexual orientation. If we cannot turn to our churches, where many of us grew up and to which many of us look as an extension of our families, then we will continue to live in denial.

---

[505] Mars & Venus On A Date: A Guide For Navigating The 5 Stages Of Dating To Create A Loving & Lasting Relationships (emphasis added by author).

~Let Your Day Begin With Christ, Day 25~

Let your Day Begin Activity: Men, today take the time to write down all the things you have done in the past to belittle a woman and eliminate them immediately. Even if it is something you did when you were four years old. Write them down and vow to never do them again. Women, what have you done to belittle yourselves in the past? Write them down and vow to never see that side of life again.

Today's Questions:

What are some things that attract a man?

What are some things that attract a woman?

Review to Begin your Day with Christ:

We need to educate what a man wants and what a woman wants. Moreover, what does God wants for our relationships as a couple.

Day Begins 26: Courtship Dating Leads To Marriage

Courtship is a biblical process in finding and choosing a mate, while glorifying God. *Courtship* is also honoring and respecting each other. Moreover, the process of courtship leads to honoring the Lord in the matrimony of marriage, which is a *sacred covenant*. Without God's consent on a future mate, there may be past and present heartbreaks as a result. There can be emotional and/or mental distress from broken relationships, in which someone was caught cheating or simply walking out of your life when things do not work out. This is a form of dating, not courtship. Overall, courtship is focused on a loving and lasting relationship. As for dating, it is a combination of broken hearts and emotional or mental baggage, including sexual insecurities.

During courtship, many couples see their personality differences as complimentary. We have to be alert to ways your personality type may be a sources of irritation to your mate. Furthermore, Nathan Bailey explains on his website, www.polynate.net/books/courtship/part1.html, that our teen years are to build skills such as interpersonal, social, and economical and character. Instead, we are distracted into the quagmire of relationships and dating. We are to be focusing on developing a deep, intimate and personal walk with God, as young warriors in this world today to overcome the Evil One.[506] Moreover, our culture teaches singles to engage in multiple dating relationships, as if it is a normal and useful practice. Modern dating has been around less than a century. Modern dating is also far away from God's original plan. Ideally, our primary purpose in life is to seek and serve God, and fulfill our destiny with Him.

Dating is man-centered. *Dating* is a cultural, social way of meeting new people who you can imagine yourself with, either intimately or in a serious relationship. However, dating only leads to a 'disaster,' since most couples are seeking self-gratification, instead of 'happily ever after' marriage. Primarily, dating leads to intimacy, but not necessarily to commitment. Most dating relationships skip the 'friendship' stage of a relationship, and often mistakes a physical relationship for love.

Additionally, dating often isolates a couple from other vital relationships. Often, it distracts young adults from their primary responsibility of preparing for the future, which can cause discontentment with God's gift of singleness and creates an artificial environment for evaluating another person's character. Usually, the scope of dating develops a self-centered feeling-oriented concept of love. Dating also teaches people to break off difficult relationships, conditioning them more towards divorce than marriage. Some of us develop an appetite for variety and change, creating dissatisfaction within marriage that causes late marriages, leaving more time for falling into sins associated with singleness.

---

[506] 1 John 2:13

Simply, the more time on one's hands with their significant other, promotes lust and moderate sexual activity. Opening the door for fornication instead of practicing celibacy, or remaining a virgin until marriage, this creates a permanent endorphin-bond between two people who will not spend their lives together. Casual dating lacks the protection and guidance afforded by parental involvement of courtship, which does not prepare children to face life's realities. Generally, dating devalues sex and marriage. Furthermore, it embarks on a romantic progression before people are ready to follow through and commit to marriage. Overall, dating encourages short-term relationships over long-term friendships.[507]

Courtship is God-centered and biblically based. Endless series of temptations: guilt, disappointment, frustration and heartbreak. Open communication and honesty, while exploring their career goals, expectations, and daily lives, including meeting their families afterwards, can give you an inclination if you can see a future with this person. Before marriage, it's a good thing to check out their family and friends since the old saying is, 'the apple doesn't fall too far from the tree.'

By learning how to build solid friendships is a way of preparing us for marriage. Friendships and non-romantic relationships are showing a mutual interest by building trust and understanding. There is a difference between quick fix versus intimacy with God. A relationship with God is to be able to hear His voice when God speaks to you. Develop oneness. Prayer is intimacy with God, not quick answers.[508]

The Bible never mentions *dating* or *courtship*. However, it gives principles and guidelines for male and female relationships. Therefore, we are to save ourselves physically, emotionally and spiritually for the one person God would have us marry. When we put our needs aside, it demonstrates faith in God's will. Wait for God to reveal His choice of a mate. Concentrate on being with the right person, instead of finding the right person. Intimate friendship with the intended person can lead to marriage as the result. No need to try out people, like dating encourages.

Courtship is like looking through the rearview mirror, the pathway to marriage at the end of the road. Enjoy the *season of singleness* since God is preparing us for our ultimate soul mate and for the foundation for His blessing. Courtship is to have full of knowledge and approval from either parents, and moreover succumb to spiritual accountability as a couple. Godly couples provide protection, correction, and direction. In addition, while courting, one is able to determine if this person is marriage material, or someone to spend the rest of his or her life with. Most believe, while courting, there are no romantic interactions until after a commitment to marriage (www.polynate.net/books/courtship/part1/html).

---

[507]Extracted from *Dating: Is It Worth the Risk?* by Reb Bradley; *I Kissed Dating Goodbye* by Joshua Harris; *Dating, Betrothal and Courtship* by Dr S. M. Davis; *Dating vs. Courtship* by Paul Jehle and various posts to the "Courtship Ring" mailing list.
[508] John 15:5

Early stages of courtship are limited amounts of time together or very little one-on-one time alone. *Dating* equates to possessiveness about being together, isolated locations, and approval addictions. *Courtship* equates to fostering the relationship, where one spirit seeks for emotional oneness such as an engagement period, and physical oneness can unite once married.

Engagement is the shortest period when choosing a mate, but a start to laying a good foundation for marriage. *Engagement* is the time to prepare for your wedding and final preparation for marriage. In addition, courtship is sacred to you and your partner as to co-habilitation, kissing, intimate hugging, sex, and raising children. These topics should be brought up to decide if this person is the ideal person to undertake in a marriage. Recognize not only your physical bodily desires, but also your emotions over your spirit, which are dedicated to that one partner for the rest of your lives, known as sacred vows. In addition, check with your Heavenly Father for confirmation that this is the ideal man or woman to spend for the rest of your days together on earth with.

Two people physically involved with each other are a difficult time discerning God's will by disregarding His rules for a godly relationship.[509] God also informs us in the Scriptures, not to be unequally yoked.[510]

> *2 Corinthians 6:14, NKJV: "Do not be unequally yoked together with unbelievers. For what fellowship has righteousness with lawlessness? And what communion has light with darkness?"*

Paul urges believers not to form binding relationships with non-believers because this might weaken their commitment, integrity, or standards. He also explained that this did not mean isolating oneself from non-believers.[511] Paul even tells Christians to stay with their non-believing spouses.[512] He wants believers to be active in their witnessing for Christ to non-believers, but not to lock themselves into personal or business relationships that could cause them to compromise their faith. Believers are to avoid situations that could force them to divide their loyalties.

Courtship can fail by not establishing a relationship with a godly person who is held 'accountable' for their actions. Courtship can fail by not receiving blessings from parents or a godly couple. By not listening to God and waiting for His direction. By not completing preparation steps, are viewed as *dating*. During the courtship, some people expect the person they are dating to be perfect, and even their parents expect their child's significant other to be perfect.

How courtship leads to a lifetime with God's chosen, is by focusing on Christ, not each other or the relationship itself. Avoiding warning signals or dangers such as

---

[509] Luke 16:10
[510] 2 Corinthians 6:14
[511] 1 Corinthians 5:9, 10
[512] 1 Corinthians 7:12-13

physical, emotional, and spiritual oneness, which are usually involved in dating relationships. One is willing to establish and enhance communication. See the virtues and faults in a future mate, and encourage and correct them. Courtship preparation before *courtship* begins, which is a commitment, and is the main focus -- building a solid foundation for a lifelong marriage and preventing divorce.

Moreover, it takes faith and courage to wait on God.[513] Patience and waiting for God is not easy. Often it seems that He is not answering our prayers, or does not understand the urgency of our situation. This type of thinking implies that God is not in control, or God is not fair. *Lamentations 3:24-26*, calls us to hope and wait for the Lord because often God uses waiting to refresh, renew, and teach us. Make good use of your waiting times by discovering what God may be trying to teach you. We are to pause for further instructions because troublemaking decisions impulsively without waiting on God's timing and thinking can lead to a disaster. Prayer for purity -- God saves His best for those who are willing to wait.

Courtship process or steps:
1. Identity in Christ
2. Ministry involvement
3. Foundation building
4. Friendship levels: acquaintance, casual, close, and intimate
5. Courtship and accountability
6. Engagement
7. Marriage

Alternatively, dating is a self-centered focus. Here are some reasons for breaking up:
1. Excitement gone; relationship is boring and/or demanding
2. Someone more attractive, or someone better comes along
3. Dating other people
4. One is ready for marriage and the other is not
5. Arguments and constant fighting or debates
6. The romance gone, and do not care anymore
7. Someone does not meet the other needs
8. Never involved seriously in the first place.

Dating for women is usually fantasy-based. For example, she portrays herself as Cinderella, where she gets her prince and lives happily ever after. It is similar to lustful feelings and thoughts. First, it starts with a simple fantasy of belonging to someone and falling in love, and then sexual images play in the mind. Once it starts in the mind, it can lead to sexual activity or masturbation, and continue to fantasize on these lustful thoughts.

---

[513] Psalm 27:14

On the other hand, for men, it is physical. What they see with their eyes, glazing at a woman's physical or physique, how she wears those jeans or tight outfit or sexy dress, and how she walks in it. He imagines what she looks like with her clothes off, naked, and what she would be like in the bed. After speaking to my closest and long time friend, he mentioned that men could view a woman and want to marry her; yet, women want to hold out on sexual contact, nothing serious, and learn this person before giving her all to him. Then, he will lose interest and sleep around with his ex-girlfriends until she is ready to lay down with him.

Once a woman is ready, after her one month to six month rule, she wants it steady and all the time. He is trained not to have sex all the time or everyday as she wishes. When he desired to have sex with his woman, she was not ready. Instead, she assumes he has to be cheating and respond, "You must be cheating on me." After hearing this notion, most men, will go out and cheat. Therefore, we have to ask certain questions to conclude who we will be with.

On the other hand, if a woman does give into a sexual relationship right away, she worries about a man calling her a 'hoe' and other degrading names. If she sleeps with a man, and he does not satisfy her, she will dump him. He will be left wondering what just happened. He wanted it, and she did not, but she gave in to it, and is not pleased with the goods and what he is dishing out. Therefore, men have to be careful what they ask for too.

Dating can counterfeit oneness like marriage, but lack of commitment and responsibility. One usually dates for intimacy, wants to be loved or seeking for love, to be accepted. Woman is viewed as suitable helper, completeness, and oneness.

Male's view: physical→emotional→commitment→spiritual
Female's view: emotional→physical→commitment→spiritual

1 Thessalonians 4:3-8: The temptation is to engage in sexual intercourse outside the marriage relationship has always been powerful. We find ourselves giving in to that temptation can have disastrous results. Sexual sins always hurt someone such as individuals, families, businesses, and churches. Besides the physical consequences, there are also spiritual consequences. Why sexual sins are more harmful, look at *1 Corinthians 6:18*. Sexual desires and activities must be placed under Christ's control. God has created sex for procreation and pleasure, and as an expression of love between a husband and wife. Sexual experience is limited to the marriage to avoid hurting us. The Holy Spirit works in us and conform us into the image of Christ.[514]

God's job is finding you a mate and revealing to you His choice in His time. Prepare yourself to be someone's mate while you wait for God's revelation. However, what you hunger for, you will attract. The type of man you want will be attracted to the

---

[514] Romans 8:29

type of women you are. Alternatively, religion does not disservice us, when it teaches us to kill our desires since there is a misunderstanding with the flesh, and the spirit implies that we avoid everything that refers to the flesh. God created us to have these desires, but also to learn how to master them by bringing our minds, will, emotions, and body under control of the Holy Spirit and by living a spirit-led life.

Spiritual maturity is inner faith and deep beliefs you have intimacy with God. Godly character displays the *Fruits of the Spirit*.[515] God would not allow you to marry someone that you are not attracted to outwardly. God loves you. We are to love and celebrate the person you choose to spend the rest of your life with. However, there is a difference between attraction and respect such as being attracted to someone you do not respect.

Moreover, as followers of Jesus Christ, are told not to be with someone that is an unbeliever. We are to be equally yoked in relationships, which consist of the passion from God on how He views relationships; giving our time and energy in the relationship; politics; money; how to raise children; standards of living; how men and women relate; the role of a man; the role of a woman; and so forth.[516] Once God reveals His revelation, write it in a journal or on paper, write your dreams or visions, and establish your future in your mind.[517] It may be difficult to stay away from your own standards. Your vision will also help you set boundaries, where you will and will not go.[518]

Courtship is a definite direction. Commitment is trust, not even love will hold or save a marriage together, when trust is broken. On the other hand, most single people have the fear of commitment. The Bible talks about the 'spirit of fear' in *2 Timothy 1:7*. Here, Paul speaks of three characteristics of the effective Christian, of which are power, love and a sound mind (wisdom). These are available to us through the Holy Spirit that lives in us. Follow God's lead each day so that your life will move fully to exhibit these characteristics. We cannot live in fear and trust God at the same time. Fear is from Satan and not of God.

As believers of Jesus Christ, we are 'set apart' of which a biblical appropriate behavior would not compromise your integrity or defraud another person. Single tendencies view dating as looking for a marriage partner. Furthermore, dating online sites and phone services are a tool to meet and know other available singles. Yet, courtship is allowing God to do the seeking and searching. He will bring the right person into your life and reveal that choice to you. If a man is willing to make it through the waiting period, he is a serious contender. If you choose to marry him, remain steady. In addition, one that has a willing heart and wisdom to discern God's choice will know when the time is right.

---

[515] Galatians 5:22-26
[516] The Unspoken Love: What Women Don't Know and Men Don't Tell You.
[517] Habakkuk 2:2
[518] Proverbs 29:18

Isaiah 55:9: "For as the heavens are higher than the earth, so are My ways higher than your ways, and My thoughts than your thoughts."

Just like the Israelites, we can foolishly believe we know what God is thinking and planning. We need to get out of our comfort zones by thinking we are in control. At times, it may appear like we are, but God is our creator, and knows us better than we know ourselves. God's knowledge and wisdom are far greater than man's is. We are foolish to try to fit God into our mold -- to make His plans and purposes conform to ours, but instead, we must strive to fit into His plans. We usually do not turn to Him until we are down and out, and have nowhere else to turn to or no one else to call. We can seek God sooner and allow God always in our lives.

Patience is a desire to benefit from one another at your own expense and to become the preeminent force in the relationship. Love holds a relationship together, not infatuation, attraction, or even desire. Love will allow a couple to endure through the hard times, even when things threaten the long-term relationship. Love is worth waiting for. There are three sides to a story: his side, her side, and God's point of view. Prayerfully ask God to reveal this man or woman to you. Do not ask unless you are willing to accept God's answer. Be prepared to act on it and desire to know, and do all for the will of God. God is willing to make his purpose known – do not show it unless you are considering doing it. God will shape and mold you into the person He called you to be, and will speak His plans in your life. Submit your situation to Jesus. God does not shout or shake you up. God whispers and we are able to hear His voice when we are quiet, without any distractions.[519] God desires a spiritual unconditional commitment to Him before matching you with one of His sons or daughters.

Differences Between The Sexes (Choosing God's Best):

Man	Woman
Does not link sex with love	Love & sex inextricably linked
Stimulated by sight & touch	Intuitive
Objection	Subjective
Impersonal	Personal
Steady (sometimes inflexible)	Changeable (adaptable)
Things (centered)	People (centered)
Straight to the point	Sensitive to other's responses
Looks for essentials	Looks for aesthetics
Future-minded (long range goals)	Present-minded (short goals)
Needs significance in life	Needs security
Egotism	Jealousy
Soul modest and body free	Body modest and soul free
Desires sex	Dreams of love
Neglects tasks	Nags partner (neglecting tasks)
Defeated by discouragement	Defeated by loneliness

---

[519] Psalm 46:10

There are **twelve steps** to recognizing God's mate:

1. *The Test of the Word.*[520] Many answers we seek about relationship choices have already been provided in the Bible. The Word has been carefully and prayerfully searched with the faith and expectation that God will reveal His will. There are wise and unwise choices for marriage mentioned in the Bible. Some of these wise choices are a suitable mate, which is one who pleases God.[521] A *suitable mate* is one who can experience anger without being controlled by it and prevents harsh feelings to continue.[522] A *carefully selected mate* is one who has a job. Love is a wonderful thing, but love alone will not buy groceries. A lazy mate is a burden, but an industrious mate is a blessing.[523] On the other hand, *unwise choices* are an ill-chosen mate who is sexually promiscuous. Marriage alone will not automatically reform a loose person's ways. Although behavior changes are possible, it must be demonstrated before marriage.[524] A *tactless mate* is one who has an argumentative and complaining spirit. A person who always has something negative to say will be a pain to live with for the rest of one's life.[525] An *insensitive mate* is one who is not compassionate and does not strive to understand one's partner. Understanding is mandatory for an effective marriage.[526]

2. *The Test of Prayers.*[527] Have I immersed myself in a serious labor of prayer to understand God's direction? God desires to provide us with answers to life's questions, even more than we do desire to receive those answers. For us to hear from God, we must throw aside our worldly weapons of selfishness and pride, so that we can come out with hands raised high in sweet surrender to the authority of God's love.

3. *The Test of Peace.*[528] Is there a serene flow of peace, trust, and contentment about the relationship and its circumstances? Each person has a built in *'early warning system'* for relationships. The purpose of this system is to alert us to any dangers lurking within our decision-making process. If we consistently heed the prompting of this system, it becomes even more sensitive and accurate. If we ignore our inner warnings, the system becomes weaker, less accurate, and eventually mute.

4. *The Test of Communication.*[529] Is it easy to discuss both tough and tender topics, and to address problems together through open discussions in a grudge-free atmosphere? Every relationship encounters those 'hot potato' topics that instantly raise the pressure. The question is not whether a relationship will encounter

---

[520] Psalm 119:105
[521] Ecclesiastes 2:26
[522] Ephesians 4:26
[523] Proverbs 13:4; 2 Thessalonians 3:10
[524] Proverbs 6:25-35
[525] Proverbs 21:9; 27:15-17
[526] 1 Peter 3:7-9
[527] Matthew 7:7
[528] Philippians 4:6-7
[529] James 1:19-20

these threats to good communication, but how they will be handled when they arise. Good communication is crucial to a healthy relationship. Stifled communication hinders growth.

5. *The Test of Complimentary Value.*[530] Are we compatible with each other? Do we regard each other with a sense of value and worth? No more thinking about is he or she as Mr. or Mrs. Right: it is all about our future and long-term goals. Can we compromise our issues, can we get along, and are we able to work the differences out together as a couple? Do not just look at their physical appearance; it is what lies beneath or on the inside.

6. *The Test of Gain or Drain.*[531] Does this person to build me up. Do I have neutral feelings towards them? Do I feel as if I am always giving or always getting? Do I leave this person's presence edified or petrified? We are to look for how they bring the best out of us, to edify and encourage one another. Not someone that is negative, thinks negatively, and speaks negatively, it will only bring out the negative side in us. God wants us to have unspeakable joy.

7. *The Test of Commitment.*[532] Is my partner at the very top of my priority list, above my parents, siblings, friends, former lovers, and possessions? Am I willing, without reservation, to commit myself wholeheartedly to this person, and to wake up next to him or her every morning for the next fifty years? It may seem hard at first, or the thought may seem devastating, but we have to trust in God to choose our mate for us, and lead us in the right direction to them.

8. *The Test of Time.*[533] The relationship may seem 'right' for me, but is it also 'ripe' for me? Timing is important. In addition, the secret to peace with God is to discover, accept, and appreciate God's perfect timing. The danger is to doubt or resent God's timing. This can lead to despair, rebellion, or moving ahead without His advice.

9. *The Test of Finance.*[534] Have both of us lived within our financial means, and handled money well during our life as singles? Are we financially prepared for the expenses involved in marriage? We should look at these questions before jumping into marriage. Once you are married, you may have a joint account, and will have to learn how to take care of you, your spouse, and soon to be family. If one is unable to get their bills under control, this is something that you will bring in the marriage, which can cause much frustration and stress that can be eliminated at an early stage. Take charge and learn to handle your money efficiently. You may consider getting financial counseling or advice from a financial advisor, or take a course or godly counsel from seminars. Be willing to be open for change and change for a future to be financially secured.

10. *The Test of Chemistry.*[535] Do we click? Do I feel physically and emotionally drawn to my partner, and am I pleased by his or her presence and touch? Would

---

[530] I Corinthians 12:14-23
[531] 2 Corinthians 6:14-18
[532] Matthew 19:4-6
[533] Ecclesiastes 3:1-8
[534] Luke 14:28-30
[535] Proverbs 30:18-19

I be easily motivated to satisfy my partner unselfishly? Would I hold back from any sexual activity because of emotions? It is one thing to click, but what does it take to make this relationship work. Most people believe to restore a relationship is through compromising instead of arguing. Moreover, it is more than physical and sexual, but to be able to work things out by learning when to listen instead of talking, to be able to read your partner's emotions without causing conflict, learn how to have intimacy with God and to be filled spiritually, and relate to each other intellectually.

11. *The Test of Godly Counsel.*[536] Have I taken the time to expose my relationship and marriage plans to the caring examination of a trusted and competent counselor? In this relationship, are we able to be real with one another? Are we able to share our future goals, plans, and ambitions with one another? We can support each other, and come to some agreement in the relationship. We could be in love blindly, however, be careful on who we choose. They can be jealous, envious, and wish they were in your shoes. If you think about separation, the best counselor to ask for advice is from God. Be able to hear His voice, see His signs or visions for our lives, or feel God's presence when this person is around us.

12. *The Test of Agape Love.*[537] Am I a selfish person? Would I rather please my partner more than I would like to please myself? Am I willing to do all I can to help my mate reach his or her potential? Do we love each other just as we are, without expecting each other to change? Think about that person or parent that loved you unconditionally. The day you were born, how they nurtured you, talked to you in a soft sweet voice, singing lullabies in your ear, and holding you so close. Kissing on your cheek, whispering *'I love you'* in your ear, and praying that God will have his Guardian Angels to watch over their baby. Imagine how much they loved you and wanted the best for you. Imagine how much Jesus loved all of us, no matter what we did or what we said or how we lived, He died for us on the Cross. Suffered and gave His life up for you and me…this is unconditional love. We may not be expected to lay down our lives, or to be nurtured in a relationship, but hope that our love will be treasured forever.

---

[536] Proverbs 11:14
[537] I Corinthians 13

~Let Your Day Begin With Christ, Day 26~

Let your Day Begin Activity: Today's activity consists of two parts:

The first part is to review the *courtship* steps in the book, take the time to evaluate your previous relationship. Write down how long you did each step in the relationship. Write down what went wrong in the relationship and how long did you as a couple stay in each step. Was it too long or not enough time to grow as a partnership or build the relationship?

The second part of the activity is to take the list that causes 'break ups' and write down 5 things for each point that will keep your relationship from suffering these issues now.

Today's Questions:

What are you seeking after in a relationship? Name the positive and negative behaviors you have seen in past and recent relationships, what would you like to see change? Are you willing to view yourself as the problem in the equation?

Will you be with someone unequally yoked? Why or why not.

Review to Begin your Day with Christ:

Review the 12 steps to recognizing God's best.

1 Thessalonians 4:3-8.

Know the differences between dating, courtships, celibacy, seasons of singleness, and engagement.

Day Begins 27: Singles Building A Healthy Dating Relationship

Do not let a relationship move too fast in its infancy. Romantic affairs that begin frenzy, frequently burn themselves out. Take it one step at a time. Do not discuss your personal inadequacies and flaws in detail when the relationship is new. No matter how warm and accepting your friend may be, any great revelation of low self-esteem or embarrassing weaknesses can be fatal when interpersonal valleys occur. Remember that respect precedes love. Do not call too often on the phone, or give the other person an opportunity to be tired of you. Do not be quick to reveal your desire to get married, or that you think you have found Mr. Wonderful or Miss Marvelous. If your partner has not arrived at the same conclusion, you will throw him or her into a panic.

Cautious lovers who like to nibble at the bait before swallowing the hook are constantly testing relationships. This testing procedure takes many forms, but it usually involves pulling back from the other person to see what will happen. Many weeks pass without a phone call. Sometimes flirtation occurs with a rival. The question, "How important I am to you, and what would you do if you lost me?" The person wants to know, "How free am I to leave if I want to?" Do not grasp the other person and beg for mercy. Some people remain single throughout life because they cannot resist the temptation to grovel when the test occurs.

Extending the same concept, keep in mind that virtually every dating relationship that continues for a year or more, and seems to be moving towards marriage, will be given the ultimate test. A breakup will occur, motivated by only one of the lovers. The rejected individual knows that their future together depends on the skill of how he or she handles that crisis. If the hurting individual can remain calm, the next two steps may be reconciliation and marriage. It often happens that way. If not, then no amount of pleading will change anything. Do not depend entirely on one another for the satisfaction of every emotional need. Maintain interests and activities outside that romantic relationship, even after marriage. Guard against selfishness in your love affair. Neither the man nor the woman does all the giving. Beware of blindness to obvious warning signs that tell you that your potential husband or wife is disloyal, hateful, spiritually uncommitted, hooked on drugs or alcohol, given to selfishness, etc. A marriage is far worse than the loneliest of singleness.

Beginning early in the dating relationship, treat the other person with respect and expect the same in return. A man can open doors for a woman on a formal evening, and a woman can speak respectfully of her escort when in public. If you do not preserve this respectful attitude when the foundations of marriage are being laid, it will be virtually impossible to construct them later. Do not equate human worth with flawless beauty or handsomeness. If you require physical perfection in your mate, he or she may make the same demands of you. Neither of you will keep it for long. Do not let love escape you because of the false accusations. If genuine love has escaped you thus far, do not begin believing 'no one would ever want me.' That deadly trap can destroy you emotionally. Millions of people are looking for someone to love. The problem is finding one another.

Regardless of how brilliant the love affair has been, take time to 'check your assumptions' with your partner before committing yourself to marriage. It is surprising how often men and women plunge toward matrimony without ever becoming aware of major differences in expectation between them. Sexual familiarity can be deadly to a relationship. Besides the many moral, spiritual, and physical reasons for remaining virgins until marriage, there are numerous psychological and interpersonal advantages as well. Men do not respect 'easy' women, and often become bored with those who have held nothing in reserve. Likewise, women often disrespect men, who have only one thing on their minds. Both sexes need to remember how to use the word, 'No.'

If the commitment between a man and a woman is given insufficient importance in their lives, it will wither like a plant without water. Fewer lovers seem to realize that extreme dependency can be just as deadly to a love affair. It has been said that the person who needs the other will normally be in control of the relationship. In romantic interactions, marriage does not eliminate his or her need for freedom and respect. Keep the mystery and the dignity in your relationship. If the other partner begins to feel trapped and withdraws for a time, grant him or her some space, and pull back yourself. Do not build a cage around that person. Instead, release your grip with confidence, while never appeasing immorality or destructive behavior.

Whether we are dating or abiding to courtship, we must follow God's model on relationships. Courting happens only once and ends in a lifelong covenant relationship. On the other hand, dating happens many times that result in heartbreaks, hurtful feelings, and can leave emotional scars. In addition, there are emotional attachments that appear to be acceptable in dating. They engage in rampant emotional promiscuity, giving pieces of their heart, and performing in sexual activities, which one wonders what we have left for our lifelong partners.

Statistical Information *(Americans):*
     83% have zero to one partner per year
     75% of married men are sexually faithful
     85% of married women are sexually faithful

     1/3 Americans have sex two or more times a week
     1/3 Americans have sex a few times a month

     95% of men always or usually reach an orgasm during sex
     75% of married women always or usually reach an orgasm during sex
     62% of never married women, not living with partner always or usually reach an orgasm during sex

1 in 10 men seek help
1 in 5 women seek help

Biblical reasons to wait for *sexual fulfillment*:[538]

> *"Marriage should be honored by all, and the marriage bed kept pure, for God will judge the adulterer and all the sexually immoral."[539]*

> *"And don't you realize that if a man joins himself to a prostitute, he becomes one body with her? For the Scriptures say, "The two are united into one..."[540]*

Some people promise to marry just to 'get with you.' Ultimately, they never really plan to marry you.[541] You cannot have sex outside of marriage and grow as a Christian. Do not feel pressured to have sex by anyone. Moreover, some of us have engaged in sexual activities, but we can be forgiven and remain celibate until marriage.[542] Jesus loved and ministered to sexually immoral people, and told them to stop sinning. Regardless of our sinful nature, we can allow the Holy Spirit to give us peace.[543] If we love and obey God, we will have life, peace, and even our troubles will turn out for good. Fornication and adultery are a sin. You hurt people you love, you bring emotional turmoil and unrest into your spirit.[544]

There are things we can avoid if we focus on courtship leading to marriage, instead of engaging in sexual relationships first. There are nearly one million teen pregnancies reported annually. There are many venereal diseases or STDs. Some of the STDs have been identified as incurable. There are over 16,000 deaths in a year caused by fatal disease like AIDS. In addition, you can avoid cervical cancer, pelvic, inflammatory disease, and infertility by not having sexual intercourse. However, if you decide to be intimate with your partner, it is best to both go to the clinic or doctor's office to avoid any sexual transmitted diseases.[545]

Abstinence is the only 100% reliable method of prevention since any birth control method, not even condoms will guarantee safety from pregnancy or diseases. Abstinence is becoming increasingly popular. More than 50% of high school students have never had sex. Celibacy is increasing, even among those with previous sexual experience.

---

[538] Whitelaw, Daniel. *Health and Emotional Reasons for Waiting for Sexual Fulfillment.* Sermon at Family Conference in 2001, emphasis added by author.

[539] Hebrews 13:4, NIV

[540] 1 Corinthians 6:16 NLT, also review verses 18-20

[541] Refer to other Scriptures Acts 15:20; Proverbs 5:3-13; 6:32

[542] John 8:11; Luke 7:48; Hebrews 4:15

[543] Psalm 37:3-9 and Romans 8:6, 28

[544] Ephesians 5:3

[545] Whitelaw, Daniel. *Health and Emotional Reasons for Waiting for Sexual Fulfillment.* Sermon at Family Conference in 2001, emphasis added by author.

People who have sex before marriage, and those who live with their partners before marriage, have a greater chance of getting divorced. Waiting on marriage can avoid heartbreak, regret, and anger that sex outside of marriage brings. Many people regret it. They feel used and worthless because they gave away something precious. To maintain healthier dating relationships, admit that having sex has ruined the relationship. They stopped getting to know each other and focused on sex instead. We can make better decisions about a marriage partner, but it is harder to break up with someone, even if he or she is not right for you, if you have had sex. Furthermore, we can grow in emotional maturity. Do not use sex as an escape from life's problems.

~Let Your Day Begin With Christ, Day 27~

Let your Day Begin Activity: For today's activity, we will turn a few pages back in the book on finding a carefully selected mate. There are **twelve steps** for recognizing God's mate. With each step, write down what you can do to improve yourself to be a godly mate.

Today's Questions:

What will you do until God reveals or brings your mate to you?

What are you doing to improve your unhealthy relationships to make them healthier?

Review to Begin your Day with Christ:

Not to move too fast in a relationship during the 'infancy stage,' and do not jump into romantic affairs if you want a long lasting relationship.

Discussing flaws, shortcomings, and personal failures can be a turn-off before the relationship begins in the early stages.

Practice abstinence or celibacy until marriage.

Day Begins 28: Soul Mates

Thought you met the man or woman of your dreams, however, the romance blew up in your face. Then, you discover things about the person you never knew while in the relationship. God requires us to stay in the relationship once married and change comes.[546] Moreover, people believe that the way to finding their soul mate is solely by chance, fate, luck, magic, good fortune, or God's grace because they do not realize how it is actually done. Everything is done with God's help, but God helps those who help themselves. Without knowing, we put ourselves in the right place at the right time, and it miraculously happens. We can feel immediate chemistry.

There are different elements creating chemistry. Potential soul mates have many shared interests, but relatively often have other interests. Try looking in places where people have interests different from yours. When a man finds what a woman needs, she feels chemistry. When a woman needs what a man has to offer, he feels chemistry. Emotional chemistry allows us to be aware of any unrealistic pictures of what our ideal partner looks for. Another element of chemistry is maturity. Soul mates have similar levels of maturity. Automatically feel chemistry with someone who reflects a similar or greater level of maturity. Maturity does not necessarily have to do with age. We cannot fully recognize our soul mate until we are ready. We need to know ourselves before recognizing this compatible person for us. Each time we experience a higher stage of dating, our maturity and discernment increases. As we mature, we gain greater wisdom and self-control.

Chemistry equals resonance. Soul mates have similar values that resonate, which inspire us to be the best we can be. When we are with our partner, what is most important to him or she resonates with what is important. Your partner's values concerning God, family, work, and marriage, resonate within you and inspire you. We can focus on the good attributes we see in our mate, to respect and admire his or her values. Not having similar values does not mean you do not think or feel the same way about topics brought up in a discussion. We can also respect your partner's point of view and admire where he or she is coming from.

Resonance creates soul chemistry, which is a combination of different interests, complimentary needs, maturity, and resonance values you share as a couple. However, when resentment builds, then different interests become extreme. When we love our partners, we actually start becoming more interested in their interests. Resonance of values creates a base from where we can work through the differences and find fair compromises. This helps the soul mates harmonize their differences. We are attracted to someone who is different to satisfy the deep yearning of our soul, to expand and embrace that is beyond ourselves. When a man needs chemistry, his experiences tends to be healthy, but when a man is primarily motivated by the possibility of getting his needs met and wants satisfied, then the chemistry he feels is not necessarily healthy. If

---

[546] Ephesians 6:14-15

he thinks about what he can get, then it is unhealthy. When chemistry is unhealthy, it does not mean anything about the ultimate potential of a relationship.

To find a soul mate, not just a secure partner, requires new insight, education and much practice. Although some of us have faced loneliness and struggles in past relationships, we can succumb to our differences and challenges when we desire a quality relationship through communication, honesty, and commitment.

Originally, God created woman for man, Adam knew her.[547] He knew that Eve was not only his woman, but also his other half, his soul mate for life. This woman was what he was missing in Paradise. Adam called her 'woman' since she received a rib from his side -- woman created happiness in Paradise. Remember that marriage is not to please you, but to serve God. Yes, God wants us to be happy. Furthermore, God created Eve as a helpmate to help Adam perform his duties in the Garden of Eden, such as working in the garden, and taking partnership in dominion over the earth before the fall. God's purpose for marriage is a team, fulfilling His call together, not only to be pleased with each other. There is firm conviction that the recreational dating scene is not in God's plan for finding a mate. [548]

---

[547] Genesis 2:25
[548] http://www.polynate.net/courtship/part1.html and emphasis added by author.

~Let Your Day Begin With Christ, Day 28~

Let your Day Begin Activity: To make a relationship work, you have to be honest with yourself and mate. Today's activity is to use the list of qualities that you looked for in a mate in the previous activity and see if the person who you are dating now, possess those qualities. If they do not, get them out of your life immediately. You are looking for a mate to walk with the Lord. If your mate lacks these qualities, it is time for you to move on.

Today's Questions:

> How do you react when you have chemistry with a significant other? Will you be able to contain your emotions to not engage in any sexual activities?

> What do you look for in a soul mate (potential husband or wife)?

Review to Begin your Day with Christ:

> *Soul mate* takes new insight, education, and much practice. Practice in learning and building the relationship by looking at their interests and goals—see if it is workable and willing to build on that as his rib, as his other half.

> *Spirit mate* is when a couple becomes as 'one,' 'togetherness,' and 'unity' under God's covenant. When a man seeks after a woman's heart for God, where he seeks after God first, and then his spirit mate will come. Their spirits harmonize with the Word of God, and love for God is the center focus of their relationship.

Day Begins 29: Generational Plans For Families

The home is a primary setting for the restoration of the image of God. The home is also a place where the principles of real Christianity are put into practice, and its values transmitted from one generation to the next. In forming the first humans, first family, God established the basic social unity for humanity, to have a sense of belonging, and providing them with an opportunity to serve God. Therefore, God created man in His own image and in His likeness.

After God created Adam and Eve, God gave them dominion over the Garden of Eden and all living creatures that roamed the earth.[549] Adam was allowed to name every creature and animal that lived, but none was compatible with him. Yet, God work was not completed until He created woman. Adam further realized since woman was created from his bones and flesh, she was called 'woman.' Moreover, the rib taken from Adam or man symbolizes marriage, 'symbolically becomes one flesh.' The main goal in marriage is more than friendship or companionship, but oneness. In *Genesis 2:21-23*, God forms and equips men and women for various tasks, but the entire task lead to one goal -- honoring God. Man gives life to woman (rib taken from Adam's flesh) and woman gives life to the world (birth).

There is no room for thinking that one sex is superior to the other. God gave marriage as a gift to Adam and Eve. They were created perfect for each other. Marriage was not for convenience. However, God established it. There is three basic aspects. First, man leaves his parents and marries his wife publicly, and vows himself to his wife.[550] Second, man and woman are joined, also taking responsibility for each other's welfare and loving their mate above all others. Third, two become one flesh in the sense of intimacy and commitment of sexual union, in which is reserved for marriage.[551] *One flesh* shows that any physical or sexual bonding is a lifelong relationship between two people, but is together as one.[552]

The foundation of marriage can be found in *Matthew 19:5* and *1 Corinthians 6:16*. However, some people will confuse *Genesis 4:1* as the first sexual experience between Adam and Eve. It is referring to procreation and does not mean this is their first sexual experience. Furthermore, Adam and Eve were the only human inhabitants on the earth, God commanded them to be fruitful and multiply.[553]

We are to be comfortable with our soul mates. For example, Adam and Eve were not ashamed of each other and did not acknowledge that 'they were both naked.' As married couples, we are to love each other unconditionally, and not focus on their downfalls or shortcomings, changes in weight or any physical changes, faults, and any

---

[549] Genesis 1:18-26; 2:15
[550] Genesis 2:24
[551] Life Application Study Bible, NKJV on Genesis 2:24-26.
[552] Ephesians 5:31
[553] Genesis 1:28

negative aspects concerning your mate. Moreover, we will see how Adam and Eve handled labor, family, and relationships. Thereafter, we will see other characters in the Bible that also showcases their gifts, family, and how they handled relationships under a sovereign God.

Adam

Adam was the first and only person on earth. Adam was lonely and never knew another living being. He had no childhood, no parents, no family, or friends. He had to learn to be human on his own. Fortunately, God did not let him struggle too long before presenting him with an ideal companion and mate…Eve. Adam and Eve love was complete, innocent, and open to oneness, without a hint of shame.

His strengths and accomplishments were to name all the animals in the Garden of Eden, the first zoologist, and first landscape architect since he had to tend to the garden. He is the father of our human race and the first person made in the image of God --sharing an intimate relationship with God. Alternatively, his weaknesses and mistakes were avoiding responsibility for his own actions, and he blamed his wife, Eve. He chose to hide rather than to confront the issue at hand with God. In addition, he made excuses, rather than admitting to the truth. Our human race would not be in this situation if he did not touched the forbidden fruit, or told God the truth instead of covering it up. These greatest mistakes, teamed up with his wife, Eve, brought sin into the world, and we are all born into a sinful nature. Only Jesus Christ can save us from death, and give us life. Yet, as Adam's descendants, we all reflect in the image of God and His likeness. We cannot blame others for our faults and we cannot hide from God.

Adam's livelihood was a caretaker, gardener, and a farmer. His relatives were Eve, his wife, sons, Cain, Abel, and Seth, and numerous children not mentioned in the Bible, and the only man who did not have an earthly mother and father.[554]

> *Genesis 3:12, NLT: "[Adam said], 'It was the woman you gave me who gave me the fruit, and I ate it.'"*

> *1 Corinthians 15:22, NLT: "Just as everyone dies because we all belong to Adam, everyone who belongs to Christ will be given new life."*

Eve

Eve is the first woman in the world; also she is the mother of us all. She was the final piece in the intricate and amazing puzzle of God's creation. Adam had another human being with whom to fellowship with, an equal to share in God's image.

---

[554] Can read Adam's story in Genesis 1:26-5:5; 1 Chronicles 1:1; Luke 3:38; Romans 5:14; 1 Corinthians 15:22, 45; and 1 Timothy 2:13, 14. Moreover, men can learn from women and how to treat women with respect and love in Romans 12:9, 10, 16; Philippians 2:1-15 (NIV); I John 4: 20, 21 (NIV); and I Thessalonians 5:11, 13 (NIV).

Satan approached Eve, where she and Adam lived. He questioned her contentment. How could she be happy, when she was not allowed to eat from one of the trees? Satan helped Eve shift her focus from all that God had done and gave in to the one thing God had withheld. Eve was willing to accept Satan's viewpoint, as Satan was speaking through the serpent, without checking with God first. Do we check with God first? We get that, 'I've got to have it' feeling. Eve was typical of us all. We consistently display that we are her descendants by repeating her mistakes. Our desires, like Eve's, can be easily manipulated. They are not the best basis for actions. We need to keep God in our decision-making process always. His Word, the Bible, is our guidebook in decision-making.

Eve strengths and accomplishments were being the first mother and wife. Additionally, she was the first woman alive on earth. She shared a special relationship with God, had co-responsibility with Adam over creation and displayed certain characteristics of God. Her weaknesses and mistakes allowed her contentment to be undermined by Satan, in which she acted impulsively without talking to God or to Adam. Not only did she sin, but shared her sin with Adam, and when confronted, she blamed the serpent.

The necessary ingredients for a strong marriage are commitment to each other, companionship with each other, complete oneness, and absence of shame.[555] The basic human tendency to sin goes back to the beginning of the human. However, Eve's occupation was as Adam's wife, helper, companion, and co-manager of the Garden of Eden.[556]

> *Genesis 2:18, NIV: "The Lord God said, 'It is not good that man should be alone; I will make him a helper comparable to him'."*

Abel

Abel was the second child born into the world, but the first one to obey God. Abel was a shepherd. He presented pleasing sacrifices to God and his short life was ended at the hands of his jealous older brother, Cain. However, the Bible does not tell us why God liked Abel's gift and disliked Cain's, but both Cain and Abel knew what God expected. Only Abel obeyed. Throughout history, Abel is remembered for his obedience and faith, and he is called *'righteous.'*[557] Like Abel, we obey, regardless of the cost, and trust God to make things right.

Abel's strengths and accomplishments was the first member in the 'Hall of Faith.'[558] He was the first shepherd and first martyr for truth.[559] Lessons we can learn

---

[555] Genesis 2:24-25
[556] Her story can be found in Genesis 2:19-4:26 except her death is not mentioned in Scripture. *Wife Roles:* Proverbs 11:22; 12:4; 21:9; 27:15 (NIV); Proverbs 9:13; 14:1; 30:21, 23 (NJKV).
[557] Hebrews 11:4
[558] Hebrews 11

from his life, God hears those who come to Him and recognizes the innocent person -- eventually punishes the guilty. He resided outside of the Garden of Eden. His parents were Adam and Eve; his twin brother is Cain, including numerous siblings not mentioned in the Bible.[560]

> *Hebrews 11:4, NLT: "It was by faith that Abel brought a more acceptable offering to God than Cain did. Abel's offering gave evidence that he was a righteous man, and God showed his approval of his gifts. Although Abel is long dead, he still speaks to us by his example of faith."*

Cain

While we do not know many details of this first-born child's life, his story can still teach us. Cain got angry. Both Cain and his brother, Abel, had made sacrifices to God, except his offerings had been rejected. Cain's reaction gives us a clue that his attitude was probably wrong from the start. Cain had a choice to make. He could correct his attitude about his sacrifice to God. His decision is a clear reminder of how often we understand opposite choices. We may be choosing to murder, but we are still intentionally choosing what we should not. The feelings motivating our behavior cannot always be changed by simple thought-power. However, we can experience God's willingness to help by asking for His help to do what is right, which can prevent us from setting into motion actions that we will later regret.

Cain was the first-born human child, following in his father's profession of farming. However, when he was disappointed, he reacted in anger by taking the negative approach instead of a positive one that was offered. His anger is not necessarily a sin, but actions motivated by anger can be sinful. Anger can be the energy behind a good action, not evil. What we offer to God must be from the heart of which is the best we are and have. The consequences of sin can last a lifetime. Cain was the first murderer recorded in the Bible and history. For some, it is hard to believe that he killed his very own brother. He lived near Eden (in the present day is Iraq or Iran), and after the murderer of his brother, he became a wanderer.[561]

> *Genesis 4:7: "If you do well, will you not be accepted? And if you do not do well, sin lies at the door. And its desire is for you, but you should rule over it."*

Noah

The story of Noah's life involves not one, but two great and tragic floods. The world in Noah's day was flooded with evil. The number of those who remembered the God of creation, perfection, and love had dwindled to one. Of God's people, only Noah was left. God's response to the severe situation was a 120-year long change, during

---

[559] Matthew 23:35

[560] Abel's story is told in Genesis 4:1-8; Matthew 23:35; Luke 11:51; Hebrews 11:4; 12:24.

[561] You can read more about Cain in Genesis 4:1-17; Hebrews 11:4; 1 John 3:12; and Jude 1:11.

which he had Noah build a graphic illustration of the message of his life -- nothing like a huge boat on dry land to make a point. For Noah, obedience meant a long-term commitment to a project. Many of us have trouble sticking to any project, whether God directs it. It is interesting that the length of Noah's obedience was greater than the lifespan of people today. The only comparable long-term project is our very lives. Nevertheless, the great challenge Noah's life gives us -- to live in acceptance of God's grace, an entire lifetime of obedience and gratitude.

Apparently, Noah was the only follower of God left before the flood. He was the second father of God's human race -- a man of patience, consistency, and obedience. He was the first major shipbuilder, an amateur, who created the ark that did not crash into a disaster like the titanic built by professionals. However, his weakness was getting drunk and it embarrassed him in front of his sons. Furthermore, we can learn from his life that God is faithful to those that obey Him. God does not always protect us from trouble, but cares for us despite trouble. Obedience is a long-term commitment. A man may be faithful, but his sinful nature always travels with him.

Noah was a farmer, shipbuilder, and preacher. He was the grandfather was Methuselah, his father was Lamech. Noah's sons were Ham, Shem and Japheth.[562]

Genesis 6:2, NLT: "So Noah did everything exactly as God had commanded him."

Bible Nations Descended from Noah's Sons: Shem, Ham and Japheth

Shem	*Ham*	*Japheth*
Hebrews	Canaanites	Greeks
Chaldeans	Egyptians	Thracians
Assyrians	Philistines	Scythians
Syrians	Amorites	
Shem descendants were called 'Semites.' Abraham, David, and Jesus were descendants from *Shem*.	*Ham's* descendants settled in Canaan, Egypt, and the rest of Africa.	*Japheth's* descendants settled for the most part in Europe and Asia Minor (now Turkey).

--Life Application Study Bible, NKJV

Lot

Some people simply drift through life. Their choices, when they can muster the will to choose, tend to follow the course of least resistance, which is following the way of the world. Lot, Abram's nephew, was such a person.

In his youth, Lot lost his father. Although this must have been hard on him, he was not left without strong role models -- his grandfather, Terah, and his uncle,

---

[562] Noah's story told in Genesis 5:29-10:32; 1 Chronicles 1:4; Isaiah 54:9; Ezekiel 14:14, 20; Matthew 24:37, 38; Luke 3:36; 17:26, 27; Hebrews 11:7; 1 Peter 3:20; and 2 Peter 2:5.

Abraham, who raised him. Still, Lot did not develop their sense of purpose. Throughout his life, he was so caught up in the present moment that he seemed incapable of seeing the consequences of his actions. It is hard to imagine what his life would have been like without Abraham's careful attention and God's intervention. Later, Lot drifted out of the picture because his life had taken an ugly turn. He had so blended into the sinful culture of his day that he did not want to leave it. Then, his daughters committed incest with him. His drifting finally took him in a very specific direction -- destruction.

Lot, however, is called 'righteous' in the New Testament by Peter.[563] Ruth, a descendant of Moab, was an ancestor of Jesus, even though Moab was born because of Lot's incestuous relationship with one of his daughters. Lot's story gives hope to us that God forgives, and often brings about positive results from evil. For example, he was a successful businessman. However, when faced with decisions, he tended to put off deciding, and then chose the easiest course of action. When given a choice, his first reaction was to think of himself.

Lot lived first in UR of the Chaldeans and then moved to Canaan with Abram. Eventually, he moved to the wicked city of Sodom. His occupation was as a wealthy sheep and cattle rancher, and city official in Sodom. His parent was Haran, as mentioned in the Bible, who was later adopted by Abraham after his father passed. His wife was not named in the Bible, who turned into a pillar of salt.[564]

> Genesis 19:16: "And while he lingered, the men took hold of his hand, his wife's hand, and the hands of his two daughters, the Lord being merciful to him, and they brought him out and set him outside the city."

Our human race is a family that shares one flesh and blood: descendants of Adam and the last Adam known as Jesus Christ. Remember, 'we are all of the body,' when prejudice enters your mind or hatred invades your feelings. Each person is a valuable and unique creation of God. Yet, by Adam and Eve's disobedience, after sin, God told woman, "Your desire shall be for your husband, and he shall rule over you."[565] God changed the basic equality of the man and woman, to benefit both married couples thereafter. Today, the original principle was distorted.

---

[563] 2 Peter 2:7, 8
[564] Lot's story is told in Genesis 11-14; 19 also mentioned in Deuteronomy 2:9; Luke 17:28-32; and 2 Peter 2: 7-8.
[565] Genesis 3:16

~Let Your Day Begin With Christ, Day 29~

Let your Day Begin Activity: Do you treat your spouse as equal? Are you ashamed of anything that your spouse does? Today's activity serves two purposes. The first one is for you to realize that you and your spouse are equals. The second is not to feel ashamed of anything your spouse does. Today, write down all the things that makes you feel ashamed about your spouse and take the time to eliminate these things together. You take the lead, for them to get rid of these issues; they need your support.

Today's Questions:

How can you break a generational curse?

Are you instilling godly character and qualities in your home? With God in the home, this can be passed down to generations to come? What is your legacy to share with other family members and/or children?

How much does family mean to you? How can you show love to those you dislike at family affairs?

Which character best suits you? Or who you can relate to? View their strengths or career choices while on earth. How can you improve your family values, beliefs, and morals?

What are your spiritual gifts or accomplishments?

Review to Begin your Day with Christ:

Family: Genesis 12:3; Jeremiah 31:1; Zechariah 12:12; Acts 3:25; Ephesians 5:21-23.

Day Begins 30: Signs Before Marriage

Myths To Reality Before Becoming As One

Before getting married, some typical myths are many people confuse the intense feelings of sex with true love, or believe great sex is love. *Good* sex is physical stimulation performed with or without love. Usually there are selfish motives, where some suffer from emotional or physical abusive relationships. Others believe if they have sex with their partner, they will never be lonely again. Moreover, they are mistaking sex for love. Likewise, marriage makes one happier than they were before. These are all myths that most people believe will happen before marriage.

After the sparks of romance, it fades. Marriage takes plenty of work, sacrifice and compromise. Statistics shows that younger couples that marry are more likely to divorce. Teen marriages end in divorce by 78%. Do not marry someone that you hardly know, try to learn more about them for at least a year. After a one year acquaintance, you will be able to judge how marriage will be since you will be able to judge compatibility, see if they are financially stable before raising a family, and evaluate important issues.

Some key factors why people get married for the wrong reasons: pregnancy or already have children as a couple; someone hoping marriage will cure loneliness, depression, and/or leaving their unhappy life; and their primary reason for marriage is to have sex. There are red warning signs to look out for in a relationship. The ability to love is to observe how your mate treats their parents, friends that are of the opposite sex, and family members. Furthermore, ask the family, co-workers, friends, and neighbors, to see if they have any problems or issues with your mate that you should be aware about.

Then you are able to evaluate the relationship for any 'danger signals' of possible violence or infidelity towards you. Verify if they abuse alcohol or any type of drugs, and beware of anger that is uncontrollable, or they are unable to work through. What are their hopes of change after marriage and ask how many times they have broken relationships with the opposite sex before courting with you?

Conversely, you can wait for improvement within six months to a year while dating, to see if this is the person for you, and praying to God for discernment to know if this is the one. In addition, many people natively think that marriage will solve all their problems. Here are some problems that marriage will not solve: sexual temptations, satisfaction of one's deepest emotional needs, and elimination of life's difficulties.

Marriage alone does not hold two people together, but commitment does of which is the commitment to Christ and to each other, despite conflicts and problems. As wonderful as marriage sounds, it does not automatically solve every problem. Whether married or single, we must be content with our situation and focus on Christ, not on loved ones to help address the problem.[566]

Before considering someone as your soul mate or the person you will spend the rest of your life with, review their political, social, and cultural views, on guidance, rules, and individual affections. Regardless of our estrangement of affection, human rebellious mannerisms, or we are following our divine will (purpose), God desires obedience from His children to follow His will and purpose. Through obedience, intuition guides us; sense of any situation; helps resolve conflicting feelings; alternative images of the future; assures character in relationships; and furnishes creativity.

God also speaks on *convictional character*, which generates the courage to choose and act. In addition, the experience of hearing God's will, which empowers the action that God wills. However, God's words can be distorted and perverted by our own desires or peculiar circumstances of our own hearing. Yet, it is known that God speaks with clarity and wisdom.[567]

Some single people feel tremendous pressure to be married. They think their lives can be complete only with a spouse. However, Paul underlines the one advantage of being single is the potential of a greater focus on Christ and His work. In other words, if you are unmarried, you have the special opportunity to serve Christ wholeheartedly.[568]

When Paul says the unmarried person does even better, he is talking about the potential time available for service to God. The single person lacks the responsibility of caring for a spouse and raising a family. Singleness, however, does not ensure service to God. Involvement in service depends on the commitment of the individual. Paul's advice comes from the Holy Spirit, who guides and equips both single and married people to fulfill their roles.[569] He clearly distinguishes his words of Christ when he speaks to virgins and unmarried widows.[570] Although Paul is concerned with both celibate men and women, the attention here is on the women.

By the second century, the church had developed important offices for virgins, widows and deaconesses. They were able to help the pastors and deacons in baptizing, ministering to the sick, and other works of mercy. In addition, a virgin would have lesser family responsibilities, and would not be deterred by the possibility of repercussions affecting her husband or children. Paul does not want to be understood as prohibiting marriage altogether. However, married couples are to dedicate themselves to God's work.

Another interpretation of Verses 36-38, any man has to speak to the father of an unmarried virgin. When she is past the *flower of youth,* shows that the virgin is

---

[566] Life Application Study Bible, NKJV, 1996.

[567] 1 Corinthians 14:33

[568] Life Application Study Bible, NKJV, emphasis added by author.

[569] 1 Corinthians 7:40 –Life Application Study Bible, NKJV, 1996.

[570] Nelson Study Bible, NKJV, I Corinthians 7:25-40.

approaching age at which marriage would be unlikely. It also refers to a fiancé, who is maintaining a celibate state. The Greek term, *she is past the flower of her youth,* is translated, he has strong passions. On the other hand, if he can control himself (has power over his own will), he should maintain his celibacy. If the man can control himself and keep himself from immoral action, he should stay single. However, if the man's will is weak, he should go ahead and marry. Paul urges all believers to make the most of their time before Christ's return. Every person in every generation should have a sense of urgency about telling the Good News to others. Life is too short -- there is not much time.

~Let Your Day Begin With Christ, Day 30~

Let your Day Begin Activity: Marriage is a sacred event. Today, write down all the things that could cause you to leave your spouse and make a vow to discuss the issue with them in depth. This way, everyone understands that the relationship is not to be taken lightly. Communication is the key. Discuss what you will and will not tolerate. Use God's Law, the Bible, as your reference. This is the time to put everything out in the open. Do not hold your tongue.

Today's Questions:

What is Paul's perspective on *unmarried and widows* and those that are *married*?

What are the danger signs of an unhealthy relationship? What are you willing to do to get out of this relationship or work on it?

Name several problems that can happen to married couples.

Review to Begin your Day with Christ:

Convictional character = courage to choose and act. God can give us clarity and wisdom.

Some couples marry for all the wrong reasons, but we are still under a sacred union under God's covenant. We cannot jump to divorce when things are not right for us, only if it is for good intentions e.g., physical abuse, infidelity, etc. Their attitude, interests, and so forth is not a legitimate reason for divorce.

Some of us are not meant to be married -- we are to remain single.

Day Begins 31: Marriage And Children

Living Under God's Standards, Not The World's

A perfect mate is compatible, lovable, and comprehensive to each other's needs. Moreover, the Holy Word describes our roles as husband and wife: to be a working relationship, where the husband is to love her, comfort her, honor and keep her in sickness and in health, and forsaking all others to keep only into her as long as they both will live. Duties and expectations of a good spouse are located in *Romans 3:10-18*, which further explains that no one is righteous, not one. Therefore, do not expect the perfect mate.

We are to be thankful for His gift bestowed on you. *His gift bestowed on you* is a person He has chosen for you. Moreover, marriage is to glorify the Lord. God blessed us with the gift of matrimony.[571] Evidently, God has a divine lifetime plan: one woman and one man committed to each other for life.[572] God's solution for man's loneliness is marriage, not dating. Marriage is viewed as a monogamous relationship when we become 'one flesh' as described in the Bible. .

Additionally, Scriptures describe marriage as a decisive act of both detachment and attachment. One will leave his father and mother, and cleaves to his wife, and they will be one flesh.[573] Furthermore, *leaving* means a marriage relationship is to supersede that of the parent and the child. Leaving one's relationship with one's parents allows one to 'cleave' to another. Without this process, there is no firm foundation for marriage. *Cleaving*, the Hebrews term, *cleave* means to stick to, to fasten, to join, and to hold onto. Closeness and strength of this bond illustrates the nature of the bond of marriage. Any attempt to break up this union, can emotionally damage the couples in love.

Covenanting is a promise, in which married couples are bound together, and is spoken as a *covenant* binding agreement known in God.[574] The relationship between husband and wife is connected with God's everlasting covenant with His people and the church.[575] Their commitment to each other is to take on the faithfulness and endurance that characterize God's covenant.[576] God and the couple's family and friends witness the covenant, which is also ratified in heaven.[577] The Christian couple understands that marriage is covenanted to be faithful to each other for as long as they both will live.

Biblically speaking, *becoming one flesh,* figuratively states that a married couple walks together, stands together, and shares a deep intimacy. *Oneness* refers to the

---

[571] Elisabeth Elliot
[572] Genesis 2:24
[573] Genesis 2:24, KJV
[574] Mal. 2:14; Proverbs 2:16, 17
[575] Ephesians 5:21-23
[576] Psalm 89:34; Lamentations 3:23
[577] Matthew 19:6

physical union of marriage. In addition, it refers to the intimate bond of mind and emotions that under grids the physical side of the relationship.

> "To become one **flesh** means that two persons become completely one with body, soul, and spirit, and yet there remain two different persons."

Intimacy in becoming *one flesh* involves sexual union: "Adam knew Eve, his wife, and she conceived."[578] Since the days of Adam and Eve, each couple reenacts the first love story. The act of sexual intimacy is the closest thing to a physical union, of which represents a closeness the couple can experience emotionally and spiritually too. Christian marriage is a mixture of love, warmth, joy, and delight.[579] Marriage is honorable among all and the bed undefiled.[580]

The Scripture clearly states that the joyous sexual expression of love between husband and wife is God's plan. *Undefiled* means not sinful and bed not soiled. It is a place of great honor in marriage, where husband and wife meet privately to celebrate their love for each other. It is meant to be both holy and intensely enjoyable. Moreover, sex is worship, it is a communion, and it is a martial duty ordained by God. To withhold sex to punish your mate is a sin.[581] Talk. Let your mate know your needs. Influence him or her to become a better lover. With unity of spirit, soul, and body -- God is well pleased and glorified. "Can two walk together, without agreeing?"[582] Clearly, requires believers to marry only those that believe in Jesus Christ too.

True oneness demands an agreement such as one's beliefs and practices. To achieve the oneness according to the Scripture, people must marry others within their own communion. To become one flesh, two people must become completely loyal to each other. When one marries, one risks everything, and accepts everything that comes with one's mate. Those who marry proclaim their willingness to share their mates' accountability, and to stand with their mates against anything.

However, differences in religious experience lead to differences in lifestyle that can create deep tensions and rifts in the marriage. Marriage requires an active, pursuing love that will not give up. For instance, two people share everything they have, including not only their bodies, or material possessions, but also their thinking and feelings that project in the relationship as a whole, which is not limited to their joy and their sufferings, hopes and fears, and successes and failures.

Marital love is an unconditional, affectionate, and intimate devotion to each other. It also encourages mutual growth in the image of God in all aspects of the person: physical, emotional, intellectual, and spiritual. The *types of love* that operate in marriage

---

[578] Genesis 4:1
[579] Proverbs 5:18, 19
[580] Hebrews 13:4
[581] Ephesians 4:26-27, NIV
[582] Amos 3:3, KJV

are romantic, passionate times; highly sentimental times; comfortable times; companionable and sense-of-belonging times. The *agape love* comprises the foundation of true, lasting marital love.

Jesus manifested the highest form of this type of love when accepting guilt, and the consequences for our sins when He went on the Cross. Describing this type of love, Paul talks more about it in *1 Corinthians 13:4-8*, which means, one loves no matter what. No matter how unlovable the other person is, agape can keep on flowing. *Agape* is unconditional as God love is for us. It is a mental attitude with a deliberate choice of will. Individual spiritual responsibility, as marriage partners, they must bear the responsibility for the choice they make.[583] Taking such responsibility means that they will never blame the other person for what they themselves have done. They must also accept the responsibility for their own spiritual growth since no one can rely on another's spiritual strength.

On the other hand, everyone's relationship with God can serve as a source of strength and encouragement to the other.[584] According to *Healing the Hurt in Your Marriage*, God's Word is full of instruction, admonition, and encouragement about our relationship on every level. The Bible provides clean instruction for resolving conflict and healing from hurt. A healthy fear of God is manifested in our trust with God. It will help deliver us from other fears that can damage our lives and marriage.[585] There are two types of controllers known as active and passive.

Active controller is someone that is in charge, controls the decision-making process, determines the course of action, and dominates what happens in his or her relationship. P*assive controller* has a low need for control and high need to please. During conflict, they have opinions, needs and suggestions, but tend to back off to keep the peace and make the spouse happy. Furthermore, they allow their partner to dominate the relationship, simmer under the surface. Learn to express yourself unequivocally, instead of struggling for dominance or power in the marriage.

Paul gives rules for three sets of household relationships for husbands and wives; parents and children; and masters and slaves (bondservants). In each case, there is a mutual responsibility to submit and love; to obey and to encourage; working hard and being fair. Examine your family and work relationships. Christian marriage involves mutual submission, subordinating our personal desires for the good of the loved one, and submitting ourselves to Christ as Lord. Consequently, children are to be handled with care. They need firm discipline administered with love. Do not alienate them by nagging, deriding, or destroying their self-respect so that they lose heart.[586]

---

[583] 2 Corinthians 5:10
[584] Seventh-Day Adventists Believe
[585] 2 Timothy 1:7
[586] Life Application Study Bible, NKJV, 1996.

Diagram 1   **Diagram 2**

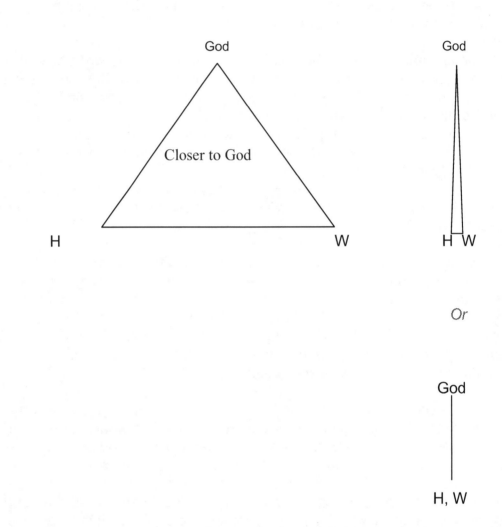

*H-Husband, W-Wife, God are the descriptors in the diagrams above.

Diagram 1: Shows if your marriage is under God, this is what our Heavenly Father wants. God is our priority in what we do, even in our marriage or union. God desires us to be equally yoked with our mates. *Equally yoked* means that we are to be with someone that believes in what we believe in. Regardless of opposites attracting, we do not need to start out our relationship in confusion on different religions. For example, one couple worships Allah (Muslim, Nation of Islam), and other couple worships Jehovah (Jehovah Witness). Do not you think these two different religions would cause confusion among members in a marriage?

Diagram 2: This diagram demonstrates how our relationship is stronger, focused, and relying on God.

Diagram 3   **Diagram 4**

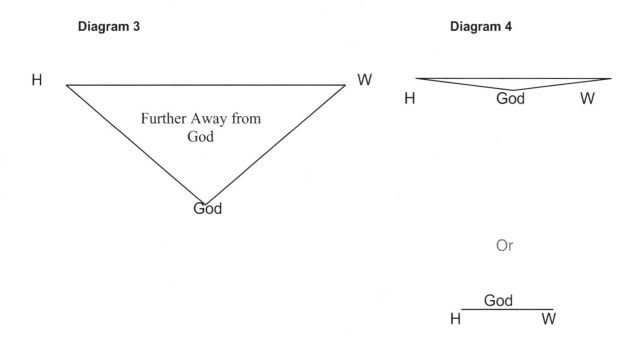

*H-Husband, W-Wife, God are the descriptors in the diagrams above.

Diagram 3: Displays someone or both parties in the marriage are not making God first, or falls further away from God's guidance and wisdom in their marriage, which shows that God is on the bottom of their list of priorities and their focus is more on each other. Once we start to focus on each other, it depends on 'self.' You find 'self' making demands in the relationship can end up in divorce, or fighting and/or cheating. One will blame the other for not meeting them halfway, or not doing the things to keep the relationship working. Marriage is a job and takes time to make it work, however, without God you will refer to each other. Self can demand, 'you need to do this for me,' 'I want this out of the relationship.' Whatever happened to, 'I want to please you and submit to you,' 'I love you so much, that I am willing to lay my life down for you,' or 'we need to study the Word of God, and pray to keep our marriage in harmony, rely on God in all that we do.'

Diagram 4: Is an overview of selfish ways usually found in a marriage, and not having God in your lives at all. Only focus on self, and lose the meaning of matrimony completely. Similar to Diagram 3, one can change and confess their sins, to get back on track. However, this diagram means you do not have God in the first place, and never expect having Him at this point.

Submitting to your mate is very important. As his wife, a godly woman, the man feels his heart, his results, and his emotions are safe with you. A woman contributes to regulating his emotions and decisions by cooling him down when he is upset. The flame would stir up his passion for God, in his ambitions, and in his home. *Consistency* is a wife who is always there, and someone he can always count on. This way, he knows what to expect from you because your character is sound and known. Not to come home to an emotional roller coaster, a different woman everyday. He needs to have access to your heart, your softness and comforting words, reassurance as you counsel him, always his side, and vice versa.

Furthermore, Paul urges believers not to regard marriage, home or financial security, as the goal of life. We live unhindered by the cares of this world, not getting involved with burdensome mortgages, budgets, investments, or debts that might keep us from doing God's work. A married man or woman, as Paul points out, must take care of earthy responsibilities, but making every effort to keep them modest and manageable.[587]

> *1 Corinthians 7:33-34, NIV: "But a married man is concerned about the affairs of this world -- how he can please his wife[34] -- and his interests are divided. An unmarried woman or virgin is concerned about the Lord's affairs: Her aim is to be devoted to the Lord in both body and spirit. But a married woman is concerned about the affairs of this world -- how she can please her husband."*

Usually happy marriages display honesty, open communication about conflicts by negotiation, compromise, and problem solving. Communication uncovers areas to make relationships stronger and deeper. One should be able to have humor and acceptance, forgiveness, treat one another as equals in decision-making and certain areas in life, and to be reliable and responsible adults in the marriage.

> *Proverbs 19:14, NKJV: "Houses and riches are an inheritance from fathers, but a prudent wife is from the Lord."*

A *prudent wife* is a woman who demonstrates wisdom or skill. Finding the right spouse is a blessing from God, which further demonstrates that it is good to be married.[588] Today's marriage tends to emphasize on an individual's freedom. Strong individuals are important, but strong marriages are important too. God created marriage for our enjoyment and views it as good.[589]

---

[587] Life Application Study Bible, NKJV, 1 Corinthians 7:33-34.
[588] Proverbs 18:22
[589] John 2:1-11 and Genesis 2:21-25

~Let Your Day Begin With Christ, Day 31~

Let your Day Begin Activity: Review the diagrams (Diagram 1, 2, 3 and 4), write down which one you are. Our focus is to have a closer relationship with God. The husband is the head of the household, where he loves his wife as he loves himself and demonstrates the same love as Jesus Christ loves the church [His people]. The wife is to be submissive to her husband, and he is the vessel to become as one flesh to serve and worship God. Children are to honor their parents. Today as a family, form closeness with God that is out of the ordinary. Think of something special that can bring the family closer as well and forming a closer bond with God.

Today's Questions:

What are the five most basic needs in a marriage for a man and woman? Do you agree or disagree? According to the book, *Five Love Languages*, what is the five ways love is expressed? Which one is yours?

If you are married, why did you join in this union? If you are not married, what are some reasons you would like to get married? What is God's view on marriage?

Review to Begin your Day with Christ:

Read *1 Corinthians 7:33-34; 13:4-8* and *Ephesians* 5. Review other Scriptures in the Bible on marriage and love.

Submission: Ephesians 5:21-33; Colossians 3:18; and 1 Corinthians 12:1, 4, 8-10.

Happy marriages: Proverbs 5:18-20; 19:14.

Day Begins 32: Set Boundaries In Marriage

In marriage, it requires discipleship. For couples to abide in discipleship, they first must understand the analogy of bridegroom and the bride. The husband is the maker and the wife is the bride. Likewise, Christ love for His Bride, His leadership, and her submission. No bride or groom can enter marriage without surrendering the right to self.

Instructions	1 Corinthians 7:1-9
Christians that never marry	1 Corinthians 7:6-9
Unbelievers divorce, one becomes a Christian may remarry	2 Corinthians 5:17
God's sexual relationships (not homosexuality)	Romans 1:26-32
Christian men to love their wives as the Church	Ephesians 5:25-29
Divorce if spouse committed adultery	Matthew 19: 8-9
Christians are not free to marry once divorced	1 Corinthians 7:10-11
Divorced, unable to remarry first spouse	Deuteronomy 24:1-4
Never loved his or her spouse and wants a divorce	Matthew 5: 31-32
Believer wants a divorce, and unbelieving spouse wants out of marriage	1 Corinthians 7:13-16
Test everything	1 Thessalonians 5:21-22
Sex before marriage	1 Corinthians 6:9-10
Desire someone else other than spouse (committing adultery without physical sex)	Matthew 5:27-28
Marriage does not concern age group (e.g., 30 and 40 year old)	1 Corinthians 7:2
Married couples abstain from sex	1 Corinthians 7:3-5
Forgive spouse of adultery instead of divorce	Matthew 19:8-9
Responsibility	Romans 5:3-4
Forgiveness	Hebrews 12:11
Equality	Ephesians 5:28-33
Unequally yoked	2 Corinthians 6:14-15
God's grace	Ecclesiastes 7:20; 1 John 3:4
One woman and one man	Genesis 2:22-24

Marriage is not only a contract -- it is a covenant between couples and God, as *one flesh* or *union*. Marriage was God's idea.[590] Love is a decision consciously made, an act of will (emotion), and a sacrificial commitment.[591] The commitment level is that God is leading in this relationship on a spiritual or emotional oneness, which usually starts as intimate friendship before marriage after discernment. God brings spiritual power into a future marriage that will require commitment to being 'set apart, holy and sanctified' in a personal relationship.

Marriage is an *unconditional commitment* to imperfect people:

> I will love you until one of us dies.
> I will honor you until one of us dies.
> I will cherish you until one of us dies.
> I will not be involved with any other substitute mate.
> I will perform all the duties of a spouse until one dies.
> I will be loving and faithful through every circumstance, for as long as the two of us live.

God's covenant is to abide to his plans for marriage. Are you committed to your mate? Are you willing to sign your name on the dotted line, and did God lead you into this matrimony? If so, God will fulfill and bless this marriage. This covenant signed and honored by our Lord, Jesus Christ. Amen.

According to *Boundaries in Marriage*, when two people are free to disagree, they are free to love. When they are not free, they live in fear, and love dies. Marriage is one of God's greatest gifts to humanity. However, we seem to overlook this gift as marriage being convenient, something to take away loneliness and depression, for financial support, or for all the wrong reasons. *Marriage* is also a lifetime of love and commitment to one person with whom we can share a life as one. *Marriage* is bonded together by caring, needing and companionship, and values shared between two people, who can overcome hurt, immaturity and selfishness, to form something much better than what a person can do alone.

There is a triangle of boundaries: freedom, responsibility, and love.[592] In essence, we live free, take responsibility for our own freedom, and love our Heavenly Father. Cloud and Townsend state that love only exists where there is freedom and responsibility are operating. Love creates more freedom that leads to more responsibility, in which leads to a greater ability to love. In a marriage, some will view it as evil since there are members that will gossip and spread rumors in the church and outside of the church to destroy the love you share for one another, or that bond that you share as a couple. In addition, people continue to try to come between the marriage, like facing temptation and engaging in a sexual act with someone that is not

---

[590] Philippians 2:3
[591] John 15:3
[592] Boundaries in Marriage

your marriage partner because of an emotional rollercoaster. Satan will set up other traps to lunge you in.

The book, *Boundaries in Marriage,* is teaching married couples how to set boundaries to protect your relationship and learning more about yourself. It is not about setting boundaries for the other person. If we are setting boundaries for our mate, this is a controlling situation. Communication is the key factor in any type of relationship such as reading body language, gestures, facial expression, and verbal comments expressed. Truth is another important boundary. God is the truth. Examples are: not lying to one another; love one another faithfully and sacrificially; not committing adultery; not to desire another person or what they have, will not covet; learn to give to others; to be more compassionate; and most of all, to be able to forgive.

You cannot make your spouse grow up since it is between him and God. We do not have the power to change our spouse, nor their destructive behaviors and attitudes.[593] However, we do have some power and choices. We can choose to tell the truth about our faults and bring those faults in the light of the relationship. We can choose to repent for these faults, work them out, and mature from them. Pray to God, instead of seeking gratification from your mate. Submit to God's authority by staying connected to the life of God.[594] Stay in God's love, His presence in our lives to limit sin and temptations. Overall, when we do not admit the truth about who we are, we give our spouse no chance to connect with us.[595] Testing your faith develops perseverance; it requires work to mature. Without seeing your own faults and shortcomings, you are not able to give it to God.[596]

Obviously, the structure of marriage is to be anti-selfish. Yet, emotional absence exposes our weaknesses and failure to relate to the other person. From time to time, couples struggle with judging, criticizing, and condemning each other. It becomes difficult in accepting these differences from others by misreading the person's actions out of a need to be loved and accepted. One might be disgusted with the sinful nature, but may also hate the sinner. This will eradicate the love in a marriage if one becomes so judgmental. God is the only Judge who can control our decisions, except God does give us the freedom to choose. The requirement in marriage is for oneness, in which requires two complete people.[597]

Instead of bringing up differences, we are to focus on one's talents, abilities, good qualities, experiences, and other gifts, of which reflect and enhance the relationship that is forming into a partnership. Each person is responsible for developing these character imbalances. In other words, we are to make sure we are completely on track in the relationship to help our mate.

---

[593] Romans 7:15
[594] Romans 6:13
[595] 1 John 1:8
[596] James 1:25
[597] Boundaries in Marriage.

For instance, if your mate is arguing over past incidents to start a conflict or confrontation, you are to remain calm and de-escalate the situation without causing more irritation. If you feel it is out of your hands, call the relationship to our Heavenly Father, to free us. Even if one has to sleep on the couch until the heat of an argument has settled down. You do not need to reply angrily to get your point across. It is not about you, it is about you and your spouse making the relationship mends through compromise and understanding each other's feelings. Moreover, God designed human beings not to go through their life alone. God will meet our needs for a deserving relationship, no longer wishing for someone to walk into your life.

Don't fool yourself that marriage is 'peaches and cream,' since there are times you are on 'rocky road.' Marriage has its difficult moments, conflicts, years spent and old experiences. In addition, there will be rejections, arguments, and feelings hurt. It can be a difficult task of accepting imperfections and immaturity. However, deception damages the relationship by lying to one another. Usually this can be worked out, unless one denies there is a problem. Sometimes, it is hard to be honest about their feelings, disappointments, desires, likes or dislikes, pain, anger and hatred, sex, sins, failure, needs and vulnerabilities. However, falsehood is not a way to protect or save the relationship since it can destroy any chance of a real relationship.

Faithfulness is to trust one another in all areas, where one can be depended on what was promised, and to follow through on what your spouse has entrusted to you. As a couple or marriage, we are to be faithful with our bodies and our heart. Sexually faithful, also not to stray from the one you love. *Emotional adultery* is an affair with the heart, when you desire someone in your mind and heart. God remains faithful. Do not let your spouse's failures of love be an excuse for your unfaithfulness. Having an affair will destroy many people who need to be rescued.[598] Remain faithful until the end. No failure is larger than God's grace.[599] You can expect failure even from the best people. God designed both spouses to invest continually in their love for each other. God says that you are equal in His eyes.[600]

Overall, boundaries are to protect love, freedom, and allow people to be who they are, and to stay connected as a married couple. Enter the process of boundary building as a team. Develop self-control and patience to be more humble and self-connecting to your partner. Appreciate your mate for who they are instead of using them. Furthermore, respect the freedom from your spouse, and avoid withdrawing from your spouse, or attacking them with complaints, or making them feel guilty.

God does not want you to come into a relationship to set limits. He wants you. Confessing your needs and faults to loving people, you will grow spiritually and emotionally. Forgive and let go of things in the past, do not masquerade with your broken dreams or promises, or continue to carry unnecessary baggage. People have a

---

[598] Proverbs 2:16-19; 5:3-20; 6:23-25
[599] Ecclesiastes 7:20; 1 John 3:4
[600] Ephesians 5:28-33

difficult time changing when their feelings are neglected and dismissed. God is the answer to proceed with change. Validation and grace softens the burden of change. You may need to change even if your spouse does not.[601] Boundaries were not designed to end relationships, nor to preserve and deeper them, nor to escape from suffering or responsibility.[602]

Ironically, 50% of new marriages in America end in divorce. African-American marriages have a higher separation and divorce rate than Caucasians. Usually 63% of women get custody of the children and two-thirds of the divorces are filed by women. Statistics show that children are better off with a happy single parent then in an unhappy household. If you think about divorce or separation from your spouse, it is best to talk to a divorce lawyer on financial and other legal matters. Alternatively, seek professional help from a counseling psychologist, or licensed counselor, or therapist, or even a psychiatrist before completing your divorce. Additionally, there is striking evidence shows that 50-70% of child mental health referrals show that emotional distress is caused from parents divorcing or separating. There are 21-52% divorced fathers, who had no contact with children at all. Before resorting to divorce, there is a six-stage process for restoring your marriage:

1. Prepare your heart
2. Diffuse your anger
3. Communicate your concerns
4. Confront your conflicts
5. Forgive your spouse
6. Rebuild your trust

Communicate your concerns is a process of healing and to express your hearts to each other is another solution. We are to connect with her or his heart; connect with the facts; and connect with a solution. Forgiveness is the key to conflict in marriage. Consequently, if you refuse to acknowledge the hurt or pain, you will take it out on your spouse without acknowledging all the pain built up inside. Instead, give it to God.[603] Remember that resentment only feeds anger. Resentment impairs the sense of understanding, undermines the healing of our hearts, and destroys the working of a gracious God in our lives. Forgiveness is requested, and then forgiveness is granted.

To rebuild the walls of marriage, we have to cry out to God through prayer by speaking honestly and wholeheartedly. We have to be willing to commit to healing. We can evaluate the damage caused, and then formulate a plan to restore the relationship. Once we have formulated a plan, we have to put this plan in action. Moreover, we have to trust God to bring forth the inevitable solution until it has been completed.[604]

---

[601] Cloud, pp. 217, 221, 222, 223
[602] Romans 5:3-4
[603] Matthew 11:28; 1 Peter 5:7; 2 Corinthians 5:19
[604] www.divorceproof.com or call 1-888-ROSBERG Divorce-proofing America's Marriage.

~Let Your Day Begin With Christ, Day 32~

Let your Day Begin Activity: Today's activity is to take the unconditional commitment list and write down 5 things on each point on why you will do this for your spouse. Why will you love them? Why will you honor them? Why will you cherish them? Make sure that no reason is repeated. Have a fresh new answer for every point.

Today's Questions:

What are some steps to divorce-proof your marriage?

Review to Begin your Day with Christ:

Marriage is an *unconditional commitment* to imperfect people. Couples are to grow as one flesh, edifying, and help each other in their calling. Overall, it is a covenant signed and honored by God.

In marriage, we are to have freedom, responsibility, and love.

Day Begins 33: Raising Children

Pregnancy is a blessing for happily married couples that want children, especially those with financial resources to raise a family. Anyone who becomes pregnant, or decides to raise a child, needs to understand the enormous psychological and behavioral consequences. On another note, mothers that breastfeed will satisfy the baby needs for intimacy, touch, interaction and affection. In addition, breastfeeding will regain a mother's physique, and the uterus will return to its normal size quicker. Infants are able to fight infections and diseases, have less constipation and diarrhea, and spit up less, and have smaller stools and fewer allergies than bottle-fed babies have. Breastfeeding also increases intelligence and avoids being obese. Breastfeeding is usually done six to twelve times a day.

Conversely, parents can choose a name together, or the father or mother chooses a name for the child. Sometimes, a family member will select a name for the child who has meaning, or the name of a deceased relative. In the ancient times, names could not be separated from character. Today, we use nicknames to classify someone, or a characteristic about a person. Names can bring a certain idea to mind such as Judas, Delilah, Jezebel, Hitler, Billy Graham, Martin Luther, Sadaam Hussein, Martin Luther King Jr., etc. What do people think about your name when they hear it?

Yet, Jesus still changes names. For example, God gave Pharaoh's sister the name for Moses, which means drawn out of the water. The name Jehovah is translated Lord, from YHWH or Yahweh. However, deeply religious Jews feared of violating God's name based on Scripture *Exodus 20:7*, and would not pronounce the sacred name or the primary name for God accurately. So, Jews submitted *Adonai* as God's sacred name. God is concerned about His name. Conversely, we are to protect the name of our children.[605]

Some names can give you power or a reputation. A person's death may be better than the day of birth, if the name of that person has merited a lasting reputation and influence. For instance, names were given to both men and women in the Bible to provide a sense of connection to God. Children need definition. If people mispronounced their names, or laughed at them, children had to defend their names and identities. A name is a 'spoken definition' of who you are and spiritual realm.[606] Naming children must be aware of what they are creating. Lay the foundation by entering a relationship with God, or reconnect with God. God will rename us to redefine our identity. Names also show how much God values us, specific significance, and to obtain a personal sense of value and purpose. Allow our Heavenly Father to name you. Picture your value and quiet out those negative voices inside your head. Several times in the Bible, God changed names to signify a change in calling, appointment, destiny, and even a change in nature.

---

[605] Ecclesiastes 7:1 and Proverbs 22:1
[606] Proverbs 18:21

For example, my name is very difficult to find on babynames.com and other websites that gives the meanings of your name. However, I finally was able to find a site with a close spelling to my name – "Adrienna," meaning 'dark and mysterious' derived from the name Adrian. I did not find this name to fit my character. Now, they have spelling of "Adrina," which means 'happiness' derived from Italy.[607] Yet, everyone calls me "Drina" or my nickname, "Deo." Drina means 'watchful,'[608] however, on another site I researched over five years ago this name meant 'helper and defender of mankind.'[609] Deo meaning 'godlike, To God,' derived from the Latin phrase, *DEO Optimo Maximo*, meaning, 'To God, the greatest and best.'[610] Now, you can see the meaning of names, and how it translates or refers to a person's personality, characteristics, or behavior. I have come to realize that my name gives me purpose, true value, and an explanation of my characteristics as I have grown older and matured. I cannot wait until I enter the gates of Heaven, and God gives me a *new name* that I am worthy of, and clothed in my heavenly body for all eternity.

>*Ecclesiastes 7:1, NKJV: "A good name is better than precious ointment, and the day of death than the day of one's birth."*

Abraham means the *father of nations* before he even had children.[611] Jacob, *deceiving one, supplanting* was changed to *Israel*, which means he prevails because of his change nature. God transformed Saul, who later was known as the *persecutor of the church* to Paul. There can be a shift in one's calling, functions, duties, and nature.[612] The Bible renames you when you are born again and allows you to see yourself as God sees you. Your name is a sense of well-being and an accurate opinion of yourself. Allow God to show you just how much you mean to Him and to give you the proper image.

>*Proverbs 22:1, NKJV: "A good name is to be chosen rather than great riches, loving favor rather than silver and gold."*

The Proverb points out that a reputation has more value than possessions or wealth. A name cannot be replaced easily. Please consider when naming your children, to be aware of the meaning of the name since it will represent the child's character and brings forth life. Do not let others call you by a different name other than the one that God gave you. Others must address you by your surname or the name your parents gave you. God knew you, before the foundation of this world, and knows your name. Walking in agreement with Him, and your actions, naturally correspond with your new identity. It identifies a perception of your behavior. Know your name. Introduce yourself. It is not by accident. God has a divine purpose for you. Remember, we are saved by

---

[607] Babynames.com
[608] http://www.babynamesworld.com, author found name meaning on site 11.15.2007.
[609] http://www.babyhold.com, author found name meaning on site 11.15.2007.
[610] Webster Collegiate Dictionary, abbreviations and meanings.
[611] Genesis 17:4-5
[612] Acts 13:9

faith, not by works. God love for us. A name is establishing a relationship with the Lord.[613]

When a child knows who he or she is, and whom he or she belongs to, their confidence shines through. They know what their parents will expect from them. Confidence in God delivers you from needs, since you have God, you will no longer think about that need for others to make you whole. An object of God's love is the creation of what He had in mind.[614]

Children are to obey their parents. However, if your parents ask you to do something that is opposite of God's commandments, it is best to obey God. Parents are representatives of the Lord. Remember the *Fifth Commandment*: *Honor your father and your mother,* and the *First Commandment* with a promise. You need to leave things that are undone, which follows with a reward. The reward or promise is to 'live long upon the earth.' Furthermore, this promise is for 'all children' who obey their parents. Honor increases esteem, value, reverence, respect for one another, and 'love.' Obey your guardians since you are in the household of your parents, or until you pay your own bills in your own home. Even if you are a child who helps pay bills in your parents' household, does not mean that you have some control or power in the home. You still have to follow your parents' rules and regulations, but you are able to voice your opinion and try to compromise with your parents' wishes.

Despite parents' efforts and worries, conflicts between children in a family seem inevitable. Sibling relationships allow both competition and cooperation. Usually, a mixture of loving and fighting eventually creates a strong bond between brothers and sisters. It is not unusual, though parents might say, "They fight so much. I hope they don't kill each other before they grow up." Cain is an example of brotherly rivalries, where the troubling potential became a tragedy. Primarily, a parent or guardian ought to praise their child/ren daily and certain behaviors that are pleasing or appropriate to their parent(s). In addition, parents should have good communication with their child/ren. Most of all, parents can focus on encouraging words, instead of bashing their children's negative behaviors. Show faith in your child/ren abilities, to develop their talents or gifts that God has blessed them with.

In contrast, anyone who made a *Corban* vow was required to dedicate money to God's temple.[615] It was a way to neglect parents, even though you are giving money to God and disregarding the care of needy parents. The *Corban* vow allowed children to disobey God's commandment, 'honor your parents.' In other words, they were respected for their earnings and not helping others, as Jesus requires of His followers. If children are excusing themselves from helping because their resources are already dedicated to God, this is also saying that children will not take care of their parents in their old age. Wouldn't you want to raise your children to be responsible adults, so when

---

[613] Nelson Study Bible, NKJV.
[614] Psalm 139:16-17
[615] Mark 7:11, was the practice of Corban, an offering

you get old, they will turn around and love to take care of you for all that you have done for them? This is one fine example of how a religious tradition governed people.

Overall, parents are prone to train our children the way it should go. The importance of parenthood is to love and nurture your children in the Word of the Lord. Later, your child will take care of your in return out of love and respect. *Parenting: The Ins and Outs*, will speak further on how to raise your children in the eyes of the Lord.

~Let Your Day Begin With Christ, Day 33~

Let your Day Begin Activity: Today's activity is to take the time to raise the children together. Do not make one decision without consulting your spouse or mate first. Raising children is a group effort. If the mother or father is not living in the house, but is still around, involve him or her in the child's activities as well.

Today's Questions:

What are some standards or rules you put in your household for your children?

What do you do to discipline your children? Is it effective? If not, what are some other options you can do to get your children to respect and obey your household rules?

Review to Begin your Day with Christ:

Children: Psalm 127: 3-5; Ephesians 6:1-8; Deuteronomy 21:18-21; Proverbs 19:18; 22:15; 15:20.

Day Begins 34: Parenting: The Ins And Outs

Parenting (www.christiannet.com):

Parenting Resources	Scriptures
Children heritage and blessings from God	Psalm 127:3,4
Children can teach adults	Matthew 18:1-4
Children's personality	Proverbs 22:15
Reasoning with children removes foolishness	Proverbs 22:15
Parents responsibility for their children to live for God	1 Thessalonians 2:11-12
Discipline our children	Proverbs 13:24
Wise child accepts reproof from father	Proverbs 15:5
Children are joy	Proverbs 23:24-25
Children's obedience brings blessings	Ephesians 6:1-3
Children enter covenant with God	Deuteronomy 29:10-12
Discipline: child on the right path	Proverbs 22:6
Authority and pacify conflict through strict words	Proverbs 15:1
Do not provoke anger or aggravate	Ephesians 6:4
Obey parents	Ephesians 6:1-3
Parent bear children's burdens	Galatians 6:5-9
David's sin hurt his family	2 Samuel 12:9-10
God's warning: not to follow in your parent's footsteps	Ezekiel 20:18
Jesus taught	Matthew 18:5-6
Passing Christian heritage to our children	Psalm 78:4-7
Parents provide	2 Corinthians 12:14
God has given us children: bless them	Genesis 48:8-10
Fatherly love	Genesis 37:3-4

Psalm 34:11-14, NLT: "Come, my children, and listen to me, and I will teach you to fear the Lord. Does anyone want to live a life that is long and prosperous? Then keep your tongue from speaking evil and your lips from telling lies! Turn away from evil and do good. Search for peace, and work to maintain it."[616]

Parents are very busy all day long, when family life tends to become busier. As parents, we have to prepare meals, chores, help children with their homework from school, and other extracurricular activities. Parents carry the heaviest load, making sure everyone is clean and ready for the day, fed, and other time constraints. However,

---

[616] Also can refer to Psalm 34:11-22, on teaching your children from right and wrong

children tend to take their parent(s) for granted by bickering and complaining.[617] Even though your work as a parent is difficult at times, maybe even exhausting and frustrating, God values our great efforts to parenthood.[618] Your parents are holding the family roles, and as a child, you will honor our Lord of the universe.[619]

Paul further talks about how faith is required in the household.[620] He is referring to the family head, usually the father. In this Scripture, he was also speaking directly about the material needs of the family. In today's world, the head of the household will face many obstacles. Economic hardship can consist of layoffs, high unemployment rates, and the rising costs of living. Moreover, a provider does well to remember that he or she is carrying out an assignment from God. Paul's inspired words gives us hope in obeying God's commandments, if we refuse to abide to them has disowned the faith. However, many people today have 'no natural affection.'[621]

God also gives the woman a dignified role as helper to her husband.[622] Today, there are many single parent families, which tend to be more common than married couples are. Many single Christian parents are doing an admirable job of providing their household. It is ideal for a family to have both parents and the father taking lead. *Father,* also known as husband, has the responsibility of being head and priest of the household.[623] The father represents Christ in his home, just like Christ is the head of the church. Husbands love your wives, just as Christ also loved the church. Christ gave Himself for us (church), so that He might sanctify and cleanse us with the washing of water of His Word. Also, Christ can present Himself a glorious church, not having spot or wrinkle, but that we are to be holy and without a blemish. Therefore, husbands ought to love their own bodies. He who loves his wife loves himself.[624] Treat her individuality with utmost respect. The husband is to lead his family sacrificially.

> *"Christ's rule is one of wisdom and love. When husbands fulfill their obligation to their wives, they will use their authority with the same tenderness as Christ uses toward the church. When the Spirit of Christ controls the husband, the wife's subjection will require from her to obey and honor her husband, and in the same way that Christ requires submission from the church...Husbands are to study the words of Christ on how he may have the mind of Christ. Then, he will become purified, refined, and fit to be the lord of his household."[625]*

The wise father spends time with his children. A child may learn many lessons from the father such as the love for God, the importance of prayer, love for other people,

---

[617] Proverbs 22:15
[618] Ephesians 3:14, 15
[619] 1 Corinthians 10:31
[620] 1 Timothy 5:8
[621] 2 Timothy 3:1, 3
[622] Genesis 2:18; Proverbs 31:13, 14, 16
[623] Colossians 3:18-21; 1 Peter 3:1-8
[624] Ephesians 5:23-28
[625] Seventh-Day Adventist…, paraphrased by author

modesty, love for nature, and things God has made. If the father is never home, the child is deprived of this privilege and joy, and which is forced on the mother to try to take the place of the father's role. The Bible urges fathers to avoid exasperating their children that they do not become downhearted.[626] Fathers who are reluctant to express their feelings can look at Jehovah's example. Children draw much strength and courage from their parents' honest expressions of love and approval. Indeed, countless fathers who shirk their responsibility, leaving their family in a lurch.

On the other hand, some women are messing around with different men, and make it difficult to determine who fathered their children. From time to time, women appear on television shows like Maury (paternal testing) or court shows to perform paternal tests to verify who fathered their children.

Inheritance	Proverbs 13:22
Encourage children to learn God's commandments	Deuteronomy 6:6-9
Fear the Lord	Proverbs 14:26
Corrects his children	Proverbs 22:15; 3:11-12; 29:17
Wild friends bring shame on the parents	Proverbs 28:7
Foolishness of a child affects the father	Proverbs 17:21
Building home	Psalm 127:1
Troubled Home	Proverbs 15:27
Joy	Proverbs 23:24
Bore child in old age	Genesis 17:17-19; 22:15-17
Birthright	Genesis 25:29-33
Love one child more than the rest	Genesis 37:3-4
Twelve Tribes of Israel	Genesis 49:28
Sons death, still worshipped God	2 Samuel 12:19-20
Footsteps of God	Ezekiel 20:18-19
Stepfather	Matthew 1:18
Evil in the sight of God	2 Chronicles 33:22-24
Courageous Father	Mark 5:22, 24, 41
Honor Parents	Deuteronomy 5:16

--Fatherhood on www.christianet.com

Motherhood is the closest thing on earth to being in partnership with God. Somebody in the family must bear the ultimate responsibility for the character of the children. Child training cannot be delegated to others, for no one feels quite the same about a child, as its parents does. God created the mother with the ability to carry the child within her own body, to suckle the child, and to nurture and love it. However, extenuating circumstances of severe financial burdens or being a single parent, causes

---

[626] Colossians 3:21

some mothers can to be verbally and/or physically abusive to their children, instead of nurturing in love.

Today, both parents are working, even though the mother is supposed to be in the home to raise her children. However, most mothers are challenged to be a nurturer, express love to the children, and secure her finances in the household. Children are her priority besides her mate. Mothers have to balance work, playtime if any, children, husbands, and finances. Furthermore, Paul writes in *1 Corinthians 11: 2-16,* the roles of a woman in a marriage and worship. In addition, I suggest picking up *Excellent Wife: Biblical Perspective* by Martha Peace. This book is also extremely helpful for single women thinking about marriage, and even better for those that are married.

Some believe a woman's role is her covering. For example, Jewish women always covered their heads in worship. For a woman to uncover her head in public was a sign of loose morals. On the other hand, Greek women may have been used to worshipping without head coverings. In this letter, Paul had already spoken about divisions and disorder in the church. Both are involved in this issue. Paul's solution comes from his desire for unity among church members and for appropriateness in the worship service. He accepted God's sovereignty in creating the rules for relationships.[627]

"The head of woman is man." Head is not used to show control or supremacy, but to lead her as Christ leads the Church. Because man was created first, the woman derives her existence from man, as man does from Christ, and Christ from God. Submission is a key element in the smooth functioning of any business, government, or family. God ordained submission in certain relationships to prevent chaos. Submission is not surrender, withdrawal, or apathy. It does not mean inferiority because God created all people in His image and because all have equal value. *Submission* is mutual commitment and cooperation. God did not make man superior; He made a way for man and woman to work together. Jesus Christ, equal to God, the Father, submitted to God to carry out the plan for salvation. Just as Christ and God are equally divine, men and women are equal beings. Just as Jesus had to carry out different roles from the Heavenly Father, men and women have to share different roles. Submission is by choice not force. Submission is not inferiority, but subordination. We serve God in these relationships by willingly submitting to others in our church, to our spouses, and to our government leaders.[628]

Man is not from woman, but woman came from man (Adam's rib): concept of 'helper' in *Genesis 2:20.* This does not mean the woman is inferior to the man. It refers only to the purposes of God for man and woman in the creative order.[629] God created the lines of authority, for His created world to function smoothly. In the lines of authority, even in marriage, there should not be lines of superiority. God created man and woman

---

[627] 1 Corinthians 11:2
[628] 1 Corinthians 11:3
[629] 1 Corinthians 11:7-9

with unique and complimentary characteristics. In other words, one sex is not better than the other is. We must not let the issue of authority and submission becomes a wedge to destroy oneness in marriage. We are to use our unique gifts to strengthen our marriages and to glorify the Lord.

In many cultures, long hair on men is appropriate and masculine. In Corinth, it was a sign of male prostitution in the heathen temples. Women with short hair were labeled prostitutes. Paul was referring to the Corinthian culture -- Christian women should keep their hair long, if short, would be hard to be a believable witness for Jesus Christ. Paul was not saying to accept all practices of the culture, but avoid appearances and behavior that detract from our goal of being believable witnesses for Jesus Christ, while demonstrating our faith.

There are proper attitudes and conduct in worship, including in marriage relationships, or the role of women in the church. Specific instructions are timeless, like respect for spouse, reverence, and appropriateness in worship and, focusing all of your life on God. If anything you can do easily offend members and divide the church, then change your ways to promote church unity. Paul told the women who were not wearing head covering to wear them, not because it was a scriptural command, but to keep the congregation from dividing over a petty issue that served only to take people's minds off Christ.[630]

Family heads may also find it helpful to contemplate Jesus' perfect example. Jesus is our *Eternal Father.*[631] Jesus is metaphorically signified as the last Adam, as the father that mankind who exercised faith.[632] Unlike Adam, who turned out to be a selfish, self-serving father, Jesus is the ideal father. The Bible speaks about Jesus in *John 3:16.* Jesus willingly offered up His own life for others. He also, on a day-to-day basis, put the needs of others ahead of His own. Your parents are able-bodied to imitate that self-sacrificing spirit like Jesus Christ did.

Parents can learn about selfless love from Jesus' words on defiant people in *Matthew 23:27.* Jesus painted a vivid picture of a mother sheltering her young with her wings. Parents may learn from the protective instincts of a mother bird. Just like the mother bird, she will readily put herself at the risk to protect her young from harm.[633] We would rather suffer harm than allow any harm to come to our children. Further, we willingly make daily sacrifices to provide for our own. Many of us will rise early for work, at exhausting and frustrating jobs, to put food on the table, provide suitable shelter, and struggle to make sure our children have clean clothing and adequate education. In addition, we keep this up day after day, and year after year, until they are able to tend for themselves. Even sometimes, when they are able to spread their own wings, we are

---

[630] 1 Corinthians 11:2-16; 1 Peter 3:17
[631] Isaiah 9:6, 7
[632] 1 Corinthians 15:45
[633] Proverbs 30:24

still there when they need us most. Self-sacrifice and endurance pleases our Heavenly Father.[634]

Jesus even speaks about providing for our children on a spiritual level.[635] What can parents do to teach their children about Jesus and commandments?[636] Parents are first to cultivate their own spirituality, building their love for God, and taking His words to heart. We are students of God's Word, to develop a real understanding of and love for Jehovah's ways, principles, and laws. Our hearts will be full of fascinating Bible truths that will move you to feel joy and love for God. You can provide and will have an abundance of good things to impart to your children.[637] Spiritually strong parents are prepared to apply the counsel and to inculcate God's Words in their offspring at every opportunity.[638]

To *inculcate* means to teach and impress by the means of repetition. For example, when Jesus taught His disciples to be humble, instead of proud and competitive, He found various ways to repeat the same principle. He taught reasoning by illustrating, even demonstrating to those that were willing to listen.[639] Jesus never showed impatience. Therefore, parents need to find ways to teach basic truths to their children, patiently repeating Jesus' principles until the children absorb and apply to their lives.

Furthermore, *Deuteronomy 6:7* shows, there are many occasions when parents can discuss spiritual things with their children. Whether traveling together, doing chores together, relaxing together, you may find opportunities to provide your children's spiritual needs. A regular, happy family Bible study is a mainstay of family spirituality. Try to keep your family conversations on a positive tone to build one's spiritual man or woman. Parents are engaging in conversations with your children will meet his or her spiritual need. Children can also effectively share their faith with peers. These discussions develop greater interest in sharing what they are learning about Jesus. They may also see the ministry as happy and interesting work, producing great satisfaction and joy.[640] Through examples, your children are learning obedience: 'training a child in the way he or she should go, and when he or she is old, he or she will not depart from it.'[641]

---

[634] Hebrews 13:16
[635] Matthew 4:4; 5:3
[636] Deuteronomy 6:5-7
[637] Luke 6:45
[638] Deuteronomy 6:7
[639] Matthew 18:1-4; 20:25-27; John 13:12-15
[640] Acts 20:35
[641] Proverbs 22:6

Honor parents	Deuteronomy 5:16
Respect mothers	Leviticus 19:3
Love God more than parents and children	Matthew 10:37
Virtuous woman	Proverbs 31:10
Beauty in vain	Proverbs 31:30
Blessing and Praises	Proverbs 31:28
Household	Proverbs 31:13-15
Training (raise a child)	Proverbs 22:6
Pain in childbirth	Genesis 3:16
Birth of child	John 16:21
Elders	Titus 2:3-5
Death or cursed parents	Exodus 21:15
Discipline	Proverbs 1:8
First twins	Genesis 25:21-23
Adoption	Exodus 2:10
Nurse child (breastfeed)	Exodus 2:5-9
Prayed for a child	1 Samuel 1:11
Child not his	Matthew 1:19
Movement in womb	Luke 1:41-42
First miracle	John 2:1-5
Death of son	John 19:25
Mother taken care of	John 19:27

--Motherhood on www.christianet.com

Other than commitment to the Lord and their spouses, parents have no higher responsibility than to the children that they have brought into the world. Put their children's interests before their own advancement and comfort, for children did not choose to come into the world, and are given the best start in life. Moreover, a parent's love is unconditional and sacrificial. Children that demonstrate agape love will establish a positive self-image and emotional health throughout life. Children who have to win love, or who feel rejected and unimportant, will try to obtain their parents' love through undesirable behaviors that become ingrained and habitual. Children who are secure in their parents' love will reach out to others and teach how to glorify the Lord.

Christian parents are to dedicate their children to God's service at the earliest possible moment of life. In this service, the parents also dedicate themselves to educate the child in the way of the Lord, so that the image of God will be formed in the child. To reach this goal, parents will bring their children to church and religious school. Consistency with spiritual teaching from the parents is a continuing process that enters every phase of the child's life. Knowing God as a loving parent is vital to the children's Christian growth. In addition, parents are to teach morals, guidance, education, and learn how to adapt to their environment.

Discipline implies far more than punishment. *Discipline* is a process in which the child is apprenticed to the parent for training, guidance, and teaching important principles such as loyalty, truth, equity, consistency, patience, order, mercy, generosity and work.

Parents also provide for their children's spiritual needs when praying. Jesus taught His disciples how to pray and He prayed with them on many occasions.[642] They learned by joining in prayer with God's own Son. Children can learn a lot from your prayers. God wants us to speak to Him freely from the heart, approaching Him with any concern that we might have. Your prayers can help your children to learn a vital spiritual truth. They can have a relationship with their Heavenly Father.[643]

Most language development is developed through socialization, which is when children learn the basic skills within their society. The language used in our homes and in schools needs careful monitoring since our children pick up the words we use, building up their vocabulary. Moreover, we need to control our tongues since it is like a sword and can verbally destroy self-esteem of others. Furthermore, our communication, or words spoken, can reveal our godly character. Children that hear frequent joyous and spontaneous expression of affection among family members will learn to praise to God.

Adults can teach them the beauty of their developing sexuality through correct and appropriate information. It is parents' responsibility to protect their children from sexual abuse.

Children also have emotional needs. God's Word tells parents how important it is to provide for them and to be mentally sound.[644] It is sensible to show a child love, which teaches a child to love, and brings lifelong benefits. In contrast, a failure to show a child love is senseless. It causes great pain, and represents a failure to imitate God, who shows us immense love, despite our imperfections.[645] *1 John 4:19* says, *"He first loved us."*

Take this initiative to build a loving bond with your children. A child learns family's values and religious concepts from their parents or elders, so we need to be consistent. Since the family is the very soul of the church and society, Christian families responding to His call, will build strong churches that reveal real Christianity. The churches made up of those families will grow, where their young people will not leave and they will portray to the world a clear picture of God.

God created our children for His purpose, not for ours. In *Psalm 127:3-5*, children are a heritage in which defines children as God's gifts.[646] In ancient times, having many

---

[642] Luke 11:1-13

[643] 1 Peter 5:7

[644] Titus 2:4

[645] Psalm 103:8-14

[646] Psalm 128:3

children was a symbol of strength (like arrows). Usually a hand of children increased the productivity of the farmer. A full quiver was a mark of God's blessing. The blessing of a home in ancient times, gave a person a measure of pride in the community. However, children want to please their parents, but controlling parents make rebellious children. Parents should not be overly rigid with their children. Our children model their parents. We need to give them more time to grow and decide what they want to be when they are mature. If your child has not learned what you knew, then give them some more time and you will be surprised what God will teach them. We cannot make our children love God or do right; we can correct them. Avoid controlling them that can only be led by the Holy Spirit. God has given us relationships with our children and/or husband for enjoyment, not for torment. Abundant life is to be content in the Lord. Do not look for the wrong in them, be encouraging and positive, look for the good in your children and magnify them. Do not focus on the negativity and harbor over it.

Overall, parental love is more than just merely words. Love is expressed primarily in action. Providing materially and spiritually is an expression of parental love, especially if love is the primary motivation. Additionally, discipline is a vital expression of parental love.[647] In contrast, a failure to discipline is an expression of parental hatred.[648] Such balance is not always easy for imperfect parents to find. It is worth your every effort to strive for that balance. Firm, living discipline helps a child grow up to live a happy, productive life.[649] When parents do the important work God has assigned you, which includes providing for your children's material, spiritual, and emotional needs, the rewards are great. Children are the best opportunity to 'choose life,' and thereafter, to 'keep alive.'[650] Those children who choose to serve God, and stay on the path to life as they mature, bring their parents tremendous joy.[651] Unspeakable joy will last forever.

For example, Joshua was a leader for thirty years. He led the nation by obeying God's Word. He meditated day and night on God's Word, so that he would be successful in all things. This is what we need to do as parents, leaders, counselors, mentors, families and communities, if children are to live a life in obedience to God. Joshua ruled a nation, raised his family, and ran an army. He led his home life to serve the Lord. A father's responsibility is to teach his family the 'Word of God.' By setting examples, this will cause our children to be the same unconsciously. Joshua spent time with the Lord, as we need to spend time with the Lord, and raise and minister to our families. Families from generation to generation need to 'break the cycle,' not allowing demonic forces to take over our family happiness. Have God shown you how to break the cycle from drug abuse, alcoholism, abusive relationships, etc.? Forgiveness is the key to getting over these hardships and demonic spiritual forces, which leaves no animosity or hostility.

---

[647] Hebrews 12:6
[648] Proverbs 13:24, Jeremiah 46:28
[649] Proverbs 22:6
[650] Deuteronomy 30:19
[651] Psalm 127:3-5

~Let Your Day Begin With Christ, Day 34~

Let your Day Begin Activity: Today's activity may be a little time consuming, but not impossible. If it takes too long for one day, keep going with it and don't move on to the next activity until this one is complete. Take your Bible and review the Scriptures in the charts in *Day Begins 34*. With each Scripture, take the time to write down what each Scripture means to you. Have your spouse do the same and discuss these Scripture viewpoints throughout your day. After discussing the Scriptures, see if you got the same objective out of it for parenting.

Today's Questions:

What have you learned from the Scriptures you read? What practices will you put in place in your household?

How effective are the parenting skills derived from the Holy Scriptures?

Review to Begin your Day with Christ:

Those without fathers or the fatherly roles can refer to *Psalm 10:14; Psalm 146:9;* and *Isaiah 1:23; 10:2.* Review in the NKJV or KJV.

Review the motherly roles and expectations from children.

Day Begins 35: Satan's Plan

How did Satan wreck the first home? Adam and Eve sinned by disobedience to God. The first person God originally called was 'Adam.' He is the leader of the household. 'You have not chosen me, I have chosen you.' Remember that God will choose us.[652]

Doubt	Makes you question God's Word
Discouragement	Makes you look at your problems rather than at God
Diversion	Makes the wrong things seem attractive so that you will want them more than the right things
Defeat	Makes you feel like a failure so that you don't even try
Delay	Makes you put off doing something so that it never gets done

How much is too much? God's will be done (not my will). Jesus paid for our sins on the Cross: suffered, been humiliated, and showed that nothing is too much.[653] Moreover, Pastor Malone mentions that people are blaming God, when it is all about 'learning the lesson of our lives.' We are put through a test. Once we pass the test, we are to move on, and not faint over the suffering and pain we experienced through this trial. We are not to live or stay in the past.[654] Also, believers are to endure the chastening of the Lord.[655] In addition, our elders, guardians and/or parents, can do the chastening. *Chastening* is teaching, educating, disciplining, and a learning process. Enough is enough. The purpose of chastening of the Lord is that believers are to be a part of God's holiness; to live in the Spirit; and to be children of the Lord, and not of Satan.[656]

---

[652] Pastor Julius Malone sermon on *All Things That Created Are For God's Purpose*, June 6, 1998.

[653] Mark 10:17-32; Acts 4:12; John 14:6

[654] 1 Peter 4:12; 1 Peter 5:10

[655] Ephesians 3:11, 13, 16-21; 2 Corinthians 4:16; 2 Timothy 4:5; James 1:12; Jeremiah 29:11, 16; Isaiah 43:1, 2

[656] Pastor Julius Malone sermon: *All Are Created By God, But Not All Children Of God,* August 2, 1998.

~Let Your Day Begin With Christ, Day 35~

Let your Day Begin Activity: Today's activity could be a little challenging. Write down anything that is attacking your household, marriage, spouse, children…etc. Have your spouse do the same and talk about them openly to each other to come up with a solution. Do not let Satan come between your families. After discussing these attacks, take them to the Lord in prayer. He is the healer of all things.

Today's Questions:

How is Satan attacking you?

What are your weapons against Satan and his tactics?

What is *chastening?* How can we get right with God?

Review to Begin your Day with Christ:

Satan uses attacks: Review the chart in Day 35.

Day Begins 36: Keeping The Romance Alive

Most marriages fall apart when partners have not developed godly qualities such as the ability to love your mate, to serve, and the willingness to make sacrifices. God bestowed these qualities on you the moment you say 'I do.' You are able to develop these qualities by having a close relationship with God. His love flows through you once you are 'born-again.'

Usually men and women differ in many areas, like the usage of offensive words, and their views on sexuality. Men are more quickly aroused and satisfied sexually than their wives. In the book, *Love is a Decision* by Gary Smalley and John Trent, it says that men are fully enjoying the sexual experience, but a man should desire to meet a woman's emotional needs too. At times, men are stimulated and aroused by what they see (physical attraction), of which causes his manhood to stiffen. They may not be sensitive to a woman's feelings and emotions, just ready to meet their own sexual needs, instead of focusing on her needs. Usually, a woman longs to be kissed, sensual touching, and some form of foreplay to get her sexually aroused before his manhood enters inside of her.

Wives do not minimize your husband's need for physical expression of sexual intimacy, even when he is slow to meet your emotional and relational needs. Try to open up to him, entice him, and show him what you want to be done in the bedroom. If he is not listening to your gentle words, or body language on how you desire to be aroused, most women will retaliate by using harsh words of bad-mouthing their mate. This can make him think that he is unable to please you, unable to meet your fantasies and wildest desires, and most of all, that he is unable to satisfy you. He wants to be all the man who you desire, and to please you sexually, financially, mentally, and emotionally. Women, please respect that some men are not as emotional and sensitive to meet your needs, but try to find other avenues to reach him.

According to **His Needs Her Needs** by William Harley, Jr., he says that the man's five most basic needs in marriage tend to be (1) Sexual fulfillment, (2) Recreational companionship, (3) Attractive spouse, (4) Domestic support, and (5) Admiration. The woman's five most basic needs in marriage tend to be (1) Affection, (2) Conversation, (3) Honesty and openness, (4) Financial support, and (5) Family commitment. In the book, *The Five Love Languages*, love is expressed by (1) Words of affirmation, (2) Quality time, (3) Receiving gifts, (4) Acts of service, and (5) Physical touch.

Marriage requires other ingredients to grow and thrive, like freedom and responsibility.[657] It is about promoting the relationship as a loving couple by learning your partner's good and bad behaviors and characteristics to avoid conflict. It is not about fixing, changing, or punishing your mate. Spouses must take full responsibility for

---

[657] 1 John 4:18

their actions and what is conversed that can make the relationship go sour.[658] Some things to look at in the relationship, when taking full responsibility:

Feelings	Choices
Thoughts	Love
Attitude	Behaviors
Desires	Limits
Talents/Gifts	Values

God gave Adam and Eve the responsibility to meet the needs of the earth, animals, and themselves. In addition, God empowered them to have the life all of us desire -- one filled with love, beautiful surroundings, and many opportunities to use our abilities, talents, and spiritual gifts. God also gave them the ability and opportunity to make the life they chose.[659] We need to take responsibility for our hearts, our love, our time, and our talents. We are to own our lives, and live in God's light, growing up, and maturing of our character along the way.[660] We have to take the responsibility for growing our marriages. We are completely responsible to God for developing our souls -- responsible for half of the marriage and all our soul, so set boundaries for yourself between you and God.[661]

On the other hand, if intimacy is lost then so is love. Love and truth must exist together for the relationship to last. However, most couples are in denial, and deny that the intimacy is gone. Instead, they turn to someone else or something else for comfort and intimacy. When they should be able to confront their partner and truthfully tell how they truly feel. You can open up with one another about anything. Usually, impure hearts will cause impure thoughts that eventually will cause this person to act these feelings out.

On another note: Some may ask will I see my mate in Heaven? Will I still be married? We do not need to be afraid of eternal life.[662] However, we can concentrate on our relationship with Christ right now because in the New Kingdom, we will be with Him. If we learn to love and trust Christ now, we will not be afraid of what He has in store for us then. Jesus' statement does not mean that people will not recognize their partners in the coming kingdom. It simply means that God's new order will not be an extension of this life, and that the same physical and natural rules will not apply. In other words, we will not be married once we go to heaven. Jesus' comments His final word on marriage in heaven, which was His response to Sadducees' riddle. Jesus did not want to fall into their trap. Therefore, sidestepping their question about the much-married woman, Jesus gave a definite answer to their question about resurrection. The Sadducees' real question was not about marriage, but about the doctrine of resurrection. The Sadducees

---

[658] Cloud, *Boundaries in Marriage*, pp. 9, 11.
[659] Cloud, *Boundaries on Marriage, p.* 22.
[660] Ephesians 4:15
[661] Cloud, *Boundaries on Marriage,* pp. 64, 66.
[662] Mark 12:18-25

were an elite group of religious leaders, who denied the existence of angels, immorality of the soul, and the resurrection. God's covenant with all people exists beyond death.

Overall, successful marriages are by following God's principles and God's design for marriage. Ironically, if we focus on God's principles instead of pleasure, we end up having a very satisfying and pleasant marriage.[663]

---

[663] http://www.polynate.net/books/courtship/part1.html

~Let Your Day Begin With Christ, Day 36~

Let your Day Begin Activity: In *Day Begins 36,* locate *His Needs, Her Needs.* For each person, write down those 5 points and make a list of things that you can do to improve on these points in your relationship. Be honest with yourself. If you know you will not fulfill those needs, do not write them down.

Today's Questions:

Will you see your husband or wife in heaven? Will you still be married in heaven?

What makes a successful marriage?

Review to Begin your Day with Christ:

We have to reevaluate what marriages are built on. We have removed godly qualities: love your mate, serve, and making sacrifices. Moreover, we are to meet our mate's physical, emotional, spiritual, and mental needs.

Ephesians 5:21-33 (Roles for Marriage or Relationships).

William Harley, Jr, *His Needs Her Needs:*
Man's five basic needs: sexual fulfillment, recreational companionship, attractive spouse, take care of household, and admiration.

Woman's five basic needs: affection (intimacy), intellectual conversation, honesty and openness, financial stability, and commitment.

Read *The Five Love Languages* by Gary Smalley to find your love language: communication (words), quality time, receiving gifts, acts of service, and physical touch.

Day Begins 37: Do You Bring God To The Workplace

First, those of us that have jobs, whether it is one, two or even three, we tend to forget who gave us the job in the first place. Second, we tend to complain about our boss, staff, employees or co-workers, and other issues relative to the job itself. Lastly, we need to ask ourselves, do we take God to the workplace? Do we pray and thank God for this job? By work of your hands, labor, and dedication, we are able to value our accomplishments, promotions, and salary increases. In addition, your work glorifies the Lord, which depends on your choice of profession and whether you are sharing the gospel with others at your workplace.[664]. *Beauty* refers to the pleasantness of God. In other words, it is a divine blessing to have a job.

In Proverbs 14:23 shows that all labor includes a profit. However, useless chatter only leads to poverty. *Useless chatter* is usually someone that talks about doing things, working on projects, and bragging about entrepreneurship. However, not seeking a position or employment opportunities leads to poverty. Furthermore, one can end up homeless because of only speaking about working, but not bringing any money in the household.

In *Proverbs 20:4*, it speaks about laziness (*sluggard*). If you are a *sluggard*, you will not have anything to harvest. In other words, any money to replenish in the home is to pay bills and take care of the family, but if you are lazy, you may not seek work at all.[665] However, sometimes when we are fired from our jobs or laid off, we try so hard to find another job that pays more. After a month or two passes, even several months to years, we tend to get lazy. We pray. We hope. Moreover, we try, but we tend to give up and become lazy to the point that we no longer look for work. We give up on ourselves. We become sluggish, no enthusiasm when searching for a job, which causes us not to be able to pay the bills.[666]

Paul explains how others worked hard, buying what they needed, rather than becoming a burden to any of the believers. If we do not work, we will not eat. There is a difference between leisure and laziness. Relaxation and recreation can be balanced throughout our weeks, but when it is time to work. Believers should work. We must make the most of our talent and time, doing all we can to provide for our dependents and ourselves.[667]

The Bible speaks on laziness versus diligence. Minister Moore focuses on the Scriptures from *Proverbs 30:24-31*. *Nelson Study Bible* points out that these Scriptures refer to one's behavior. Each of these small creatures has a behavioral trait from which wise people can learn. *Life Application Bible* points out that these Scriptures demonstrates how the ant teaches us about preparation; badgers about wise building;

---

[664] Psalm 90:17, also can see Job 14:15, NKJV
[665] also can see Nehemiah 3:5
[666] Also refer 2 Thessalonians 3:7-10
[667] Life Application Study Bible, NKJV.

locusts about cooperation and order; and spiders about fearlessness. Minister Morgan stated a vital part of wise living is by the work of our hands.[668] To serve God, it requires work on our part. There are two kinds of people: diligent and lazy. Which one are you?

The four behaviors or characteristics that each animal demonstrated in the *Proverbs 30:24-31*, which shows us how we can be diligent workers to God:[669]

1. *Preparation:* We are busy doing our Father's business, just as the ants are prepared to gather food during the hot months since they will hibernate during cold. We are to be prepared to do God's will at any cost.
2. *Wise Builders*: Badgers are wise and able to protect themselves from their enemies. God can instill wisdom in us when we obey His Word and comprehend what He has set us to do. Whether it is ministry, evangelism or to serve others, let us have open ears and willing to carry the task God has placed on our hearts. We are not to have 'deaf ears.' Believers of Christ are set out to speak the Word to others who are lost and dead to God's existence.
3. *Cooperation and Order:* Locusts are leaders, even without a leader in charge. We have to be self-starters, and go out to preach God's Word, even if others are not standing behind and helping you in your walk. Your calling may not to be preaching, but our Heavenly Father will bless you with such gifts to get His message across. In addition, if your pastor is visiting other churches, it does not mean that you need to leave and wait on your pastor's return. Members can still go to church and receive God's message.
4. *Fearlessness:* Spiders are known to be in the king's palace and the owner of his own place. He does not show any fear of this occupancy. We need to believe and trust in the Lord to spread His word to each person and not fear such an outcome. Satan may fill your mind of doubt and fear, but you can overcome by trusting in God, just like Moses trusted in God when he was to deliver Israelites from slavery. He was afraid or feared for what was to come, a place he once knew and lived a life in luxury, but now has to go to Egypt to set his Hebrew people free. God assured Moses by saying, "I am the one that gave you the mouth to speak." When asked who God was, He replies, "I am who I am." Therefore, we can do it...no matter what it appears to look like, and imagine how God can move and change a person's life in an instant.

Remember what we sow, we will reap. This is the season for sowing and reaping. How do you think we make the wrong turn? To make the wrong turn is by allowing the fleshly desires take over us, even if God showed us the right way. God spoke to me through a dream -- in reference to taking the wrong or right turns in our spiritual walk.

---

[668] Minister Moore, *Changing Your World Ministries*, July 31, 2005.
[669] Minister Moore, *Changing Your World Ministries*, July 31, 2005, emphasis added by author.

At the Woman-to-Woman conference in Milwaukee, WI and gave my testimony. My dream can be titled, "Which Path Are You Taking?"

I was wandering down this unfamiliar road, where others walking back and forth. Then, I noticed traffic on a busy street, while I was walking on a sidewalk near a bridge and water below. Suddenly, there was a fork in the walkway, and decided that I might get to my destination quicker if I make a 'right turn.' After making a right turn, I see a couple of people ahead of me, laughing and appearing friendly, but we do not speak. Overhead, I see green pastures, plentiful homes next to each other, and a beautiful place. I wonder why I have never seen this roadway before. Before traveling further ahead, I stopped and was afraid maybe I am going the wrong way and would end up lost. However, I wavered back and forth, one foot forward and the other foot back to my previous destination. Finally, I decide to go back.

The meaning of this dream can take many forms. What path are you taking? Will you make the right turn or many wrong turns in your life? Will you turn back or stay forward on your journey? There is narrow road, which few will take or follow. On the other hand, there is the wide road, which many will take. Today, we live in a society, where we focus on what our peers or the crowd is doing. We get lost in a mindset of worldly ways and thoughts, to think it is okay to do it. Just do it. Do what makes you feel good, will cause you to lose sight of God's path. In God's path, we are promised to live a life in abundance, peace, and obedience.

Earlier I mentioned that I started a path, wandering, and wondering what I will do, and where I will go. There are so many twists and turns, undecided in decision-making and no sense of direction. God says, if we follow His path in a life of obedience to do His will, we will see a life of green pastures, still waters, and abundance. Instead, I hesitated like most of us do and turned back in the dream. Don't turn back from the path God has you on to fulfill your dreams, visions, and final road of your destination. Will you take the detour?

Proverbs 6:11, warns us of the traps of laziness.

Diligent worker	Lazy worker
To be profitable	Experience poverty
Work when not convenient to receive or reap the reward	Full of excuses
Set yourself up to prosper	Want much, but reap little
Hard worker and makes wise decisions	Refuse to work and believe you are thinking wisely (Proverbs 26:13-16)
Leaders	Never will succeed or failures
Love to give, will be successful	Desire things, but refuse to work for them
Will stand before Kings	Do not dare to stand up for God

Sometimes, we can find ourselves in a heap of debt, seeking for debt counseling, or other means to pay our debts. No matter how long or how hard the situation is, God will open or close the doors for His children. He knows the job for you, if you believe and continue to pray to Him. I am a witness to how you can be at your lowest, and how God can bless you. I was out of work for ten to eleven months because of my supervisor jealous spirit after completing a master's degree, thinking I would take her position. At the time, I had a volunteer position and part time job, of which barely paid the bills. I continued to look for work, and started to become sluggish, not wanting to look for a job. I felt I had all these qualifications and degrees, but could not find a decent paying job with benefits. I did not give up on praying and trusting in God with other family members and friends praying too. I finally did get a job as a Youth Development Specialist, however, no benefits were available at that time, but I still trusted God. If He had something else for me, I would be waiting with open ears to what He felt He had for me. The Lord told me that I would be blessed three-fold.

Although, I was down and out, bills steady on my mind. I used all my savings, took out a second loan, and suddenly my Chevy Metro car engine was blown. I prayed and cried, and then the heavens opened a blessing for me. My grandmother, Maxine Battle, was praying and then God spoke to her heart. He told her that I would see change within two weeks and God sticks to what He promises. I am blessed that people trusted and believed in God as much as I did. I know that God has a better plan for me. Later, God spoke to my heart, saying counseling. I continued to pray by asking God for insight. Finally, I was able to understand what God was trying to tell me. I thought that I would seek a doctoral degree in Psychology and understood why I was not getting accepted in the PhD Counseling Psychology program at University of Wisconsin-Milwaukee. One night, God woke me up from my sleep to look in a Thesaurus on the term *counsel*. It was a breakthrough for me, where I realized that my true calling is to become an attorney. This was my original plan after completing my master's degree, until I was unemployed for over ten months. Now, I am allowing God to move me into a challenging and competitive degree, and pray for financial stability before seeking a law degree. God also promised me that I would be financially secure by staying in His will for my life.

Because our days are numbered, we want our work to count, to be effective and productive.[670] We desire to see God's eternal plan revealed now and for our work to reflect His permanence. If we feel dissatisfied with this life and all its imperfections, remember our desire to see our work established is placed there by God.[671] However, our desire can only be satisfied in eternity. Until then, we must apply ourselves to loving and serving God.[672]

> *Ecclesiastes 3:13, NLT: "And people should eat and drink and enjoy the fruits of their labor, for these are gifts from God."*

---

[670] see Psalm 104:23
[671] Ecclesiastes 3:11
[672] Life Application Study Bible, NKJV, 1996.

Your ability to find satisfaction in your work depends on your attitude. You will become dissatisfied if you lose the sense of purpose God intended for your work. We can enjoy our work, if we remember that God has given us *work* to do,[673] and the *fruit of our labor,*[674] is a gift from Him. Review your labor like God does by finding a way to serve God.[675] *Unless the Lord builds*, psalmist asserts that life lived apart from God is not worth living. Even *building a house* is useless if the Lord is not in the process. The phrase *bread of sorrows* captures the essence of those of which removed a sense of the Lord in their lives. The food gave them strength for life and a zest for living, instead of being in their miserable state.

In *Nehemiah 6:15*, the job was too big and the problems were too great. Nevertheless, God's men and women joined for special tasks, solved huge problems, and accomplished great things. Do not let the size of a task, or the length of time needed to accomplish it, keep you from doing it. God has *put eternity* in our hearts. This means that we can never be completely satisfied with earthly pleasures and pursuits. Because we are created in God's image, we have spiritual thirst, and we have eternal value, and nothing but the eternal God can truly satisfy us. God has built in us a restless yearning for the perfect world that can only be found in His perfect rule. He has given us a glimpse of the perfection of His creation. However, it is only a glimpse since we cannot see into the future or comprehend everything, unless God reveals Himself through a vision or speaks to us in a dream. Therefore, we must proceed with His *work* on earth.

On the other hand, we do not want to be gossipers or busy bodies.[676] The *Life Application Study Bible* states that a *busybody* is someone who gossips. An *idle person*, who does not work, ends up filling his or her time with less than helpful activities, like gossip. Rumors and hearsay are tantalizing, exciting to hear, and make us feel like insiders. Conversely, they tear people down. If you often find your nose in other people's business, you may be unemployed. Furthermore, *2 Thessalonians 3:6-10* speaks against idleness or laziness and those who do not want to work.

> *2 Thessalonians 3:6-10, NLT: "And now, dear brothers and sisters, we give you this command in the name of our Lord Jesus Christ: Stay away from all believers who live idle lives and don't follow the tradition they received from us. For you know that you ought to imitate us. We were not idle when we were with you. We never accepted food from anyone without paying for it. We worked hard day and night so we would not be a burden to any of you. We certainly had the right to ask you to feed us, but we wanted to give you an example to follow. Even while we were with you, we gave you this command: "Those unwilling to work will not get to eat."*

---

[673] See Ecclesiastes 3:10
[674] See Ecclesiastes 3:13
[675] Psalm 127:2
[676] 2 Thessalonians 3:11-12

However, some religions forbid those from working on the Sabbath.[677] Another Scripture is *Exodus 16:23*, shows that the Israelites were not to work on the Sabbath -- not even to cook. You may be asking yourself why. God knows that the busy routine of daily living could distract people from worshipping Him. It is so easy to let work and family responsibilities, even recreation, to crowd our schedules that we do not take time to worship the Lord. Carefully guard your time with the Lord. Check with your place of work for religious observance to request off from Friday sundown to Saturday sundown for Sabbath-observance. This does not mean to rest, chill, or sleep that day. The purpose of Sabbath is to worship with the Lord and to give our Heavenly Father praise. In addition, we are not to cook, only heat up food, and not to buy or sell on the Sabbath day to glorify the Lord.

In *Exodus 5:6-18*, talks about how the Israelites had double workload. To punish Moses and Aaron for the insolence, Pharaoh imposed severe measures on the Hebrews workers, who needed straw to strengthen the sun-dried bricks they were making. With no reduction in their daily quota, the people had to gather straw during their off-hours. Until now, the Egyptians had provided it for them. Pharaoh felt that they had too much time on their hands--*free time*.[678] Hebrews leaders of the work gangs, subordinate officials, complained about the new work rules. Pharaoh repeated his excuse that the people were idle and ordered them to continue. Hebrews crew chiefs were in a more precarious position than ever. Instead, they turned all their anger and complaints from Pharaoh on to Moses and Aaron. *Let the Lord look on you and judge* is a harsh curse. They felt that Moses and Aaron's words to Pharaoh were futile and only hated them more. The word translated *abhorrent* means 'to cause to stink.'[679]

Even though Pharaoh increased the Hebrews workload, you may think that your workload has increased and expect results. When God is at work in any situation, suffering, setbacks, and hardship still occur. In *James 1:2-4*, we are encouraged to be happy when difficulties come our way. Problems develop our patience and character by teaching us to: trust God to do what is best for us; look for opportunities to honor God in our present situation; remember that God will not abandon us; and watch for God's plan in us.[680]

Perhaps you have felt caught in the middle at work, or in relationships in your family or church. Complaining or turning on the leadership does not solve the problem. For these supervisors, God had a larger purpose in mind. So, rather than turning on the leadership when you feel pressured by both sides, turn to God to see what else He might be doing in this situation.[681]

---

[677] Jeremiah 17:21-27
[678] Nelson Study Bible, NKJV.
[679] Nelson Study Bible, NKJV.
[680] Life Application Study Bible, NKJV, 1996.
[681] Life Application Study Bible, NKJV, 1996.

Another story of hard work is found in *Ecclesiastes 2:18-23.* Solomon continues to show that hard work bears no lasting fruit for those who work solely to earn money and gain possessions. In addition, it may be well cared for, and all that was gained may be lost. Hard work done with proper motives such as caring for family and serving God is not wrong. We must work to survive. Moreover, we are responsible for the physical and spiritual well-being of those under our care. However, the fruit of hard work done to glorify only us will be passed on to those who may later lose or spoil it all. Such toil often leads to grief, while serving God leads to everlasting joy.

"Be strong and courageous, and do the work."[682] Judah's people had returned to worshipping God, in which God had promised to bless their efforts. However, it was time for them to work. We are people of prayer, Bible study, and worship, but eventually we must get out and do what God has in mind for us. He wants to change the world through us. God has given you a job to do in the church, at your place of employment, and at home. The time has come to be strong and work because God is with you through discipleship.[683]

Sometimes God will give us a job to do as He did with Moses, Abraham, and Noah, just to name a few. Noah had a difficult and huge task that others found humorous since this was during a time that did not rain. He was building a large boat, ship, or ark. God took care of the details of the job Noah was called to do. For instance, Noah was required to build detail architecture craftwork with the proper equipment to build an ark, but God supplied everything that was needed for completion. Too many times, we worry about details over which we have no control, while neglecting specific areas such as attitudes, relationships, and responsibilities that are under our control. Like Noah, concentrate on what God has given you to do and leave the rest to God.

In another situation, Joseph was a prisoner and a slave in Egypt. Joseph could have seen his situation as hopeless,[684] but Joseph did his best with each small task given to him. Once Joseph was thrown into prison, after being falsely accused of sexual conduct, he was the keeper of the prison, and later promoted to prison administrator, showing diligence and demonstrating a positive attitude through his hardship. At work, at home, or at school, follow Joseph's example by taking each small task and doing your best. Remember how God turned Joseph's situation around. He will see your efforts and can reverse even overwhelming circumstance.[685]

Another example, Jehu did much of what the Lord told him to, but he did not obey Yahweh with all his heart. He had become God's instrument for carrying out justice, but he had not become God's servant. As a result, he gave only lip service to God, while permitting the worship of the golden calves. Check the condition of your

---

[682] 1 Chronicles 28:20; also can refer to 1 Chronicles 28:10; 2 Chronicles 15:7; Psalm 31:24
[683] Life Application Study Bible, NKJV, emphasis added by author.
[684] Genesis 39:21-23
[685] Life Application Study Bible, NKJV, emphasis added by author.

heart toward God. We can be very active in our work for God and still not give the heartfelt obedience He desires.[686]

Jesus is coming back -- we know this to be true. Does this mean we must quit our jobs to serve God? No, it means we are to use our time, talents, and treasures diligently to serve God completely in whatever we do. For a few people, this may mean changing professions. For most of us, it means doing our daily work out of love for God.[687] Pray for your job, for your employer to blend with your personality, to be recognized and appreciated by others and your boss, and receive promotions and advancements in line with God's will.[688]

---

[686] 2 Kings 10:30-31
[687] Matthew 25:21
[688] Proverbs 14:23; Romans 12:11

~Let Your Day Begin With Christ, Day 37~

Let your Day Begin Activity: Review the chart on the traps of laziness. Write down 5 things on each point that you plan to do, to change the laziness in your life at work. Set your goals high, no underachieving is allowed.

Today's Questions:

Do we bring God in the workplace? Do we pray before we walk in the office or start our daily duties?

Do we pray for the job we have and when we are seeking other employment? Do we trust where God will lead us? How do we show God thanks for our jobs?

Do we pray for our employers, bosses, and those in leadership? What are some other things we pray for while we are on the job? Will we see our prayers happen?

Review to Begin your Day with Christ:

If we do not work, we will not eat. We are required to work for a living to put food on the table, pay the bills, and take care of other financial responsibilities. We are to tap in to see what our career goals are, further our education, and ask God to show us what profession we are to go into. There will be entrepreneurs, politicians, missionaries, and volunteers. We are to find what best suits us, not get lazy on the job. Many of us get tired of working for someone else, then venture off and find your passion.

Review the laziness chart. Make sure you do not fall into this category.

Day Brings 38: Work Dilemma

A particular job can be based on demographics, lifestyles we portray, and background we have acquired, whether it is through experience and/or education. *Occupation* is the single pursuit that dominates our lives since we normally will take our net income to buy groceries, personal items, clothing, household items, pay bills, pay for education or other extracurricular activities, tithing and offering, and to pay off other debts. Except according to the Word, God requests our tithes to come from our *gross income*, is what we make before taxes, not our *net income*, what we bring home after taxes. However, there are those who work to live and those who live to work.

Most of us become burned out from our jobs or career choices that we have made over a span of time. We feel trapped in a job or career path, which we feel, we can neither escape nor derive psychological gratification. It can be from the long hours or stressful events while on the job. We are either workaholics or hardly workers. *Workaholics* allow work to crowd out all other aspects of life. *Hardly workers* know when to turn off the computers, to switch from work environment to personal life affairs, and are able to leave work at work and home life at home. *Workaholics* find an emotional payoff in overwork and an adrenaline high from success, as *hardly workers* only meet the needs and requirements of the position. However, medical professionals classify job stress as an *occupational hazard*. This stress can cause ulcers and deep depression that can lead to suicide. The Japanese term is *karoshi*, meaning death from overwork.

Today, our work environment requires staff to be multitasked, detail-oriented, and provide resources to save the company tons of money. Therefore, it is cost-effective to hire someone that is able to carry the load of two or more people. In the unpredictable world we live in today, a combination of industrial and technological experience work is essential and fulfilling the obligations of your employer. Qualifications for most graduates and applicants can be discouraging. In addition, we need to examine our attitudes about work. We cannot always change our circumstances. However, you have been influenced by negative attitudes toward work, and then you need to consider God's viewpoint and principles relative to our daily jobs.[689] God can measure the happiness and contentment in our work.

God is a worker. In Genesis, God created the heavens and earth.[690] Think of all the roles God had when creating the earth itself: designer, organizer, engineer, artist, developer, information specialist, project manager and developer, chemist, biologist, zoologist, programmer, linguist, and the list continues.[691] Overall, the quality of God's work is very good.[692] His creation can glorify and praise God, for His marvelous works.[693] God's work did not end with the creation of physical heavens and earth and

---

[689] Ecclesiastes 5:18
[690] Genesis 1:1
[691] Proverbs 8:12, 22-31
[692] Genesis 1:4, 31
[693] Psalm 19:1; 148:1

the first human couple. Jesus said, "My Father has kept working until now."[694] More in depth, my father: Jesus is "the only begotten Son" -- unique Son of God. He is not only a unique relationship with God, the Father, but also equality with God in nature.

Since God continually does good works without allowing Himself to stop on the Sabbath, the Son does likewise since He is equal to God. If God stopped labor on the Sabbath, nature would fall into chaos, and sin would overrun the world. In *Genesis, 2:2*, states that God rested on the seventh day, but this cannot mean that He stopped doing things. Jesus continues to work by providing His people, sustaining His creation, and saving His faithful worshippers.[695]

God even uses people, *His fellow workers*, to help with accomplishing certain tasks.[696] In other words, God's work involves many individuals with a variety of gifts and abilities. No superstars, only team members performing their own special roles. We can become useful members of God's team by setting aside our desires to receive glory for what we do. Do not seek the praise from people since it is worthless; instead seek approval from God.

In *Genesis 3:17-19*, some view that God punished Adam and Eve for their rebellion, by putting the burden of work on them. God said to Adam, "In the sweat of your face, you will eat bread until you return to the ground." Because of Adam and Eve's unfaithfulness, extension of the Eden Paradise would not happen. The ground came under God's curse. Sweat and toil were required for a person to eke out a living from the soil.[697] *Futility* means 'vanity, emptiness,' which refers to the curse on creation,[698] and creation waits for the coming glory because it also will be delivered. The bondage of corruption describes the *futility* in *Genesis 3:20*. Nature is a slave to decay and death, because of sin.

Since God is a hard worker, humans are created in His image.[699] The work assignment was given before God pronounced the words recorded in *Genesis 3:19*. If work were a curse and evil, God would have never encouraged people to engage in it. For example, Noah and his family had much work to do before and after the Flood. In the Christian era, Jesus' disciples were also urged to work.[700] However, work can be a burden caused from stress, hazards, boredom, disappointment, competition, and deception. Injustices are those 'thorns and thistles' relative to the curse bestowed on Adam and Eve, for their disobedience in the Garden of Eden.

---

[694] John 5:17
[695] Nehemiah 9:6; Psalm 36:6; 145:15, 16
[696] 1 Corinthians 3:9
[697] Romans 8:20, 21
[698] Genesis 3:17-19
[699] Genesis 1:26, 28; 2:15
[700] 1 Thessalonians 4:11

Believers are well-equipped to deal with work-generated stress. The Bible provides numerous fundamental principles to carry us through difficult times, with a positive effect on our spiritual and emotional well-being. For example, Jesus told us not to be anxious for nothing. The encouragement is to focus on today's problems, not tomorrow's. We are to avoid blowing things out of proportion; even our problems, troubles, and situations will only increase the sense of pressure and stress.[701] Christian ultimately can rely on God's strength in our dreadful and tiresome situations. When we think that we are at that breaking point, God can give us peace and joy in our hearts, and provide us with wisdom to deal with any hardship.[702] Even stressful circumstances can produce positive results. Trials can make us turn to God. It can also prompt us to continue cultivating a Christian personality and the ability to preserve under pressure.[703]

Quality and excellence in the workplace have always been praised. God does His work with excellence. For example, Bezalel and Oholiab with the wisdom, understanding, and knowledge were enabling them to carry out specific artistic and practical tasks.[704] God took a special interest in the function, artisanship, design, and other details of Bezalel and Oholiab's labor.

Perception of our personal abilities and work habits will help us see them as gifts from God. God will review our performance.[705] Since creation, God has given us work. We can perform our jobs without complaining or resentment. Furthermore, *reward of inheritance* is a strong motivation to serve someone. Our future reward is to spend eternity with Jesus Christ, which He treasures those who are faithful in His service. We normally think that we receive eternal rewards for spiritual practices such as reading the Bible, prayer, or even evangelism. Paul asserts that all work done to the honor of Christ will bring an eternal reward.[706]

We are to have a godly attitude, behavior and Christ-like perspective on the job, so that our message of the Bible will be attractive to coworkers and others we are in touch with from day to day. Remember, there is always room for improvement.[707] For instance, King Solomon, who worked hard, enjoyed all the riches and comforts that life, had to offer said, "Fear God and keep His commandments, for this are the whole duty of man." This clearly states that we must consider God's will in whatever we do, even if it is work. If we do not consider God's will, we will suffer from pain of despair, loneliness, and emptiness. Doing work that pleases our Creator will not leave us dissatisfied. To Jesus, the work Jehovah assigned Him was as nourishing, satisfying, and refreshing as food.[708] God will alert us in the areas, where we need to grow in faith.[709] Those who are

---

[701] Matthew 6:25-34
[702] Ephesians 6:10; Philippians 4:7
[703] Romans 5:3, 4
[704] Exodus 31:1-11
[705] Colossians 3:23
[706] see Colossians 1:22-23
[707] Proverbs 10:4; 22:29
[708] John 4:34; 5:36
[709] 1 Corinthians 16:13-14

working hard to serve God can look forward to the time when He will restore new earth and new heavens. Our deep-rooted faith and spirituality can supply much-needed strength. Once we learn what God's will is for our lives, and work in harmony with it, may be blessed and always see well in our work.

~Let Your Day Begin With Christ, Day 38~

Let your Day Begin Activity: Today, take the time to sit down and evaluate your job or career. Does it make you happy? Do you plan to elevate in the company? If you are unable with your current job, what career would make you happy? On a piece of paper, write down the steps needed to take to reach that ultimate happiness in your career or job.

Today's Questions:

What type of career do you see yourself doing to enhance your skills, gifts, and fulfill your accomplishments?

Are you willing to go the extra mile to do God's will and listen to His direction even if it calls you to change your career goals?

God is a worker. Can you give some examples on how God is at work?

Do you know the real reason you are working so hard? Through your workmanship, do you see yourself as Moses, Nehemiah, Noah, Joseph, Solomon, Ruth, or someone else in the Bible? Please explain.

Review to Begin your Day with Christ:

Many of us have work-generated stress and become burned out. We need to pay close attention to the jobs we have. In our economy, we find ourselves being workaholics, overworked and putting in overtime hours to pay our debts. Moreover, God desires us to give a good day's work, meaning we are to give our employer quality and excellence.

Genesis 3:17-19=rebellion, burdened with work.

Find the career, job, or business that best suites you. Check your local library on career, employment, and education books or online sites to take personality tests that will pick what jobs best suites your choices.

Day Begins 39: Faith And Works

Are You Working To Please God Or Allowing God To Work Through You?

Corinthians continued steadfast in the work of Christ because of the resurrection. Your *labor is not in vain* is stating that all the work that we do for Christ will be rewarded.[710] Sometimes, we hesitate to do good because we do not see any results. Nevertheless, if we can maintain a heavenly perspective, we will understand that we often will not see the good results from our efforts. If we truly believe that Christ has won the ultimate victory, this should affect the way we live right now. Do not allow discouragement over an apparent lack of results keep you from working. Do good things that you have an opportunity to do and know that your work will have eternal results.[711] Moreover, Paul said that no good work is ever in vain. In *1 Corinthian 16*, Paul elaborates on some practical work that has value for all believers.

> *1 Thessalonians 1:3, NKJV: "Remembering without ceasing your work of faith, labor of love, and patience of hope in our Lord Jesus Christ in the sight of our God and Father."*

Paul commended these young believers for their work produced by faith, labor prompted by love, and endurance inspired by hope. These characteristics are the marks of effective believers in any age.[712]

Conversely, John's hearers were shocked when he said that being Abraham's descendants was not enough for God. The religious leaders relied more on their family lines than on their faith, while standing for God, which is not handed down from our parents to their children. Jesus' harshest words were to the respectable religious leaders, who lacked the desire for real change. Religious leaders wanted to be known as authoritative leadership, but they did not want to change their minds. Therefore, there lives were unproductive. Repentance is tied to action, or it is not real. Following Jesus means more than saying the right words, it means acting on what He says.[713] Everyone has to commit to God on his or her own. Do not rely on someone else's faith for your salvation. Put your own faith in Jesus and then exercise it every day.

For instance, the book of James emphasizes on faith in action. God-fearing servants living are the evidence and result of faith. The church served with compassion, speak lovingly and truthfully, live in obedience to God's commands, and love for one another. The body of believers ought to be an example of heaven on earth, and drawing people to Christ through love for God and for each other. If we truly believe God's Word, we will live by it daily. God's Word is not merely something we read or think about, but

---

[710] see 2 Corinthians 5:10
[711] 1 Corinthians 15:58
[712] Life Application Study Bible; Please read 1 Corinthians 3:7-15.
[713] Life Application Study Bible, Luke 3:8-9, NKJV.

something we do. Belief, faith and trust must have hands and feet – ours.[714] Faith without works is dead.[715]

Do not think good works will get you in the gateway of Heaven.[716] Jesus spoke against this way of thinking. Faith is to believe that Jesus Christ will come through for you, and His grace will give us salvation if we only believe. Do not think because you are a good person will get you in heaven either. We are to work as believers of Jesus Christ to help others find salvation, for we are so blessed to have, by believing and receiving Jesus Christ in our lives. Ask God what type of job He has for you, trust in Him always, and He will bring you through as He has done in the past to succeed in this task. God has blessed you with talents and gifts. If you are not sure, pray and ask Him. He will let it be known to you through either visions or dreams. His voice will speak to your heart and mind, or through others. Ask for confirmation to make sure it is a word from God.

---

[714] Life Application Study Bible NKJV, emphasis added by author.
[715] James 2:14-26
[716] Ephesians 2:8-9

~Let Your Day Begin With Christ, Day 39~

Let your Day Begin Activity: What calling do you feel the Lord has bestowed on you. Today, take the time to pray to the Lord and ask Him to allow His calling to come through to you. Once doing so, do whatever measures needed to do for the calling of the Lord in your life.

Today's Questions:

Are you too busy to see what is going on around you? If so, how are you willing to make some changes for God?

Are you volunteering your time to serve others, to allow your gifts to give God the glory, and shine in other people lives, or applying God's Word in your life? If so, please list some examples. If not, what do you see yourself doing for the Lord?

Do you believe that your good works will get you in heaven? Please explain or revert to the Scriptures on the message about "good works."

Review to Begin your Day with Christ:

Labor will not be in vain. We will receive a full reward, what we do for Christ.

1 Corinthian 16=Paul elaborates on the meaning of "work."

We work with faith, love what we do (labor), and all that is hoped for through endurance.

Faith: Hebrews 11:1; 10:38; 4:2; Romans 10:17; 1:17; 1:8; 4:19-21; Proverbs 28:20; James 1:16; Galatians 5:6; Ephesians 2:8; 1 Thessalonians 5:8; 1 Corinthians 2:4-5; 1 Timothy 6:12; 1 John 5:4; Matthew 17:20; 23:23; 9:2; 9:20-22; 15:25-28; Mark 10:49-52; 2 Thessalonians 1:4; Acts 6:8; 3:16; and Luke 17:5.

Day Begins 40: How Is Your Prayer Life?

Give God The Praise

Abba	Romans 8:15	*Advocate*	1 John 2:1 (KJV); John 14:26
Almighty	Psalm 68:14; Matthew 28:18; Revelation 1:8	*Alpha*	Revelation 22:13; 1: 8-13
Amen	Revelation 3:14	*Ancient of Days*	Daniel 7
Anointed One	Psalm 2:2	*Apostle*	Hebrews 3:1
Arm of the Lord	Isaiah 53:1	*Atoning Sacrifice of our Sins*	1 John 2:2
Author of Life	Acts 3:15	*Author of our Faith*	Hebrews 12:2
Author and Perfecter of our Faith	Hebrews 2:10	*Author of our Salvation*	Hebrews 2:10
Beginning (and End)	Revelation 3:14; 21:6; 22:13	*Blessed and Holy (only) Ruler*	1 Timothy 6:15
Branch	Jeremiah 33:15	*Bread of God*	John 6:33
Bread of Life	John 6:35, 48	*Bridegroom*	Isaiah 62:5
Bright Morning Star	Revelation 22:16	*Chief Shepherd*	1 Peter 5:4
Chief Cornerstone	Ephesians 2:20; Acts 4:11; Isaiah 28:16 1 Peter 2:7	*Christ*	Matthew 22:42; 1 John 2:22; Revelation 20:4
Chosen One	Isaiah 42:1	*Christ the Lord*	Luke 2:11
Christ of God	Luke 9:20	*Consolation of Israel*	Luke 2:25
Christ, Son of Living God	Matthew 16:16	*Deliverer*	Romans 11:26
Commander	Isaiah 55:4	*Door*	John 10:7 (KJV)
Consuming Fire	Deuteronomy 4:24; Hebrews 12:29	*Eternal God*	Deuteronomy 33:27; 1 John 1:2; 5:20
Creator	1 Peter 4:19; John 1:3	*Faithful and True Witness*	Revelation 3:14
Desired of all Nations	Haggai 2:7	*Father*	Matthew 6:9
Faithful and True	Revelation 19:11	*First Risen from the Dead*	Revelation 1:5
Everlasting Father and Counselor	Isaiah 9:6	*First Fruits*	1 Corinthians 15:20-23
Faithful Witness	Revelation 1:5	*Foundations*	1 Corinthians 3:11

First and Last	Revelation 1:8,11,13; 1:17; 2:8; 22:13		
Firstborn	Revelation 1:5; Romans 8:29; Colossians 1:15	Gentle Whisper	1 Kings 19:12
Friend of Tax Collectors and Sinners	Matthew 11:19	Gift of God	John 4:10
Gate	John 10:9	God	Genesis 1:1; John 1:1; 20:28; Hebrews 1:8; Romans 9:5; 2 Peter 1:1; 1 John 5:20
Gift of God	John 4:10	God over All	Romans 9:5
Glory of the Lord	Isaiah 40:5	Good Shepherd	John 10:11, 14
God Almighty	Genesis 17:1	Great Shepherd	Hebrews 13:20
God who sees me	Genesis 16:13	He searches the thoughts of everyone	Revelation 2:23
Great High Priest	Hebrews 4:14	He opens and closes doors, no man can shut	Revelation 3:7
He resurrects	Revelation 1:13, 18	Heir of all Things	Hebrews 1:2
He holds the seven stars and golden lamp stands	Revelation 2:1	High Priest Forever	Hebrews 6:20
He is the Seven Spirits (of God)	Revelation 3:1	Holy One	Acts 3:14; 2:27
He carries the sharp sword with two edges	Revelation 2:12	Hope	Titus 2:13; 1 Timothy 1:1
Guide	Psalm 48:14	Horn of Salvation	Luke 1:69
Head of the Church	Ephesians 1:22; 4:15; 5:23; Colossians 1:18	Image of God	2 Corinthians 4:4
High Priest	Hebrews 2:17; 3:1	Immanuel	Isaiah 7:14
Holy and True	Revelation 3:7	Jesus	Matthew 1:21
Holy One of Israel	Isaiah 49:7	Jesus Christ our Lord	Romans 6:23
Hope of Glory	Colossians 1:27	King	Zechariah 9:9
I Am	John 8:58; Exodus 3:14	King of Israel	John 1:49
Image of His Person	Hebrews 1:3 (KJV)	King of Kings	1 Timothy 6:15;

			Revelation 19:16
Jehovah	Psalm 83:18 (KJV)	*Lamb*	Revelation 13:8; 5:8,9
Jesus Christ	Revelation 1:1	*Lamb of God*	John 1:29
Judge	Isaiah 33:22; Acts 10:42	*Last Adam*	1 Corinthians 15:45
King Eternal	1 Timothy 1:17	*Leader*	Isaiah 55:4
King of the Jews	Matthew 27:11	*Light of the World*	John 8:12
King of the Ages	Revelation 15:3	*Lilly of the Valleys*	Song 2:1
Lamb slain	Revelation 5:8-9	*Living One*	Revelation 1:18
Lamb Without Blemish	1 Peter 1:19	*Living Water*	John 4:10
Law Giver	Isaiah 33:22	*Lord God Almighty*	Revelation 15:3
Life	John 14:6; Colossians 3:4	*Lord Jesus Christ*	1 Corinthians 15:57
Like an Eagle	Deuteronomy 32:11	*Lord of Glory*	1 Corinthians 2:8
Lion of the Tribe of Judah	Revelation 5:5	*Lord (YHWH) our Righteousness*	Jeremiah 23:6
Living Stone	1 Peter 2:4, 6	*Man from Heaven*	1 Corinthians 15:48
Lord	John 13:13; 2 Peter 2:20; Revelation 4:11	*Master*	Luke 5:5
Lord God of the Holy Prophets	Revelation 22:6	*Mediator of the New Covenant*	Hebrews 9:15
Lord of All	Acts 10:36	*Messenger of the Covenant*	Malachi 3:1
Lord of Lords	1 Timothy 6:15; Revelation 19:16	*Mighty God*	Isaiah 9:6
Love	1 John 4:8	*Nazarene*	Matthew 2:23
Man of Sorrows	Isaiah 53:3	*Omega*	Revelation 22:13
Mediator	1 Timothy 2:5	*Our Passover Lamb*	1 Corinthians 5:7
Merciful God	Jeremiah 3:12	*Our Holiness*	1 Corinthians 1:30
Messiah	John 4:25	*Our Peace*	Ephesians 2:14
Offspring of David	Revelation 22:16	*Our Redemption*	1 Corinthians 1:30
Only Son of God	John 1:18 (KJV); 1 John 4:9	*Power of God*	1 Corinthians 1:24
Our Great God and Savior	Titus 2:13	*Prince of Peace*	Isaiah 9:6
Our Husband	2 Corinthians 11:2	*Purifier*	Malachi 3:3
Our Protection	2 Thessalonians 3:3; Genesis 15:1	*Radiance of God's Glory*	Hebrews 1:3
Our Righteousness	1 Corinthians 1:30	*Refiner's Fire*	Malachi 3:2
Potter	Isaiah 64:8	*Rider of White Horse*	Revelation 19:11

Prophet	Acts 3:22	Righteous Branch	Jeremiah 23:5
Rabboni (Teacher)	John 20:16	Rock	1 Corinthians 10:4
Redeemer	Job 19:25	Rose of Sharon	Song 2:1
Resurrection (and the Life)	John 11:25	Ruler over all Kings of Earth	Revelation 1:5
Righteous One	1 John 2:1; Acts 7:52	Savior	Luke 2:11; Ephesians 5:23; Titus 1:4; 3:6; 2 Peter 2:20
Root of David	Revelation 5:5, 9; 22:16	Seed	Genesis 3:15
Ruler over Israel	Micah 5:2	Shepherd of Our Souls	1 Peter 2:25
Scepter out of Israel	Numbers 24:17	Son of David	Luke 18:39; Matthew 1:1
Servant	Isaiah 42:1	Son of Man	Matthew 8:20; Revelation 1:13
Son of God	John 1:49; Hebrews 4:14; Matthew 27:54; Revelation 2:18	Source (of Eternal Salvation)	Hebrews 5:9
Son of the Most High God	Luke 1:32	Star out of Jacob	Numbers 24:17
Spirit of God	Genesis 1:2	Sun of Righteousness	Malachi 4:2
Stone	1 Peter 2:8	The One Mediator	1 Timothy 2:5
Teacher	John 13:13	True Bread	John 6:32
The Stone the Builders rejected	Acts 4:11	Truth and the Way	John 14:6
True Light	John 1:9	Witness among the people	Isaiah 55:4
True Vine	John 15:1, 5	Wisdom of God	1 Corinthians 1:24
Word	John 1:1	Word of God	Revelation 19:13-16

God has no correct name. God has only the name you give Him since His name changes from time to time, from place to place, and from person to person. However, God remains the same and never changes, long as you give Him the praise that He deserves. Even the angels in heaven, praise and worship the Lord to the highest, Lucifer even worshipped God. God created all things, even the angels to worship Him, but Lucifer name changed to Satan because of his pride, desiring others to worship, and praise him instead of God. Some of us want the praise and to be worshipped, we are children of Satan. Are you a child of God or child of Satan? The Bible speaks of the differences. We are all God's creation, which would make us a child of God. Our lifestyle and actions can determine which father we live under. Do you have the *Fruits of the Spirit*?

~Let Your Day Begin With Christ, Day 40~

Let your Day Begin Activity: Review the chart in the beginning of Day 40. How is your prayer life? Take fifteen minutes, thirty minutes, or however long it will take to pray to God. Pour your heart out to God, choose one of the names or titles in the prayer chart, and speak about what God has done for you. Read the Scripture(s) that follow under the title(s).

Today's Questions:

Who do you serve? What sacrifices have you made to serve God?

What are the *Fruits of the Spirit?* If you are unaware of what gifts God bestowed in you, you can take a spiritual test on www.chistianet.com.

Review to Begin your Day with Christ:

This day, we are praising and worshipping God. You can pick a name from the chart and read those Scripture(s) under the title of our Creator, Yahweh (Yeshua).

We are either children of Satan or children of God, who do you, serve. From this day forth, I will serve _____ all the days of my life.

Day Begins 41: Determining God's Will Through Prayer

Matthew 6:25-34, Verse 33, NKJV: "But seek first the Kingdom of God and His righteousness and all these things shall be added to you."

What is prayer? It is communication with God? Prayer is a two-way thing. We come to God in prayer, and He speaks to us through different means, especially through His Word. This is why it is imperative to be in the Word on a consistent basis, and meditate on it day and night.

Who can pray? The church is to pray. As believers, we are the righteous that were once sinners saved by God's grace.

When can we pray? Always and all day long, we can pray. Thanking God for our meals we eat. In the morning, noonday, and when the sun goes down. When we are sick or ill, we can pray to God for healing. Most of us, pray when we are facing death.

Where should I pray? Pray in groups, while engaged or involved in church ministries, Bible study, work, home studies, and other meetings or seminars. You can pray in one's closet, or in secrecy. You can pray in one's home. You can pray in church either publicly or corporately.

How should I pray? A.C.T.S.:
A-Adoration: Magnify God for who He is.
C-Confession: Forgiveness for our sins.
T-Thanksgiving: Personal blessings.
S-Supplication: Petitioning God's throne for others and ourselves.

What are things that can hinder my prayers? Not only limited to, some things that can hinder our prayers are sin, unforgiving spirit, and empty repetition prayer. Other ways are family problems,[717] such as husbands taking advantage of his wives submission, and spouses failing to honor and respect one another. *Hypocritical prayer* is praying with the wrong motive, self-righteous, pride just as Lucifer can also hinder your prayers.

Praying to God will change the person, change their situation, and make a difference in our lives. Ask the Lord for wisdom. After you are willing to change by allowing God in and to do His will, your situation will change. When we pray in the Holy Spirit, it will edify ourselves, a tool to build ourselves up. Prayer spoken in tongues can be in utterance.[718] Each prayer language is different, which Satan may have a problem translating. Satan will let them think it is 'gibberish.' Only God will never give us a bad

---

[717] 1 Peter 3:7
[718] Romans 8:26

gift.[719] It is diligent to seek God when we pray. *Prayer* is a deeper intimate way to reach the Lord. God will reveal Himself – manifest Himself. We have to learn to wait on Him and pray. Others are willing to fast and pray to get an answer from God. God will manifest His presence in many ways.

When we are full of ourselves, biblically speaking, we are full of death and darkness. When were full of God, we are full of light and life. Pray like Paul did, he prayed until he knew God's power and who God is. If we pray this way, it will help us from trying to manipulate people into doing what we want them to do, and from throwing fits when things do not go our way. We are able to be more patient and willing to hear from God. Furthermore, how to handle these issues that we are going through. Jesus continually intercedes for us, as He sits at the right hand of God.[720]

Keep in mind that not all of us pray alike and God created us that way. Not one of us are alike in appearance, unless you are identical twins, do not share the same DNA except for identical twins, personalities, characteristics, or behavior, so we are going to pray to our Heavenly Father differently. Whether you fast, use blessed oil or holy water, pray on your knees, standing, bow, or lie on the floor to pray to our Creator, He wants to hear from you. Some would argue that I do not have a prayer life with God. Do you talk to Him? Do you praise Him? Do you thank Him for what He has blessed you with? Do you thank Him for the food on the table? Do you thank Him for the car you drive? Thank Him for making a way out of no way to pay your bills and blessing you with a job? Do you pray to God and praise Him at the same time. However, if you do not have a relationship with God, then why would you pray? Once you receive and believe in Jesus Christ, you have a relationship with Christ. When we are praying and trusting in God's promises for our lives,[721] but first we have to seek the Word of God for the promises. We will receive all the good things that God has promised us in His Word, when we believe and obey the Lord wholeheartedly. Here are some of the promises listed in His Holy Word:

Deliverance	Healing	Peace
Prosperity	Eternal Life	Health
Guidance	Life	Protection
Abundance	Revival	Wisdom
Truth	Love	Victory
Freedom	Happiness	Blessings

To obtain these promises, we need to know God, the love of God, believe in God, live for the Lord, and pray to God. However, sometimes it requires patience.[722] Next, we need to be obedient to the Lord's Commandments and things that He requires

---

[719] 1 Corinthians 12:30
[720] Hebrews 7:25; Romans 8:34
[721] Acts 6:4
[722] Hebrews 10:36-37

from us.[723] We need faith.[724] We are to be strong and courageous.[725] We are to be active in God's Word and to do His will.[726] We are to put God first in everything we do.[727]

Prayer is an avenue that takes us from the problems to God's promise, from doubt to discovery, from the valley to the mountaintop, from giving up to hope, from discouragement to encouragement, from fear to faith, from despair to happiness, from lies to truth, from confusion to wisdom, and from losses to gains. Prayer brings life, peace, joy, and victory to every area of our lives.[728]

---

[723] Deuteronomy 11:22-23
[724] Hebrews 11:6
[725] Joshua 1:7
[726] Hebrews 6:12
[727] Matthew 6:33
[728] Praying God's Promises

~Let Your Day Begin With Christ, Day 41~

Let your Day Begin Activity: For today's activity, sit down and think of all the promises in the Holy Word. What do these promises mean to you? How many of the promises do you need answered? Today, write down all the things you need the Lord to do in your life and take them to God in prayer tonight.

Today's Questions:

Do you pray regularly?

Do you trust God in your decision-making and to bring you through difficult situations?

Do you thank God for all the blessings in your life, or only pray when you are in trouble? Please explain.

Review to Begin your Day with Christ:
Provide a written response for the following questions:
- Why is prayer important to me in determining God's will for my life?
- What will I do this week to increase my prayer time? How can I make time?
- Is there any sin in my life that may hinder my increased prayer time?
- Who can pray? Review Scriptures: 1 Timothy 2:1-8; 1 Peter 3:10-12; James 5:16.
- When can we pray? Review Scriptures: Acts 10:2; 1 Thessalonians 3:10; 1 Timothy 5:5; Matthew 14:19; Mark 1:35; 6:41; John 6:11; Acts 27:35; James 5:14-15.
- Where should I pray? Review Scriptures: Matthew 18:19-20; 6:6; Acts 12:12; 1:14.
- How should I pray? A.C.T.S.
- *A-Adoration:* Magnify God for who He is (Psalm 8, 9, 23, 46, 100, 148).
- *C-Confession:* Forgiveness for our sins (Isaiah 59:2; Psalm 66:18; 1 John 1:9).
- *T-Thanksgiving:* Personal blessings (Psalm 103:2; 136, 138; 1 Thessalonians 5:18).
- *S-Supplication:* Petitioning God's throne for others and ourselves (Philippians 4:6, 7; 1 Peter 5:7).

Day Begins 42: Six Steps To Prayer (Praying God's Promises)

1. *Step 1:* Know God's Word. God's Word is implanted in our hearts to keep us from sins, also our sword where the Holy Spirit will always slay the enemy.[729]
2. *Step 2:* Believe in God's Word. It builds faith in our hearts.[730] God keeps His Word, does not lie. No matter how dismal circumstances might seem, keep our forces clean.[731]
3. *Step 3:* Receive God's Word. Receive His promises, which it is essential to know what they are. As we read, study, memorize, and meditate on God's Word, it brings the promises to life for us.[732]
4. *Step 4:* Personalize the Word. The Bible is more personal than any other book, a message from our Heavenly Father's heart to us. It enables us to claim God's promises to meet our every need. In addition, it personalizes God's promise, being able to see everyone from a different perspective -- from the perspective of the Holy Spirit.[733]
5. *Step 5:* Pray the Promise. Once you have immersed yourself in the Word of God and allowed its truths to saturate deeply within your spirit, be ready to walk by faith and not by sight. For example, studying the Word of God opens your eyes to deeper truths of God.[734] *Spiritual freedom* enables you to believe God's Word and trust His promises implicitly.[735] God will lead you every step of the way. Personalized faith and promised prayer life (all forms of prayer to pray the promises of God -- *1 John 5:14-15*). Praying accordingly to God's will -- whole counsel of God is praying what He wants us to pray and believe, pray His Word. He hears us and answers us.
6. *Step 6: Answered prayers* are when God meets every human need. We can apply to every aspect: physically, financially, family, relationally, emotionally, mentally, sexually, vocationally, and spiritually. Furthermore, the Bible contains every need, praying His Word, actualizes those answers through faith. Through prayers, we are building faith in our hearts. *Prayer* is also a stepping-stone to new spiritual discoveries. Prayer will change your life in radical ways. All God's blessings will come to you as you enter this exciting way to pray. The promises that God wants us to claim as our own through faith and prayer.[736]

"I pray for the anointing of God. Stir your people to action. Strengthen your people! Encourage! Give us the power to overcome the appetites, which try to take control over our spiritual life. Give us purpose and direction to follow you obediently and faithfully. In Jesus Name, Amen!"—Author, Adrienna Dionna Turner

---

[729] Ephesians 6:17
[730] Romans 10:17
[731] Lamentations 3:22-25
[732] 1 Corinthians 2:9-10
[733] 1 Corinthians 2:14
[734] John 8:32
[735] Proverbs 3:5-6
[736] 2 Corinthians 1:20

~Let Your Day Begin With Christ, Day 42~

Let your Day Begin Activity: For today's activity, using the 6 steps to prayer. Write down how you can improve in each step to get closer to God. Tonight, take those improvements to the Lord and ask Him to help you succeed in those steps.

Today's Questions:

Will you pray without ceasing? What does this mean to you?

Do you pray in the Spirit? Explain.

Review to Begin your Day with Christ:

- *Yahweh protects us:* 2 Samuel 22:3-4; Jeremiah 29:12-14; Luke 10:19; and Jude 1:24-25.
- *Yahweh hears us:* 2 Kings 20:5; Job 34:28; Psalm 4:3; 9:12; 28:6; 34:4; 120:1; Proverbs 15:29; Zechariah 13:9; 1 Peter 3:12; and 1 John 5:14, 15.
- *Yahweh heals us:* 2 Kings 20:5 and Psalm 91:15-16.
- *Yahweh answers our prayers:* Psalm 91:15-16; Jeremiah 33:3; Matthew 6:8; 7:7-8, 11; 18:19-20; 21:22; Mark 11:22-24; John 11:22; 14:13-14; 15:7; 16:23, 24; Romans 10:12; Ephesians 3:20-21; 1 Thessalonians 5:24; Hebrews 4:16; 11:6; James 1:5-6; 5:16; and 1 John 5:15.
- *Yahweh will give us a long life:* Psalm 91:15-16.
- *Yahweh will draw us near to Him:* Psalm 145:18 and James 4:8.
- *Yahweh will meet our needs:* Matthew 6:8; 7:7-8, 11; and Philippians 4:19.
- *Yahweh will show us supernatural truths:* Jeremiah 33:3.
- *Yahweh will give us power over the enemy:* Luke 10:19; James 4:7; and Revelation 12:11.
- *Yahweh does exceedingly, abundantly, and beyond our expectations:* Ephesians 3:20-21 and Jude 1:24-25.

Day Begins 43: Steps To A Meaningful Meditation

Meditation is a prayerful consideration and a continuous thought to a specific Scripture.[737] *Meditation* is to get in touch with who you really are, after asking God all the questions. First, clear your mind, and then you are able to get into meditation. Then, you should forget all the questions that you wanted to address to God. Require no answers just meditate. *Meditation* is being able to go one place where the answers and questions are. If you expect an answer, you will not get one. If the answer comes to you, not out of expectation, accept the answer from God. *Meditation* is not a mental process; it is simply the absence of the mental process. In other words, it is not thinking or expecting anything, just pure relaxation and focusing on the Lord.

If you tell God to make moves in your life, in your walk, in your talk, change your ways to become more like Christ, watch God move into action. Some think that God speaks through your imagination. We need to have channels of communication open to God by talking or praying to Him everyday. This is the remedy to ward off selfish thoughts such as doubt, worry, fear or discouragement. Living without expectations, you will avoid disappointment.

Memorize   Emphasize   Visualize   Personalize

Find a prayer time and remain faithful to that 'prayer watch.'

Worship (thanksgiving)	Confession (repentance)	Intercession (others)	Petition (self)	Communion (listening to God's Word or hear His voice).

According to Stormie Omartian's book, *Lord I Want to Be Whole*, she says several steps to follow when the enemy attacks:

1. Are you proclaiming the Lord in every area of your life? Sometimes, we exclude Jesus without realizing it. Name specifically the area Satan is attacking by giving God the credit.
2. Saturate yourself with God's Word.
3. Prayer. Ask God to reveal the truth of your situation to you. Ask God for guidance, protection, and strength for whatever you are facing.
4. Continue to praise the Lord in the midst of whatever is happening.
5. Ask God to show you if there are any points of obedience that you have not taken, which the lack of obedience always opens us up in the enemy of attack.

---

[737] Joshua 1:8

6. Fast and pray, which is a powerful weapon for breaking down enemy strongholds.
7. Resist Satan since Jesus lives in you. You have full authority and power over Satan.
8. Rest in the Lord. Jesus is the victor and fights all our battles.

There are times when are prayers will not be answered, or not exactly the way we prayed for it to happen based on our timetable. If that happens, trust that God knows what is best. There can be painful consequences of unanswered prayers. This is just a matter of waiting on God. On the other hand, our prayers can be answered without realizing it. If a prayer takes so long to be answered, we tend to give up on hope. Then, we become discouraged and fear God has forgotten us. Next, you will stop praying, stop reading the Holy Word, and stop going to church. We tend to feel, what is the point of praying if they are not answered? Most of us do not like to wait a day, a month, or even years, for the answer to come.

Scriptures On Prayers, Pray

Genesis 24:15	Matthew 26:40-41; 5:43-44; 6:5-7	Genesis 18:20-33	Genesis 25:21
Exodus 14:15	Genesis 32:9-12	Philippians 4:6-7	Numbers 10:35
Revelation 15:3-4	Exodus 32:9-14	Acts 12:5	Jude 20
Revelation 8:3-4	Revelation 22:8-9	1 John 3:21-22	1 Peter 3:7,12
1 Peter 5:7	Hebrews 10:19-23	James 4:3	1 Samuel 12:23
Daniel 2:16-23	Isaiah 7:12	Isaiah 38:1-5	2 Kings 19:1-7, 15-19
1 Chronicles 17:16-20	Deuteronomy 8:10	2 Chronicles 6:19-42	2 Chronicles 20:6
2 Chronicles 7:12	1 Samuel 1:10-11	1 Kings 8:56-60	Nehemiah 4:9; 5:19
Ezra 8:23	1 Chronicles 22:7-10	Nehemiah 2:4	Psalm 5:1-3
Job 1:5	1 Chronicles 4:9-10	Psalm 4:3	Psalm 77:1-12
Psalm 10:1	Nehemiah 1:5	Psalm 55:17	Matthew 18:19-20
Psalm 122:6-9	Jonah 2:1	Matthew 6:5-8	Mark 9:14-29
Matthew 6:5-13	Matthew 7:9-11	Matthew 14:23	Matthew 14:35-36
Mark 11:22-23	Luke 1:13; 6:28	Mark 1:35; 11:25	Acts 4:23-30
James 5:13-16; 4:2-3	John 17:1, 20	Luke 6:12,19	Colossians 1:9-14
Acts 12:13-15	Romans 1:8-10	Acts 1:12-13	1 Thessalonians 1:2-3
1 Timothy 2:1-4	Ephesians 6:19-20	Galatians 4:4	Hebrews 5:7; 6:13-14
1 Thessalonians 3:10; 5:17	Philippians 1:4	2 Corinthians 12:7-10	Hebrews 13:18-19
1 Timothy 2:2, 8	1 Peter 3:9	2 Thessalonians 1:3	Psalm 18:3-6

Psalm 27:4, 8	Psalm 37: 3-5	Hebrews 4:16	Psalm 66:18-19
Psalm 69:1-3	Psalm 78:18-22	1 John 5:14-15	Psalm 85:1-7
Psalm 86:11	Psalm 88:1-2	Psalm 42:1-2, 7-8	Psalm 99:6
Psalm 103: 1-22	Psalm 106:14-15	Psalm 80:4	2 Samuel 21:1
2 Chronicles 7:14	Nehemiah 6:9-14	Psalm 91:14-16	1 Kings 8:52
Psalm 6:9	Psalm 116:1-4	2 Samuel 5:17-19	Psalm 119:62, 65
Psalm 123:1-2	Job 6:8-10	Psalm 118:5	Job 30:20
Job 33:14-17, 26	Psalm 34:17	Job 16:19; 22:12-14	Psalm 138: 1-3
Ephesians 3:12	Psalm 123:1-2	Psalm 17:6	Psalm 141:2
Psalm 145:17-19	Proverbs 10:24	Psalm 139: 23-24	Ecclesiastes 5:2
Proverbs 1:29-31	Jeremiah 7:16	Proverbs 13:12	Jeremiah 2:27
Isaiah 30:9	Isaiah 62:6-7	Isaiah 65:24	Jeremiah 12:1-6
Lam 3:8	Micah 3:4	Jeremiah 11:18-23	Jeremiah 20:7-18
Jeremiah 15:10-21	Jeremiah 17:12-18	Jeremiah 18:18-23	Daniel 10:12, 15-21
Ezekiel 36:37-38	Daniel 3:16-18	Daniel 6:5-11	Matthew 21:21-22
Micah 3:1-4	Zephaniah 3:9	Zechariah 7:13	Luke 20:47
Luke 8:56	Luke 10:1-2, 11:1	Luke 11:5-13	John 17:1-26
John 14:13-14	John 16:23-24	John 15:16; 16:24	Psalm 95:6
Acts 1:6-7	Acts 1:24-26	Acts 8:24	Romans 8:26-27
Daniel 6:6	Acts 9:40	Acts 20:36	Ephesians 3:17-21
Romans 15:31-32	Ephesians 2:18	Ephesians 3:14-21	Acts 12:5
Philippians 1:9	Psalm 62:3-6	Acts 21:5	Colossians 4:12

Jesus taught the disciples how to pray and teaches us how to pray to the Lord. Here is our daily prayer:

"Our Father in heaven.
Hallowed by Your name.
Your kingdom come.
Your will be done.
On earth as it is in heaven.
Give us our day by day our daily bread.
And forgive us our sins.
For we also forgive everyone who is indebted to us.
And do not lead us into temptation.
But deliver us from the evil one (Luke 11:1-4)."

~Let Your Day Begin With Christ, Day 43~

Let your Day Begin Activity: In this section, there are steps to use when Satan attacks, the best offense is a great defense. Take the time today to figure out how you will take these steps so that you will be prepared for the enemy when is comes to attack. Do not wait until the attack begins.

Today's Questions:

What is a meaningful meditation to you? What do you normally do?

How often do you meditate and pray to God to avoid Satan's tactics?

Are you a prayer warrior? If not, what will it take to become one?

Review to Begin your Day with Christ:
What are things that can hinder my prayers?
- *Sin* (1 John 1:9, James 5:16).
- *Unforgiving spirit* (Matthew 6:14-15).
- *Empty repetition* is a repetitious prayer to God or asking the same prayer repeatedly (Matthew 6:7-8).
- *Family problems* (1 Peter 3:7) such as husbands should not take advantage of their wives submission
- *Hypocritical prayer* (Matthew 6:5).
- *Pray with the wrong motive* (Matthew 6:5-6, James 4:3).
- *Self-righteous* (Luke 18:11-14), not to be full of yourself, just as Lucifer was too sure of himself (pride).
- *Spouses failing to honor and respect one another* (1 Peter 5:7).

Prayer Warrior: worship, confession, intercession, petition, and communion.

Day Begins 44: Does Your Social Life Seem Empty?

God wants us to enjoy life. When we have the proper view of God, we discover that real pressure is enjoying whatever we have as gifts from God, not in what we accumulate.[738] God also wants to lead us out deeper into the waters of surrender and consecration. In *Romans 6*, there is no other chapter in the Bible that gives assurance to a struggling Christian. God will never do anything in our spiritual lives that we are not willing for Him to do. He never coerces the will, or pressures us into any actions to which we have not given consent. We can disabuse our minds or forced into any life choices, which are not free and sovereign.

We become whatever we choose to be. We are not what we feel, or what we might do or say in a single impulsive moment of our life. We are what we will be. We cannot always control our emotions, but we can control our own will. God has granted us 'free will.' Usually our feelings have nothing to do with the truth of God. It is not your feelings or emotions that make you a child of God, but the doings of God's will.

Moreover, your battle is with self, and when you become willing, God will give you victory over your situation and carnal enemy.[739] Before you can have, you must give away. Before you can be full, you must be empty. Before you can live, you must die. In other words, the *old man or woman* must lie down our fleshly desires. Before you have the victory, you must surrender to God. In the weakness of the flesh, we find ourselves bound in mind and body by the superior strength of our spiritual enemy. We struggle to extricate ourselves from the bondage, but the harder we try, the deeper we sink into the mire. Without the transforming grace of the new birth, we will live our lives with a carnal mind.[740]

Fatal delusion depends on trying harder and struggling longer to get the victory over sin. The secret is trusting instead of trying. Time will only make a young sinner into an old sinner. We must admit that we are not as strong as our adversary, Satan. We are to surrender our dependence of human strength and effort to God since He provides the glorious gift of victory. Jesus stated we could do nothing without Him.[741] *Philippians 4:13* states, *"I can do all things through Christ, which strengthens me."*

Sinners do things willfully such as breaking the commandments of God. *Sin* is also the attitude of pride, arrogance of your thoughts, which starts with our minds. We ought to let the Holy Spirit be captive of our minds. Sin is not just a private matter.[742] Everything we do affects others and we have to think of them constantly. God created us to be interdependent, instead of being independent. We, who are strong in our faith, without pride or condescension, treat others with love, patience, and self-restraint.

---

[738] Ecclesiastes 3:12—Life Application Study Bible, NKJV.
[739] 1 Corinthians 15:57
[740] Romans 8:7
[741] John 5:15
[742] Romans 14:20-21

As believers, we are to *edify* or *build up* each other. Paul has already exhorted mature believers to have consideration for the weak believers. Here, Paul exhorts the mature believer to identify ways to build up those weaker in their faith. Alternatively, there is a little distinction between stumble, offended, and someone who is weak. Paul uses all three words to reiterate that a mature believer should not cause the downfall of another believer.[743]

On the other hand, Paul does not require the strong to abandon their convictions about things, not condemned by the law. Instead, he encourages them to have faith about such issues. Although believers may refrain from eating meat in front of weaker believers, they can still believe that Christ gives them the freedom to eat all types of food privately before Him.[744] Nevertheless, this does not refer that drinking wine is okay in the privacy of your home and with God. Christ is the ultimate model for the strong believer and someone to turn to for the weak, let Jesus make you strong. We try to avoid actions forbidden by the Scripture, of course, but sometimes the Scripture is silent. Then, we are to follow our conscience. When God shows us that something is wrong for us, we must avoid it. However, we are not to judge other believers who exercise their freedom.[745]

If we merely set out to please our neighbors and other people, we are labeled people-pleasures. Peer pressure can be difficult and a touchy situation, so we want to do our best to stand out with the crowd. However, Jesus was not a people-pleaser, but pleasing the will of God. As believers of Jesus Christ, we can please God instead of people. God will bless us. Paul was opposed to seeing people trying so hard to please other people.[746] Nevertheless, we are to set aside willfulness and self-pleasing actions for the sake of building others up. Our Christian convictions must be a disguise for coldhearted treatment of our brothers and sisters.[747]

Overcoming sin is the possibility rests with God and the responsibility rests with us. We begin to act against the sin, which God provides the power to break habits of sin. By yielding our will to the higher powers from above, we can be delivered from the bondage of the flesh. Then, our wholeness is captive to the Spirit of God, and we are able to think His thoughts. Paul declares that we partake of the divine nature and have the mind of Christ. The process is surrendering our will and giving up our own way.

Satan's strongest efforts are aimed at the exaltation of self. Satan can only control the individuals, who continue to feed the carnal nature. Self-related indulgences are when Satan constantly holds to the fallen human race. The most appealing subtitles are self-righteousness, self-dependence, self-seeking, self-pleasing, self-will, self-defense, and self-glory. However, counselors urge us to improve our self-worth and our

---

[743] Nelson Study Bible, NKJV, Romans 14: 20-21.

[744] Romans 14: 2, 5

[745] Romans 14:23

[746] Galatians 1:10

[747] Romans 15:2

self-esteem. Even ministers preach sermons around their interpretation of loving our neighbors as we love ourselves.

We need to recognize our value in the sight of God. The Lord has counted every one of us as more precious than His own life. God can love us despite our genetic weakness and indulged carnal appetites, but the closer we come to Jesus, we become less charmed with our own selfish ways. We enter the converted life through the Holy Spirit; the confidence we placed in the flesh will be wholly shifted to the Savior, our Lord. The truth is that egocentric nature of a baby, child, or as an adult, is to have its own way. This nature needs to be crucified, and under the new spiritual nature, affections are set on Jesus. Self is no longer important where the flesh has no control over life to fulfill its own will.

The subject of the will is not achieved by any decision since self will never make the choice to put itself to death. Only the Holy Spirit can create the desire to escape from the domination of a sin-loving nature. It can bring us to the point of being willing to give up every indulgence of that corrupt, fallen nature. Self makes the Christian path seem dark and fearsome, but when self is surrendered and crucified, the narrow road is filled with joy unspeakable. Ironically, you would think believers of Jesus Christ should be the happiest people in the world. If not, it is because self has not been surrendered and crucified.

God gives us insight and warning signs, which we need to pay attention to them to keep out of trouble. We tend to blame our unhappiness on many things that really is not the blame. Adam blamed Eve -- Eve blamed the serpent -- just the syndrome of the 'blame game.' We need to repent for each sin we have committed, to have balance. Sometimes, we are tempted to do things other than what our heart and/or mind want to do. God has been speaking to you about some changes in your life, but you are afraid whether it is minor or major, and whether you think that you are unable to proceed and accomplish this task at hand. Just because you have made many mistakes, does not mean that you have to end your relationship with God. Ask for forgiveness through repentance by confessing your sins. Do not look back at your sin, wishing you could have done things differently. If you lost your direction, where you are unable to see the full path or picture, let God lead your steps. We are appointed in due time.[748]

---

[748] 1 Peter 5:6 and Genesis 18:14 also talks about the proper time (Galatians 4:4).

~Let Your Day Begin With Christ, Day 44~

Let your Day Begin Activity: Today, sit down and determine a day to go out with other fellow believers of Jesus Christ and enjoy life. For the ladies, plan a date to have lunch or go shopping with fellow girlfriends. For the guys, plan a day to hang out and watch sports on television or at the stadium (coliseums) with your male friends. Take the time to be involved with others like you.

Today's Questions:

Have you done anything fun or entertaining lately? Do you have any friends or family members who would love to go out with you?

What do we do in our social life? Does it glory the Lord in any form or nature?

Why wait until everything else runs out before trying God? Why save the best until last?

Is this what it takes for us to believe, to see a miracle happening before our very eyes?

Review to Begin your Day with Christ:

God wants us to enjoy life. We have to be conscious of the choices we make, what we watch, and what we do. We are to glorify God with everything we do, including our social life.

Read *Romans 6* and *Philippians 4:13*.

Day Begins 45: Take Yourself For A Joy Ride

Paul tells us to test everything, to hold on to the good, and to avoid evil in the world.[749] *1 Thessalonians 5:21-22* refers to the evil scary movies that we watch, video games that we play, and sexual images or content in movies or magazines. These images can play in your mind; and act it out and your actions, including thoughts that are against God. Alternatively, Jesus warned the undiscerning people to stop judging according to mere appearance and to make right judgments.[750] For example, Harry Potter books are a facet of occult, alchemy, astrology, spells, mediums, and other pagan practices. Potter books desensitize children and others to the forbidden and dangerous world of pagan magic.[751] Besides Potter series or movies, there are other witchcraft related shows such as *Sabrina the Teenage Witch*, *Charmed*, and *Buffy the Vampire Slayer*.

There are other horror movies that showcase other deadly creatures of the night like ghouls and demons. A *ghoul*, according to the occult legend, is an evil spirit to rob graves and feed on human corpses. *Hindus (vetala)* are demons that haunt cemeteries and animate dead bodies as for *rakshasas*, are a whole order of evil demons that disturb sacrifices. *Harass* devours human beings. This generation is becoming desensitized to the occult. The Bible gives a biblical perspective on the occult, and explains how followers of Jesus Christ resist encroachment of darkness into our increasingly pagan culture. However, if we are lovers of Jesus Christ, we can walk in the Spirit's wisdom and strength, to tackle many spiritual counterfeits.[752]

Unbelievably, being entertained by evil and pornography movies can release an evil spirit in your home, in your mind, in your spirit, and in your life. We can repent to God, asking for forgiveness for watching such movies or television shows, and rebuke some evil spirits that linger. We allowed them a window to come in. Alternatively, God spiritual footwear, known as the *gospel of peace*,[753] symbolizes readiness of spirit and commandment to share God's good news of salvation. Believers of Jesus Christ will be protected from many fiery arrows of persecution. Our most potent weapon against evil is God's Word, which is the *sword of the spirit*,[754] which divides the truth from error in the most confusing situations.[755]

Some believers are inaccurate about certain things because of misinterpreting the Bible to fit their own needs and wants can be spiritually dangerous. Christians who believe and receive Jesus Christ as their personal savior will enjoy eternal bliss.[756]

---

[749] 1 Thessalonians 5:21-22
[750] John 7:24
[751] Deuteronomy 18:9-14; Galatians 5:20; Revelation 22:15
[752] 1 John 4:4
[753] Ephesians 6:15
[754] Ephesians 6:17
[755] Hebrews 4:12
[756] Romans 10:9; 1 John 5:11-13

Others will suffer eternal separation from God by not accepting Jesus Christ as their personal savior.[757] This is why the Bible explains that Christians are instructed to overcome evil with good.[758] We also must avoid seeking revenge.[759] Instead, Jesus tells us to pray for your enemies,[760] consider others more important than ourselves,[761] view all people as inherently equals,[762] and to reject lying.[763] Other habits we can turn away from are drunkenness,[764] flee from hypocrisy,[765] refrain from using corrupt and vulgar communication,[766] and to avoid activities like occultism that leads away from God.[767] Now we can live a life in honesty,[768] walk with integrity,[769] and forgive those that hurt us.[770]

Overall, we say we are followers of Jesus Christ, but want to openly watch anything and listen to everything, and feel we are strong enough to withstand all evil. *Evil* is the substance of a higher power, supernatural power, superseding from the fallen angel Satan and his demons (a third of the angels who fell from heaven). These *fallen angels* are also known as demons or devils that are deceiving and trying to steal your joy and happiness. As mentioned in the previous chapter concerning 'prayer,' if we pray to God, God's Holy Spirit points at the thing He wants you to get right. *Unconfessed sin* is prime reason we do not know God's will or purpose on the pathway of life.[771]

According to *2 Timothy 3:9*, sin has consequences and no one will get away with it forever. Live each day as if it is your last, your actions will be brought into the light. Now is the time to change anything you would not want to be revealed later. Pray during the time of temptation and difficulty, God will bring a verse or Scripture that will give you a clear indication of your sin, and how to overcome this sin by making godly choices according to His will. Amen that our Heavenly Father loves us so much, to not only overlook our sin once we confess and repent, but also willing to help us overcome our battles.

---

[757] Luke 16:19-30; John 3:16; Revelation 20:11-15
[758] Romans 12:21
[759] Leviticus 19:18; Romans 12:17, 19; 1 Peter 3:9
[760] Luke 6:27
[761] Philippians 2:3
[762] Acts 17:26; Galatians 3:28
[763] Proverbs 12:22; Ephesians 4:25; Colossians 3:9
[764] Ephesians 5:18
[765] Luke 6:42; Romans 12:9; James 3:17
[766] Colossians 3:8; 4:6; Titus 2:8
[767] Isaiah 44:25; Galatians 5:20; Revelation 21:8
[768] Hebrews 13:18
[769] Psalm 15:2; 26:1; Proverbs 11:3
[770] Matthew 6:14-15; Ephesians 4:32
[771] Isaiah 59:2

~Let Your Day Begin With Christ, Day 45~

Let your Day Begin Activity: To be a Christian, you have to live like one. Today's activity is to get rid of any ungodly things out your life. Anything that is keeping you from God is a form of idolatry.

Today's Questions:

What areas of sin do you struggle in? How can we overcome sin?

Why does Paul tell us to test everything?

Share your thoughts on Potter books and movies? Does it desensitize children to pagan religion and/or magic? Please give examples.

Do you watch pornography and/or scary movies that put God's name in vain (blasphemy)? How does it make you feel? Will you continue to watch movie that says things like 'Jesus Christ!' 'Oh my God…,' and so forth in which is considered blasphemy according to God's Word.

Review to Begin your Day with Christ:

2 Timothy 3:9=sin has consequences. We have to evaluate the movies we watch. Evil has a way of lurking in…looking for an open door. We have to be careful what we listen to (ear gate) and what we watch (eye gate). We want to spend eternity in Heaven with God, but we have to remove ungodly possessions out. We can also repent and accept God's correction.

Day Begins 46: Should We Drink Liquor, Smoke, Or Carousing As Believers?

Some would argue that Jesus drank wine, so how is it forbidden for us to drink if Jesus did it. I always thought it was fine to drink, if we did not overly indulge or get overly intoxicated -- a couple drinks would not hurt anybody. A majority would believe that one is able to drink moderately, just not excessively. The third argument is that alcohol is addictive and destructive. Therefore, followers of Jesus Christ must not drink at all. The Scripture references to Jesus' drinking wine were similar to drinking grape juice today without the sugar consumption or fermentation. It was fresh grapes crushed into a liquid.

Wine, in a biblical sense, refers to the *new* or fresh juice of grapes, and other times describes *wine* as the aged or fermented product known as alcohol. However, most translators never used 'grape juice.' The word *tiyrosh* is used for new unfermented wine, and *yayin* is used for fermented wine, but there are exceptions.[772] However, in the New Testament, only one Greek word, *oinis*, is used to describe both fermented and fresh grape juice. In *Luke 5:37-39*, it speaks about 'old and new wine.' This context is also referring to grape juice, not alcohol.

> *Mark 2:22, NKJV: "And no one puts new wine into old wineskins; or else the new wine bursts the wineskins, the wine is spilled, and the wineskins are ruined. But new wine must be put into new wineskins."*

Apparently, the *new wine* is referring to fresh unfermented wine. In addition, *Isaiah 65:8* speaks of *new wine* that is simply grape juice. In these Scriptures, some tend to think wine is what we get from the liquor store, or if served at parties and clubs is acceptable to drink since Jesus' speaks of drinking 'new wine' in some of the Scriptures mentioned above. However, He is referring to wine that has not sat out for a period to turn into alcohol, instead it is fresh grapes crushed into a liquid form and drank before fermented. Yet, others would argue that Jesus drank wine with His disciples at the Last Supper.[773] Jesus uses new wine as a new covenant with His people. He also calls wine *fruit of the vine*.

Fermentation is the identical process of leavening.[774] Bread without leaven, the leaven is a type of sin, and then we could be assured that *wine* is a symbol of Jesus blood. A symbolic illustration of Jesus' blood was conversed with His disciples at the Last Supper. The perfect, sinless blood of Jesus would never be symbolized, by corrupt and putrefying old wine.

The first time *wine* was mentioned in the Book of Genesis, story of Noah, after the flood, created the original fermented grape juice.[775] During this time, Noah drank

---

[772] Isaiah 16:10
[773] Matthew 26:28-29
[774] Exodus 12:19
[775] Genesis 9:20-23

and stumbled around naked and shamefully exposing himself to his sons. Lot also drank and was easily seduced into having incestuous relationships with his daughters.[776] His offspring of these relationships became the nations of Moab and Amnon, the mortal enemies of God's people. Usually, alcohol often leads to sexual immorality -- adultery, rape, and incest, to name a few.

At a Jewish wedding, one of the guests served as a *governor of the feast*, similar to the master of ceremonies at a banquet. The *headwaiter* was responsible for seating the guests and the correct running of the feast. Then, good wine or better wine was served first. Then, after the guests were dulled, the every day wine was served. However, this wine was so good that the master of the feast was surprised how late it was served during a celebration.

In the Gospel of John, the miracles of Jesus were called signs, showing that they pointed to His messiahship. John records seven signs in the book of Revelation. Jesus first sign (miracle) signified Christ's glory -- His deity. Jesus first miracle was when he transformed water into wine. He clearly demonstrated His power.[777] In *John 2:6*, it explains how much water it took to make the finest wine for such a feast. Each water pot held 20-30 gallons, for a total of 120-180 gallons of the finest wine.[778]

In contrast, alcohol can be classified as poisons, of which are toxins to the human body. Beer, wine and brandy are ethanol or C_2H_5OH, which is a clear, highly flammable liquid that has a burning taste and a characteristic odor. If one consumes this type of alcohol, death can occur if the concentration of ethanol exceeds about five percent. Those that drink it sparingly, there are immediate behavioral changes, impairment of vision, and unconsciousness can occur. In addition, it has the same effect as if you used heroin or even marijuana. On the other hand, Native Americans consider alcohol or liquor as *spirits* since it caused them to sin, changing their whole way of thinking--pure evil.

Strong drink is translated from the word, *shekar,* condemned by Solomon as brawler.[779] This strong drink was prohibited from the priests,[780] and Nazarenes.[781] *Shekar* is called a sweet wine or syrup. *Shechar* is a luscious, saccharin drink or sweet syrup in its fresh and unfermented state. Sugar and cider are from *shekar*. *Shekar* can be either a sweet unfermented drink or intoxicating drink. We must never interpret the Word that it is okay to drink shekar or any strong alcoholic beverage.[782] For example, the children of Israel drank alcohol, stripped naked and worshipped a golden calf.[783] Some of these stories seem exotic or nauseating, but it lets you imagine some of the

---

[776] Genesis 19:33
[777] John 2:9-11, Nelson Study Bible, NKJV.
[778] John 2:10
[779] Proverbs 20:1, also can refer to Isaiah 5:11
[780] Leviticus 10:9-11
[781] Numbers 6:2-4 and Judges 13:3-5
[782] Deuteronomy 14: 26
[783] Exodus 32:6, 25

things we could be capable of doing if we indulge in alcoholic beverages. What will be our excuse? It was only a drink.

In *Isaiah 5:8-25*, where God condemns six sins: (1) exploiting others;[784] (2) drunkenness;[785] (3) taking sarcastic pride to commit a sin;[786] (4) confusing moral standards;[787] (5) being conceited;[788] and (6) perverting justice.[789] Because of these sins, God punished Israel with destruction by Assyria.[790] A similar fate was awaiting Judah if they did not turn away from these sins. These people spent many hours drinking and partying, but Isaiah predicted that eventually many would die of hunger and thirst. Ironically, our pleasures, if we do not have God's blessings, may destroy us. Leaving God out, allows sin to come in. God wants us to enjoy life,[791] but to avoid those activities that could lead us away from Him.

Amnon, the son of David, was another strong drinker that raped his half-sister, Tamar. Because of his insidious act, he lost his life at the hands of his enraged half-brother while intoxicated.[792] Think about how many drive-bys are usually under the influence of alcohol and bad decision-making. Think about all the rape victims: the person who was violated was either drunk or influenced by the substance of drugs or psychotic reasons. Think about how many fights usually occur at house parties, college parties, clubs, and other events that has alcoholic beverages. There are other terrible repercussions involving alcohol found in the Bible.[793] How would believers of Christ argue in defense if they are actively drinking and in ungodly environments?

Think about what people do today when they drink liquor. Whether it is *moonshine*, known as a consumption of various alcohols usually made in the Southern States that sits out in the sun or in a shack. *Moonshine*, can also be considered a hard drink served at a bar or club setting. What are people thoughts or actions after consuming alcohol? For instance, some may run out on the streets naked, while blurting out bizarre things. Some may go back to someone's home and have one-night stands. Afterwards, they blame their actions on what they drank. Imagine what other excuses and things we do when we drink fermented wine or other alcoholic beverages. Ironically, people looked everywhere, but to God for excitement and true meaning. Instead, we prefer to go to the club and bars, concerts, and other special events that usually have alcohol available at our leisure.

---

[784] Isaiah 5:8-10
[785] Isaiah 5:11-12
[786] Isaiah 5:18, 19
[787] Isaiah 5:20
[788] Isaiah 5:21
[789] Isaiah 5:22-24
[790] Isaiah 5:25-30
[791] 1 Timothy 6:17
[792] 2 Samuel 13:28
[793] 2 Samuel 13:28 and Job 1:13-19

For some reason, people expected God to be dull and lifeless. Jesus saved the best wine for last at the Jewish wedding, which demonstrates that a life with Jesus is better than life on our own.[794] When the disciples saw Jesus' miracle, they believed. This miracle showed His power over nature and revealed the way to go about His ministry -- helping others, speaking with authority, and being in personal touch with people. Today, we are caught up being in touch with people in the clubs, in their bedroom, or somewhere making out with someone that is not our husband or wife, and gossiping or spreading rumors about one another. There is a difference in what God expects or wishes from us.

Woe means deep distress, or misery, which is usually caused by grief or wretchedness. Here are a few Scriptures that use the term *woe*, refer to alcohol.

> *Isaiah 5:11, NKJV: "Woe to those who rise early in the morning, that they may follow intoxicating drink; who continue until night, till wine inflames them!"*

> *Proverbs 23:29-30, NLT: "Who has anguish (woe)? Who has sorrow? Who is always fighting? Who is always complaining? Who has unnecessary bruises? Who has bloodshot eyes? It is the one who spends long hours in the taverns, trying out new drinks."*

> *Habakkuk 2:15, NKJV: "Woe to him who gives drink to his neighbor, pressing him to your bottle, even to make him drunk, that you may look on his nakedness!"*

Daniel would not defile his body with wine.[795] Sour wine mixed with gall would have dulled Jesus' pain and consciousness.[796] Jesus refused it. He wanted to drink His cup of suffering.[797] Furthermore, the wine was mixed with gall that was offered to Jesus to help His pain, but Jesus refused to drink it. *Gall* is generally understood to be a narcotic that was used to deaden pain. Jesus chose to fully suffer while conscious and with a clear mind. Therefore, as a Christian, God is making a clear statement about alcohol consumption. In other words, when in doubt, is it representing what God is all about? Consumption does not glorify the Lord. Instead, it destroys the mind and body, which is a clear violation of the *Sixth Commandment*.

In another sense, cigarette smoking and alcohol is a slow death (or suicide) in small increments such as a payment plan in installments. One puff, one more drink, is taking the life out of you and you will die sooner. Some would argue, who cares since we are all born to die because of Adam and Eve's fallen sin that messed up the entire generations to come. At least, I can enjoy my life to the fullest until that day comes. How does this sound?

---

[794] Life Application Study Bible, NKJV, 1996.
[795] Daniel 1:8
[796] Matthew 27:34
[797] Psalm 22:18-24

God is the truth, He wants you to open your eyes and see the truth. Let it be revealed in your body to convince you to stop drinking alcohol and follow the ways of Christ. Consider other good things to drink and nourish your body.

Even Abraham Lincoln quoted: "Drink is a cancer in human society, eating out its vitals threatening its destruction." What good has alcohol done in one's life? It usually breaks up homes, breaks up marriages, loose confidence and self-esteem, losing jobs and categorized as *alcoholics*. Usually, once you are labeled an *alcoholic* at your work environment, it may be requested that you attend Alcoholics Anonymous to keep your current position. In addition, it can lead to drunk driving, and destroying other people's lives and families because of the lost of a love one. Drinking under the influence can also lead to various transmitted diseases by having unprotected sex with multiple partners and other deadly measures.

Alcohol was known for destroying nations in *Jeremiah 13:12-15*. Think about all the crimes in the nation today because of the consumption of alcohol beverages or influenced by other drug substances. Imagine how many people see psychologists, counselors, and other community services for alcohol abuse and other drug substances.

Micah also warned of lying and false prophets, who condone wine and strong drinks.[798] Alternatively, some congregations or preachers teach 'moderation,' but throughout the Scriptures shows that it can be addictive and lead to many destructions. Refer to *Romans 14:21*, shows how alcohol makes you weak and stumble. If you truly love your family member, close friend, or sister or brother that is struggling with alcohol and/or other intoxicating substances, how can we tell them it is okay to drink? Paul said, he would neither eat flesh, or drink wine, or do anything to offend a brother.[799] In addition, Daniel would not defile his body with the delicacies of the King that also included wine. Let us make this simple and plain: it lowers Christian's mortality and resisting temptation. In general, we already have a hard time removing ourselves from the pleasures of the world or sin and alcohol just makes an excuse for doing it or trying it. Do you really want to make it easier for the Devil to lure his way in your life?

> *Romans 13:13-14, NLT: "Because we belong to the day, we must live decent lives for all to see. Don't participate in the darkness of wild parties and drunkenness, or in sexual promiscuity and immoral living, or in quarreling and jealousy. Instead, clothe yourself with the presence of the Lord Jesus Christ. And don't let yourself think about ways to indulge your evil desires [of sinful nature]."*

The Scriptures above, *Night* in *Romans 13:12*, is referring to present day while we live in Satan's dominion or during evil times. *Day* is the beginning of a new life with Christ in His glorious reign, or the time of Christ's return. *At hand*, means Christ can return at any time.[800] Note that Paul puts strife and envy on the same level as

---

[798] Micah 2:11
[799] Romans 14:21
[800] Philippians 4:5; James 5:8; 1 Peter 4:7

drunkenness and lusts. Put on the Lord Jesus, believers clothe themselves with Christ-like characteristics such as righteousness,[801] truth,[802] and peace.[803] Jesus sermon on the Mount, Paul considers attitudes as important as actions.[804] Just as hatred leads to murder, envy leads to strife, and lusts to adultery. When Christ returns, He wants to find His people clean on the inside, and on the outside.

How do we *put on* the Lord Jesus Christ? First, we identify with Christ by being baptized.[805] This shows our solidarity with other believers, and with the death, burial, and resurrection of Jesus Christ. Second, we exemplify the qualities Jesus showed while He was here on earth, of which are love, humility, truth, and service. We role-play what Jesus would do in our situation.[806] We must not give our desires any opportunity to lead us into sin. Avoid those situations that open the door to gratifying sinful desires. Christ should satisfy our needs and wants.[807]

A person whose life changes radically at conversion may experience contempt from his or her old friends. He may be scorned, not only because he refuses to participate in certain activities, but also because his priorities have changed and he is now heading in the opposite direction. His life incriminates their sinful activities. Mature believers can help new believers resist pressures of opposition by encouraging them to be faithful to Christ. *Dissipation* refers to wasteful expenditure and intemperate pursuit of pleasure, especially drinking to excess and partying.[808]

Some of us would go to the club on Friday and Saturday, and whether you had a hangover that Saturday, would attend church on Sunday praising the Lord as if nothing went down the night before. Some believers get drunk as a skunk. Go club-hopping and dancing, and unmarried couples are having sex on Friday and Saturday nights. On Sunday mornings, these same Christians attend church, singing hymns, and clapping their hands, which is so hypocritical to the Word. Instead of engaging in sinful acts against what the Word says, we are to be modeling Jesus Christ. This is why Peter charges us to remain sober.[809] The devil is already on our case, so we will not face Jesus Christ when He returns. Satan wants to see us suffer, struggle, and keep us from ever turning to Christ. Jesus Christ can bail His followers out and receive salvation for our past sins.

Do you intentionally leave your home wearing the shortest skirt or dress, the tightest jeans or outfit, and revealing more than meets the eye in the club scene? Sometimes men are walking out the house, trying to look thuggish or gangster by

---

[801] 1 Corinthians 1:30
[802] John 14:16
[803] Galatians 5:22, 23; Ephesians 2:14; 6:10-17
[804] Matthew 5-7
[805] Galatians 3:27
[806] Ephesians 4:24-32 and Colossians 3:10-17
[807] John 6:35
[808] 1 Peter 4:3, 4 –Life Application Study Bible, NJKV.
[809] 1 Peter 5:8

wearing sagging or baggy pants down to their knees, showing their behinds. We must put on our armor, including how we dress. Both non-believers and believers are guilty of dressing provocatively or unholy.[810] Whom are you trying to attract? The clothing you wear should draw attention to your face, not your body. This does not mean to dress appealing, but to pray and ask God to show you what the right thing you should wear. This is a challenge for all of us. The change in how you dress can be a starting point to show that you really want to live for God.

Remember when Jesus was on the cross, dying for our sins, He had wanted something to quench his thirst. The Roman soldiers offered him wine to drink, but Jesus refused. He would not risk any wrongful judgment by drinking a mouthful of wine to quench His thirst. Would Jesus expect less of us? Nevertheless, why do we continue to offer Him less of us?

If we praying to God after having a few beers to drink, would this be convincing and uplifting to the Heavenly Father? This is confusing, especially to our children since we are sending mixed signals. God tells us to come out from among them, which are people who are following the morals and rationale of the world, and to be separate.[811] If a Christian begins to drink alcohol, they show that they are not separated from worldly things. In *1 Timothy 3:2*, *temperate* means without wine, sober or clearheaded. *Sober-minded* means that an overseer must have control of his or her body and mind. It is a balance state of mind, arising out of self-restraint. *1 Timothy 3:3*, where Timothy points out, *not given to wine* means not addicted to wine. Paul speaks of not being drunk with wine, wherein is excess, but to be filled with the Holy Spirit. Most think the passage refers to not drinking too much. The word *excess* in Greek is *asotia*, which is translated as riot or riotous living.[812] In addition, we are called to be sacred vessels filled with God's Spirit.

God approves moderate use that is good for our bodies and spirit. However, gluttony, whether it is drinking or eating, is condemned in the Bible.[813] Additionally, Jesus describes gluttony as one of the primary sins of the people destroyed by the flood.[814] In contrast, moderate drinking is not God's answer–abstinence is. Jesus did not drink a portion of wine mingled with myrrh to quench his thirst while he was on the Cross, which was intended to numb the pain. Jesus refused it, choosing to suffer the complete pain.[815]

Every alcoholic sip starts their downward path with one or two drinks, which is considered as a *moderate drinker*. Drunkenness might be excusable for dying people in

---

[810] Romans 12:1-2
[811] 2 Corinthians 6:17
[812] Ephesians 5:18; 1 Peter 4:4; Luke 15:13
[813] Deuteronomy 21:20 and Proverbs 25:27
[814] Matthew 24:38
[815] Matthew 27:34; Mark 15:23

great pain, but it is inexcusable for national leaders.[816] Alcohol clouds the minds, and can lead to injustice and poor decisions. Leaders have better things to do than anesthetize themselves with alcohol.

On another note, tobacco-use injures health and defiles the body.[817] In addition, tobacco is unclean.[818] *Nicotine* is an addictive substance that enslaves people. We become servants to whomever or whatever we yield ourselves to.[819] For instance, tobacco users are servants of nicotine. In addition, it is a chemical addiction, but also a psychological addition to support the habit of smoking cigarettes. On the other hand, tobacco is a waste of money.[820] We are God's stewards of the money given us. It is required in stewards that a man is found faithful.[821] The use of tobacco never draws anyone close to Christ.

In *1 Peter 2:11, "Abstain from fleshly lusts, which war against the soul."* Tobacco-use is a fleshly lust or desire. Furthermore, the use of tobacco shortens the life span by one-third. Even though is a slow murder, it is still murder. One of the best ways to postpone your funeral is to quit using tobacco or smoking cigarettes.

Drug-using parents often transmit their weaknesses to their children. Parents drug abuse habits can be passed down to the third and fourth generation because of their unruliness.[822] The children and grandchildren inherit bad habits and weakened sickly bodies, when mother and father defy God. Ask yourself: is this what you want for your children, grandchildren and great-grandchildren? If you are using drugs, smoking or drinking alcohol, it usually follows a pattern until someone breaks the cycle or habit.

The church will not condone drinking any harmful substance. Some congregation teaches that it is permissible to drink a little wine. Instead, the church must uphold the clear position of the Word of God, knowing that Jesus is the Word that made flesh and come to dwell among us. God's issue on alcohol is clear -- it is unholy and unclean. Partaking of the worldly drink can only compromise God's high standards for our lives. If you have a problem with alcohol, seek counseling or appropriate help, but trust in God and pray that He will deliver you from this addiction.

In addition, the Bible speaks against drugs.[823] Most people are running from their problems and think getting high or drunk will eliminate their pain and misery. Overall, you will only have a hangover and became more depressed in the end, then find yourself shortchanging your budget due to buying liquor or drugs. This can lead to losing your family, home, and losing your life since it can lead to an addiction. This

---

[816] Proverbs 31:6, 7
[817] 1 Corinthians 3:16-17
[818] 2 Corinthians 6:17
[819] Romans 6:16
[820] Isaiah 55:2
[821] 1 Corinthians 4:2
[822] Deuteronomy 12:24, 25 and Exodus 20:5
[823] in Matthew 27:34 (CEV) and Mark 15:23 (LB)

addiction generally takes control over you, where you no longer have self-control over this situation since your body is craving alcohol, drugs, or any other harmful substance.

~Let Your Day Begin With Christ, Day 46~

Let your Day Begin Activity: Today, take the time to get any drugs or alcohol out of your house, the Lord's house. To get over these problems, you have to get rid of them. In addition, we have to get rid of any and everyone who are negative, leeches, and draining you dry. We have to find more positive people and like-minded people as our friends. Today is a new day for you.

Today's Questions:

Why would a Christian want to gamble or stake their health with deadly substances and miss eternal life with our Heavenly Father by arguing reasons to consume alcohol, which is a destructive substance? Even Abraham Lincoln quoted, "Drink is a cancer in human society, eating out its vitals threatening its destruction." Elaborate on this quote, how does it apply to your life?

How does it make you feel after drinking or getting high? How do you react when you drink too much or drink at all? Do you have self-control after drinking liquor? Not so much on whether you can hold your liquor, but how does your Heavenly Father views our drinking!

Review to Begin your Day with Christ:

We can repent to God for all our faults and shortcomings. He is a forgiving God. He is also a jealous God. He does not want to see us spend all our time with our fleshly desires such as partying, clubbing, drinking, smoking, and drugs. We have to reflect our time and how it is spent. Is it healthy? Will it build our spirit man or woman? Who loves you? God is love. We can show our love by spending our days with Him.

Day Begins 47: Addictions: Where Can It Take You?

With addictions, there could be an argument that psychological or medications are needed to stop addictions. However, on a spiritual level, we can fight addictions and get out of bondage.[824]

Paul was content because he could see life from God's point of view. Paul focused on what he was supposed to do, not what he felt he should have. He had his priorities straight. He was grateful for everything God had given him. He was also able to detach himself from the non-essentials, so that he could concentrate on the eternal. Often the desire for more or better possessions is a longing to fill an empty place in a person's life. How can you find true contentment? The answer lies in your perspective, your priorities, and your source of power.[825] Can we really do all things? The power we receive, union with Christ, is sufficient to do His will. Furthermore, we can face the challenge that arises from our commitment to press forward. He does not grant us super human ability to accomplish anything we can imagine without regard to His interests. As we contend for the faith, we will face troubles, pressures, and trials. When these difficulties come, ask Christ to strengthen you.[826]

Christ made us free! We do not have to be caught up in bondage with sin. In other words, Christ died to set us free from our sins, including the old laws and regulations. Even though Christ set us free from sin, does not mean that we can continue to sin because we are saved by grace. In other words, there is no excuse to go back into our own selfish desires. Those who only want to be free, yet, continue to live and fulfill our fleshly needs, will fall back into sin.

Nevertheless, it is also wrong to judge or place the burden on Christians on following God's laws. These laws ought to be laid on our hearts to obey God's commands and decrees. We must stand against those who would enslave us with rules, methods, or special conditions for being saved while growing in Christ.[827] By keeping the law and being saved by grace are two different approaches. You will not profit anything if you are trying to save yourself. We need Christ's provision and protection. Obeying the law does not make it any easier for God to save us. All we can do is accept His gracious gift through faith. Our deeds must never be used to try to earn God's love or favor.[828]

Who is weak in their faith? Who is strong in their faith? We are all weak in some areas and stronger in other areas. Our faith is strong; we can survive contact with unbelievers without falling into the same patterns. In our areas of strength, we will not fear being defiled by the world. Rather, we continue to serve God. If we have strong

---

[824] Philippians 4:13 and Galatians 5:1

[825] Life Application Study Bible, NKJV, 1996.

[826] Life Application Study Bible, NKJV, emphasis added by author.

[827] Life Application Study Bible, NKJV, emphasis added by author.

[828] Life Application Study Bible, NKJV, 1996.

faith, but shelter it, we are not doing Christ's work in the world. If we are weak, we must avoid those activities that would cause us to fall to protect our spiritual life. It is important to take a self-inventory to find out our strengths and weaknesses. In the areas of weakness, we need to be cautious. If we have a weak faith but expose it, we are being extremely foolish. Whenever in doubt, we may ask, "Can I go without sinning? Can I influence others for good, rather than being influenced by them?"[829]

Usually a sinner's conscience will drive him or her, either into guilt resulting in repentance, or flipside into sinful acts because of a refusal to repent. It is no act of kindness. The more guilt he or she feels, the more likely he or she is to turn to God and repent. Sometimes, when we continue to repeat this particular sin, we fall further away from repentance and turning to God. If we interfere with the natural consequences of his or her actions, we make it easier for them to continue to indulge in their sin. Please turn to God, trust and believe that He has forgiven you. Get out of that habit of believing that once I sin, God will forgive me without repenting to Christ anymore. Thinking, 'He sees and knows all, so He will automatically forgive me because I am saved.' Remember, God wants us to confess our sins to Him, repent, and move forward, not looking back at that sin. When you think or feel that you cannot fight addictions such as lust, sexual immorality, anger, and so forth, remember that we have a higher power looking over us and can bring us through.[830]

> Matthew 19:26, NKJV: "But Jesus looked at them and said to them, 'With men this is impossible, but with God all things are possible.'"

Non-believers cannot understand God and they cannot grasp that God's Spirit lives in believers.[831] Do not expect most people to approve of, or understand your decision to follow Christ. It all seems so silly to them. We cannot receive God's message if we continue to reject Him.

However, sometimes we can get sidetrack by mingling with things or people caught up in the way of the world. Then, we tend to fall further away from Christ, and no longer focused on the prize of our Heavenly Father. Satan would love us to be lost forever from our Savior Jesus Christ, who died on the cross for our sins.

On the other hand, it is funny how so many philosophers, religious leaders, and books like *Da Vinci Code* is questioning Christ coming and going. Where is Jesus' body? Did Jesus really die on the cross? How did He suffer? Was Jesus married? All these remarkable stories were broadcasted on ABC around March 2004. A year later, the movie on the *Da Vinci Code* was featured. The real answers lie in the Bible, and having an intimate relationship with Christ.

---

[829] Romans 14:1
[830] See also Philippians 4:13 and Matthew 19:26
[831] 1 Corinthians 2:14-16

Please do not be fooled by things or people who will influence you to sin. Even your friends may have an influence over you to do things that you know is wrong. Others will believe that other people's opinion justifies your well-being. Overall, we are to turn to God for guidance and reassurance in our decision-making, seeking wisdom in areas we are not confident in, and remain righteous.

In our social life, pray about it and search for Scriptures for answers because everything you do is viewed in the eyes of God. God will bring it to light. Do not say that 'I cannot do it.' If you gave your life to Christ, yes you can.

If you like to go to clubs to dance, then learn to dance for Christ and join a praise dance at your local church or recreation center within your community. If you love hip-hop music, listen to gospel and gospel rap artists such as Cross Movement, Canton Jones, Righteous Riders, Ton3x (was Tonex, pronounced Toe-nay), Kirk Franklin, and many others by tapping into this genre of music until one suit you. There is a variety available from Jazz, R&B, Hip-Hop, Reggae, Christian Rock, Contemporary Christian and Gospel, to name a few. If you like to drink, smoke, or get high, instead, get high on the Word, a spiritual high through meditation and prayer can take you higher than any drink, drug, or marijuana. If you crave porno tapes, or certain movies, and games to entertain yourself, we need to turn to God for the remedy. Conclude there are open doors for evilness to enter where Satan and his demons are always lurking for an opportunity, whether it is through music, videos, movies, and even pornography. This can be an outlet, Satan and his fallen angels, which is a way to manipulate and to possess your soul, unless you give it over to Christ by allowing the Holy Spirit to convict you.

~Let Your Day Begin With Christ, Day 47~

Let your Day Begin Activity: Yesterday, we took the time to get rid of drugs and alcohol. Today, we will take the time to get rid of all other addictions. Sit down, write them all down, and rid them of your life forever. As a Christian, we are to practice what we preach. We are to walk in our destiny, as Disciples of Jesus Christ.

Today's Questions:

What are your thoughts on drinking alcohol? Should it be done in moderation or not to drink at all? Share your reasons.

What are some excuses that you have made for drinking strong liquor or any type of alcohol and/or smoking? Are you willing to stop? If so, what steps are you taking to avoid alcohol, drugs, and/or smoking? Do you trust that God will remove these intoxicating drugs and liquor out of your system?

Review to Begin your Day with Christ:

Most of us turn to other things to make us happy, as others are searching for love. To remove our addictions, we have to find true love. We are to seek God. God promises us: we ask for answers, we will receive; we seek Him, we will find Him; and we knock for answers, the door will open (Matthew 7:7). We have to trust God when we ask for his help. When we seek Him, He will bring restoration and solutions to our weaknesses. He will open doors for us— opportunity is in our hands once we call on Jesus. Make just one call—our addictions will leave. Faith believes without seeing. God knew you. He knew you before the foundation of the world. He loved you when you were conceived, and loved you more when you enter this world. He still loves you through your hardships. He will greet you in open arms. Come to Him and kick back the habit.

Day Begins 48: How Do We Live A Christian Life?

There are roadblocks that keep us from living a Christian life. Some people portray themselves as followers of Jesus Christ. However, Christ does not live there. God speaks about obedience by following His commandments and rules that He demonstrates throughout the Holy Bible. We are not saved by keeping God's rules alone.[832] Trying to live a Christian life by just going to church weekly is not enough. Fellowship is essential in the Christian life. However, we need a daily relationship with God. Some of us try to live a Christian life by doing what is good. We are not saved by our ability to do good works.[833]

> *2 Peter 1:5-6, NKJV: "But also for this very reason giving all diligence, add to your faith virtue, to virtue knowledge, to knowledge self-control, to self-control perseverance, to perseverance godliness."*

We need to understand God's part for living a Christian life. God does not expect us to live a Christian life through our own understanding and knowledge.[834] In *2 Peter 1:1-14*, God has shown us what we need to do to live a Christian life. These attributes consists of faith, help, grace, peace, knowledge of God, a source of divine power from God, and promises from God. God does not expect us to live this life by being a spectator. Our responsibility for living a Christian life or prerequisites is to trust in God, which is depending on God. Another prerequisite is diligence, which is effort to do our part. Both of these must be present to live a successful Christian life.

Seven Steps for Living a Christian life:[835]
1. *Virtue -- excellence*: We cannot produce a virtuous character ourselves. Do we desire to live right and please the Lord?
2. *Knowledge -- practical wisdom*: Once we desire to do what is right, we now need to know what is right. We learn what God expects from the Scripture. What questions should we ask as we study the Scripture? What is God like? What does God disapprove and approve? What did Christ do for us?
3. *Self-control -- practice*: Knowing all the answers means nothing if our life is not in shape with Jesus. Self-control results from the Holy Spirit. Thinking and meditating on the Scripture is a start, but not enough since we have to put it to practice (action speaks louder than words).
4. *Perseverance -- endurance*: In life, we will face troubles and problems. This gives us the ability to complete what we have started. It develops character and faith through spiritual maturity.
5. *Godliness -- focus*: We live for God and not for ourselves. Our focus, therefore, is becoming more like Christ.

---

[832] Galatians 3:1-5
[833] Ephesians 2:8-9
[834] Proverbs 3:5-6
[835] 2 Peter 1:5-7

6. *Brotherly -- kindness*: Godliness requires us to do what God does. As God shows kindness to us, we must show kindness to others.

7. *Love – agape*: God's love is agape, unconditional love no matter what we do or say. We are to love people despite how they treat us. We are sacrificing ourselves for the good of others.

The results of living a Christian life is to be productive, not to be shortsighted and blinded to the point that we have foresight what Christ has done for us.[836] We will not stumble. We can look forward to greater rewards in heaven.

God must be your focus on everything you do. We are able to make choices since God has blessed us with freewill. However, this does not mean once we are saved that we are able to do what we want to do. Every time you are not sure what to do in a situation, just think, *What Would Jesus Do (WWJD)*. If fear continues to run your life, God says if we believe, we will receive. We can be delivered from 'fear' if we only ask God.

When we are asked to do something for God such as evangelism, singing in choir, musicians, and ministering to others, just to name a few, imagine what God can do to you and for you. If you do what God commands, imagine all the blessings you can receive in the Kingdom of Heaven and receive here on Earth. If we do not follow His commands, imagine a soul that is lost to the Lord and burning in Hell for eternity. Remember, you cannot force God on them either. Just plant the seed, pray that God will be the focus in their lives, and watch them grow spiritually. If you feel fear, ask God to be fearless like the 'spider' and conquer to do His will.

For instance, I feared writing this novel, but I realize that it is more important to reach and save souls by spreading God's Word then sitting back praying that someone will be saved. I will still pray for those souls, but we need to do something about it when God shows us our calling. I feel you when you have fear or doubt, you will see God purpose for your lives. If you open and let God in, you will get pass it. You may think that it is hard work to do God's business.

---

[836] See 2 Peter 1:8-11

~Let Your Day Begin With Christ, Day 48~

Let your Day Begin Activity: Today, we will take the 7 steps for living a Christian life and apply them to our lives. However, not only for today, apply them everyday. Take a piece of paper and write them out. Place them in an area that you frequently visit. Every time you visit that area, take the time to read over them to know how to live your life.

Today's Questions:

How you can save a soul through your testimony? What does God command us to do (Hint: make disciples)?

Review to Begin your Day with Christ:

Many of us want to let the world know we are believers, but still do what we want to do instead of viewing God as a sovereign God. We are carnal beings, only turn to God for 'fire insurance.' We want to live on grace and God's mercy, not His judgment and wrath.

Seven steps to a Christian life are only setting an example, but we can add to it.

Then, Jesus said *he did not come to condemn the world, but to save it*. What are your thoughts on this statement? Is this why people always refer to God's grace and mercy—'I am saved under grace' and 'God knows my heart,' therefore, it is ok if I continue to live in sin. He will forgive me. I do not have to say it aloud since he knows what I think (my thoughts) and how I feel about it (my heart). Elaborate on the terms used loosely: grace, mercy, justice, and images. Compare and contrast on these different terms and how it plays a role in your daily walk as a Christian.

Review *2 Peter 1:1-14.*

Day Begins 49: Glorify The Lord And Keep It Holy

Glory is the manifestation, or Hebrews word *doxa*, of God's excellence and goodness. We all want to experience His glory because the Spirit of Grace lives inside of us as believers in Jesus Christ.[837]

> *1 Corinthians 6:20, NLT: "for God bought you with a high price. So you must honor God with your body."*

> *Romans 8:16-17, NLT: "For his Spirit joins with our spirit to affirm that we are God's children. [17] And since we are his children, we are his heirs. In fact, together with Christ we are heirs of God's glory. But if we are to share his glory, we must also share his suffering."*

Romans 8:16, 17: Indication of believers' son-ship is that the Holy Spirit bears witness. When believers cry out to the Father in prayer, *Romans 8:15*, and the Holy Spirit intercedes for them, *Romans 15:26. Heirs:* All of God's children have an inheritance based on their relationship to God, which is incorruptible, unfilled, and reserved in heaven.[838] Their inheritance includes an expectation of eternal life.[839] As joint heirs with Christ, they share His suffering now,[840] and will share His glory later.[841] First, Christ must live in us. Otherwise, we are unable to experience the glory of God. We all want to experience God's glory on a continuous basis. If we ask, then we shall receive it.[842]

According to *Vine Dictionary, glory* means: For those of us still live under the Old covenant, rituals and formulas or follow the dead letter of the law,[843] will not enjoy life. Live a life under the grace of God, we are expecting glory and to be filled with the Holy Spirit in which we should be excited about life. If we are excited about our lives, where we are living a life for Jesus Christ, it will make things better, easier, and more enjoyable, including able to overlook the evilness in the world since we have complete joy knowing we are believers. We can experience remarkable joy, *Dancing in the Son*, a song by Ton3x.[844]

> *Psalm 119:175, NLT: "Let me live so I can praise you, and may your regulations help me."*

We are to surrender everything to God. Some refer to surrendering to God is to bow, of which is done by standing, lying straight down, or on your knees. Bowing may

---

[837] Colossians 1:27
[838] 1 Peter 1:4
[839] Titus 3:4-7
[840] Philippians 3:10
[841] Philippians 3:11-14
[842] Matthew 7:7
[843] 2 Corinthians 3:6
[844] emphasis added by the author

be in private, which is worshipping the Lord in your secret place. Worshipping God involves acknowledgment of divine perfections. *Direct address* is an adoration or thanksgiving or service to God, can be in private or in a corporate function. In reference to worship, praise, and/or glorifying the Lord, we have to fear the Lord with all our heart, mind, body, and soul. *Fearing the Lord* is another key word to 'loving the Lord.' If we love the Lord, we will follow His commandments. If we love the Lord, we will follow His will. If we love the Lord, we will read, study and meditate on His Holy Word. God is greatly to be feared in assembly of the saints and to be held in reverence by all those around Him. Moreover, to serve the Lord, God focuses on our hearts, not our physical appearance. Jesus is the way, the truth, and the light.[845] .

There are different ways of worship. God will lie on your heart and can be expressed through praise dance. Other ways is the admiration of God's creation, thanksgiving for the blessings He has administered, and through songs and hymns including poetry/lyrics. We can give God praise through our service, with our announcements or testimonies and glorifying the Lord. We can start as early in the morning, when we first open our eyes, get out of bed. It is a true blessing to see another day. We are blessed to have our health, family, and roof over our heads. We ought to worship and thank the Lord throughout the day and until the end of our day before dosing off to sleep. Give God the praise for your life by coping another day in our toxic world of sinful acts and thoughts and in the air we breathe (toxic chemicals). In addition, we can exhibit worship in a corporate setting through prophetic sermons, concerts, prayer meetings, Bible study, and church services.

Another reason for glorifying and worshiping the Lord, it gets God's attention to enlist the help of His angels. You will hear some people say, 'I know that I have a guardian angel.' Angels are prompted when God commands them to do so. God will be there for His children, when they call, and His sheep will be able to hear His voice. He will take care of their enemies. "Vengeance is mine," says the Lord. Praise God for taking care of your enemies and the ultimate enemy of them all -- Satan. Furthermore, Satan is the fallen angel responsible for first two humans to fall and lead us all into sin. Since the fall, we are all born into sin, but can be saved through our Lord and Savior. We have a second chance, but Satan and his followers do not.

For example, God released His angels when Daniel continued to praise and pray to God at the same time everyday, instead of worshipping the idol King Nebuchadnezzar wanted everyone in his kingdom to worship. Due to not worshipping and following the King's command, Daniel was thrown in the Lion's Den with hungry ferrous lions. Nevertheless, he knelt in the den to pray to God, what do you think happened? Some imagine the worse. Some just simply do not know. If you read the story, there was victory from beyond that cage he was trapped in with hungry animals that would eat flesh. The angels were inside to tame and calm down the lions, where they did not touch a hair on Daniel. Through prayer, Daniel worshipped the Lord, no

---

[845] John 14:6; 17:7

matter what the situation was. The presence of the angels was sent on God's command to slew the enemies in a war, but in Daniel's case, was to calm the lion's in the den.[846]

Another example is the good news about the birth of a child named Jesus. Joseph prayed that his fiancé would make it to his birth land unharmed. The Corinthians prayed for Peter while he was held captive in prison. After God heard their sincere prayers, He sent angels to come to Peter's rescue to release him from prison without disturbing the guards at the post. The chains fell off Peter's hands and feet as the prison gates flew open and he walked quietly pass the sleeping guards.[847] Look at what prayer can do! Remember that vague prayers will get vague answers. Tell God the desires of your heart, and wait and watch how God will shower you with blessings beyond your wildest dreams.[848]

Fourteen Reasons to Worship and Praise God

1. Forgiveness of iniquities
2. Heals all my diseases
3. Redeems life from destruction
4. Loving kindness
5. Satisfies my mouth with good things
6. Executes righteousness and justice for oppressed
7. His ways are known to us
8. Merciful and everlasting
9. Gracious
10. Slow to anger
11. Removes our transgressions from us
12. Pity on us
13. Believers who obey Him
14. Rules us all, His throne is established

We can have the *attitude of surrender*, which means putting God first, and submitting to His rulership will make all the difference. A simple prayer to God: "I surrender my relationship, my finances, my work, recreation, my decisions, my time, my body, my mind, my soul, my desires, and my dreams. I put them all in Your hands so they can be used for Your glory."[849]

> *Philippians 2:9-11: "Therefore God also has highly exalted Him and given Him the name which is above every name, that at the name of Jesus every knee should bow, of those in heaven, and of those on earth, and of those under the earth, and that every tongue should confess that Jesus Christ is the Lord, to the glory of the Father."*

---

[846] Daniel 6
[847] Acts 12
[848] John 5:14; Psalm 37:4-5
[849] Refer to the following Scriptures: Galatians 2:20; Luke 9:23-24; Romans 14:8; 1 Peter 5:6-7

Every knee: Only those who put their faith in Him will have an everlasting relationship with Him after death. *Those under the earth*: Paul refers to those who will already have died before the time of Christ's second return on earth. Those who were saved and lived a righteous life will be raised first when Christ returns. Second, He will rapture those who will still be living on earth.

Confess: Paul uses a strong, intensive verb, agree with or say the same thing. Paul is saying that everyone will unanimously affirm what God, the Father, has already stated that Jesus is Christ the Lord.[850]

At the last judgment, even those who are condemned will recognize Jesus' authority and right to rule.[851] People can choose to consider Jesus as your Lord and Savior this very day. This shows a step of willing and loving commitment to follow Christ. Or you will acknowledge Him as Lord when He returns and it will be too late for your salvation. Christ may return at any moment. Are you prepared to meet Him?

---

[850] Isaiah 45:23
[851] Philippians 2:9-11

~Let Your Day Begin With Christ, Day 49~

Let your Day Begin Activity: Today is to glorify God. Enjoy your day learning how to surrender to God. Turn your dreams, goals, and accomplishments over to Him. He will reveal new dreams and new visions that He sees you accomplishing, for the Body of Christ. We all have a job to do.

Today's Questions:

What chains we need to loosen and surrender to God?

When God's glory is manifested in your life—others will recognize it. What is glory?

What are some reasons we give God praise, worship, and glorify Him?

Are you watchful and pray and ready for Jesus Christ return? What are some things you believe you have to do to remain ready? You can also read about the "10 brides" in the Bible, to have an idea how 5 brides were ready and 5 brides were not.

Review to Begin your Day with Christ:

We are to surrender our will over to God. God will not force himself on us. We were created with freewill, to choose to serve, worship, and glorify God on our very own. We are not robots.

Review *1 Corinthians 6:20* and *Romans 8:16-17*.

Worship and praise: *Exodus 15:2; Ezra 3:10-11*.

Day Begins 50: New Creature And Growing Christian

God's Revelation (Psalm 119)

Word	Number of Occurrences	Meaning	Key Verse
Law, the Hebrews word, *torah*	25	The first five books of the Old Testament, the Torah; the Pentateuch	"So shall I keep Your law continually, forever and ever" (v. 44)
Testimonies, the Hebrews word, *edot*	22	Ordinances; God's standard of conduct according to the *Ten Commandments*	"Blessed are those who keep His testimonies" (v. 2)
Way, the Hebrews word, *Derek*	11	The pattern of life required by God's law	"I have chosen the way of truth" (v. 30)
Precepts, the Hebrews word, *piqqudim*	21	Injunction; requirement; commandment	"I will keep Your precepts with my whole heart" (v. 69)
Statutes, the Hebrews word, *huqqim*	21	Things inscribed; enacted laws	"I will keep Your statutes" (v. 8)
Commandments, the Hebrews word, *miswot*	22	A distinct, authoritative order	"I do Your commandments." (v. 166)
Judgments, the Hebrews word, *mispat*	23	A binding law; judicial decision	"I will praise You...when I learn Your righteous judgments" (v. 7)
Word, the Hebrews word, *dabar*	39	A general term for God's revelation	"Your word I have hidden in my heart that might not sin against You." (v. 11)

Source--Nelson Study Bible (chart above)

Remember: Believers are not *lucky*; we are *blessed*.

God's Law:
1. Love the Lord with all your heart, mind, soul and body
2. Love your neighbor

Law of Moses:
1. Has penalties for not following the law
2. We have to make a choice of which law we will follow
3. Lord by the Spirit: Will love your family? Will we follow and live for the Lord, regardless of the law?
4. Some people only concerned about themselves -- not the Lord
5. Satan will have you focusing on one extreme or the other
6. Learning how to fight the Adversary
7. God will not leave you alone
8. Fear and intimidation = Devil concentrates on
9. *James 4:7:* Resistance and Satan will flee from us, Devil fear
10. Head knowledge: learning and studying more, but we need personal experience

While reading, *Choosing God's Best* says that God's guidance will never go against the Scripture. The Bible is a record of God's revelation of Himself to man. If you look to the Spirit alone for guidance without the Word, you can open yourself up for possible deception. If you look to circumstances alone without the Word, you can be deceived. In seeking God's direction, in prayer, in Scriptures, through circumstances, and the counsel of other believers agree in the direction that God is leading you. You are unable to see the agreement of God's will and advice from non-believers.[852] Allow God to purify your spirit and mind to make you strong and secure in all that you do, build you up, restoring your soul and mind, to refresh your spirit, and most importantly, to grow in Christ.[853]

No athletic or competitor are crowned unless he competed with the rules of the Lord. We are conquerors. However, we need to follow God's laws to preserve and conquer any spiritual warfare or battles that come in our path. Faithful believers will receive a victor's crown, which is the royal crown that belongs to Jesus. In other words, spiritual activity must be conducted within the directives of biblical faith and doctrine.[854]

Psalm 119:165-166, 174-176 reads:
> *165: "Great peace have those who love Your law, and nothing causes them to stumble."*
> *166: "Lord, I hope for Your salvation, and I do Your commandments."*
> *174: "I long for Your salvation, O Lord, and Your law is my delight."*
> *175: "Let my soul live, and it shall praise You."*
> *176: "I have gone astray like a lost sheep; seek Your servant, for I do not forget Your commandments."*

Do we love the Lord? God says in His Word: God is love. Once we know that God loves us and we love Him, we will obey His commandments, laws, decrees, or anything He asks of us to do -- we will do. Lastly, we know that His love will never fail.[855]

---

[852] Micah 4:2

[853] 2 Timothy 2:5

[854] Nelson's Study Bible, NKJ, emphasis added by author.

[855] 1 Corinthians 13:8

We ought to be delightful to serve the Lord because He cares about the welfare of His children.

We were like lost sheep, unable to find our way to the Father, but if we seek the Lord and truly love Him, we will not forget His commandments that He set forth. Something we cannot ignore or run away from as believers of the Word. Blessed are those that keep the Word of God, who are able to hear the Word and keep it. The Word of God will set a person free from bondage. We are able to see the areas that need to be improved – *walk in holiness*. Be an anchor in the Lord. Hear the gospel so we can be doers of the Word. Doers of the Word manifest itself through service or ministry.

God will continue to bless you and show you His will through obedience and willingness to listen to Him. Obedient servants will not fall short of God's glory. We stand boldly in confidence and peace by abiding to His laws and commandments. Please Lord; show me Your steps, so I can trust Your guidance in everything.[856]

> *Psalm 119:10, NLT: "I have tried hard to find you—don't let me wander from your commands."*
>
> *Psalm 119:11, NLT: "I have hidden your word in my heart, that I might not sin against you."*
>
> *Psalm 119:15-16, NLT: "I will study your commandments and reflect on your ways. I will delight in your decrees and not forget your word."*
>
> *Psalm 119:17-21, NKJV: "…That I may live and keep Your word. Open my eyes, that I may see wondrous things from Your law. I am a stranger in the earth; do not hide Your commandments from me. My soul breaks with longing for Your judgments at all times, you rebuke the proud -- the cursed, who stray from Your commandments."*

God promises to bless our health through salvation and obedience. God will pour on the blessings that we are meant to receive. Furthermore, God wants us to pray, praise, glorify, and turn to Him in everything we do daily. We need to meditate on His law (precepts) and take in (contemplate) God's ways. In addition, *contemplate,*[857] means consider purpose, reflect on, study, think of, think about seriously, and plan. God will show us His purpose. We are to reflect on studying the Bible and having a personal relationship with God. We need to think about God's plan and take it seriously. Through obedience, we will be blessed and satisfied.

We must admit that we have sin that God is not pleased with. Otherwise, we only deceive ourselves and the truth is not in us. If we confess our sins, God is faithful and just to forgive us of our sins and cleanse us from all unrighteousness. Allow God to reveal your faults, shortcomings, mistakes, and sins to you. *Sin* is one's desires that fulfills its wants of the flesh and willingness to proceed with an act, thought, or desire to

---

[856] Philippians 4:13
[857] Roget's Thesaurus.

satisfy self. Unfortunately, some of us are bonded in chains of the world, of our flesh, and not seeking the Holy Spirit for correction and direction. Before making decisions, seek God first to direct our path, our choices, and in everything we do in the name of Jesus Christ.

Jesus is the Shepherd of His sheep, as His sheep, we hear our Master's voice and clear instructions from the Lord. Additionally, we will be able to decipher from right from wrong, especially things that is not like Jesus Christ, our Lord.[858]

---

[858] also can refer to these Scriptures—1 John 3:22-24; Luke 11:28; John 14:21

~Let Your Day Begin With Christ, Day 50~

Let your Day Begin Activity: Today is the final day of activities. Whew, you made it through the tough challenges. Rejoice with others about your experience as you became a mature believer and how God lead you to a new you, with a new view on life.

Today's Questions:

How was this adventure for you? Will you share this with another?

What is your testimony?

Review to Begin your Day with Christ:

Review the chart and closing remarks. Let it set in. Look at God's Laws and Laws of Moses (inspired by God).

Special Thanks

First, I would like to thank my Heavenly Father for allowing me the courage, and touching me with His Holy Spirit to write this book. I never imagined that I could write such a remarkable and spiritual non-fictional work. It is a blessing and privilege to write an uplifting book to touch souls, and those that do not really know You, Lord. Thank you, Lord, for allowing me to be a faithful servant, and to hear Your voice to do Your will.

Yahweh just wants us to get a closer and personal relationship with Him to hear from Him. Sometimes, God communicates with us in other forms such as dreams and visions like Daniel and Joseph; hear His voice like Elijah and Noah; feel His Holy Spirit shine down on us like Saul later known as Paul. God loves you and wants you to get you to know Him better. God already knows you before the foundation of the world.

Second, I would like to give thanks to those for the encouragement and the heartfelt emails to keep me going and trusting in the Lord that I can do it. In addition, I would like to thank Kathleen Jackson for her copyediting. Harriet Wilson was responsible for bringing my vision to life by reconstructing the book to get this book on the market for readers to see how his or her day can begin with Jesus Christ. Joey Pinkney was responsible for beginning touches on clarity of content. Thank, Rochelle Melander for her valuable opinions on writing since she is a nonfiction writer. I would like to thank Katari Campbell (spiritual sister) for praying for me during my darkest moments.

I cannot forget my family members, Sonny Turner (father) and Sarah Cunningham (grandmother) for all material/books used for research. Most of all, my mother, Diane Leslie Turner (calling the prayer line), Sonya Turner (shares the visions and dreams she gets from our Heavenly Father for my life), Gionna (Gee-Gee) Smith, Atria Davis (Mason) for believing in my true calling on my life and encouraging words left on my voicemail, my cousins who sustain me, and my grandmother, Maxine Battle (for all her love, support, and prayerful words spoken in my life…trusting and believing that one day I will be on Oprah Winfrey Show), and too many to name of which they know who they are.

You can purchase autographed copies at the author's website: www.adriennaturner.webs.com or literary site: www.dreams4more.com. Her future goal is law school (Intellectual Property) and to start a publishing company called Dream Your Reality Publications.

About Author

Adrienna Turner is an accomplished author. She writes inspirational non-fiction and fiction books. Under pseudonym names, she writes also science-fiction, fantasy or supernatural fiction, Young Adult inspirational dramas, suspense thrillers, and a new genre created by author called romance draspensedy (romance, drama, and comedy). Her previous books are *Mystery Lies Within (novella), From the Depths of My Soul: Collection of Poetry and Songs, Gospel Version;* and *Half of the Battle is to Surrender All I Have (secular poetry and songs).* Currently, she is writing an inspirational suspense-drama called Miss The Mark Series. She is also in the process of rewriting and reconstructing her first published novella, *Mystery Lies Within,* into a full-fledge novels from the stories in the book.

Adrienna has a Masters Degree in Library Information Science and Bachelors Degree in Information Resources. She also participates in law training seminars through Council for Legal Education Opportunity (CLEO). Additionally, she is a book reviewer for African Americans on the Move Book Club (AAMBC) and for Dream 4 More Reviews. She writes articles for Heavenly Magazine (http://www.heavenlymag.com). She is also the founder and President of Dream 4 More Literary Consulting Firm, a consulting firm for new and aspiring authors. Her literary site is at www.dreams4more.com.

You can keep up with her updates at her personal website: www.adriennaturner.webs.com. Her BlogTalkRadio show is www.blogtalkradio.com/Adrienna-Turner. Dream Summore website is http://dreamsummore.webs.com.

Reviews Are In

AAMBC (Africans on the Move Book Club), Gretchen Tolbert, 5 out of 5 stars.

The Day Begins with Christ puts me in the mind of a theologian properly dissecting the bible so that others can better understand Christ and develop a relationship with him. This book analysis God's relationship with his people and helps the reader to further develop and cultivate their relationship with Christ. We all are here for a purpose and for a season. That season and purpose involves God's love and guidance to properly understand and pursue. One must first be able to hear God's voice and know what his voice sounds like to you. Afterwards, one must be able to take heed and follow after Christ with passion and convection that will lead to salvation and further trust in God. As a non-fictional reader of Christian-related information for a passion, I found the book to be very informative and easy to read and non-threatening.

Christians are looking for a following guide or something to aid in their walk as they grow in God. This journal/booklet provides this ultimately to the readers. Each day provided enriching elements of what God expects from his people consistently. I agree with Adrienna Turner that without the knowledge of the expectations of Christ, his people perish or do not live life to the fullest and to their best capability.

Author Wright, Historical Romance (Lavina: The Saga of an African Princess) and Biblical Fiction (Ruth of Moab: Triumph of a Daughter's Love) gave 5 out of 5 stars.

His review is also posted on **http://www.midwestbookreview.com/rbw/aug_09.htm#rc (August 2009-August 2010)**

Often, the full impact of God's sovereign grace for fallen man is hidden in the writing style and expressions of many biblical scholars and teachers. However, the exhortation from our Lord and Savior to lead a righteous and holy life is still as relevant in our lives today as it has ever been. As Christians, we should always have God's amazing love as we walk in Faith from day to day. It is his transforming love which brings us to the true expression of his will. The Day Begins with Christ is a marvelous work of God guiding the hands and heart of his servant Adrienna. In her powerful book, she makes the power and purpose of our Lord's death abundantly clear and accessible in her lucid discussions of life and salvation. She stresses that through Jesus' death alone, the power over sin and death has been conquered. In her gracious writings, she tells her readers that mastery and dominion of sin have been broken once and forever. Then, she patiently leads them into the perfect will of God. The Day Begins with Christ, along with the Holy Bible, should be in every home so that one could learn how to live the successful walk of Faith.

Other Spiritual Books And Novels

From The Depths Of My Soul: Collection Of Poetry And Songs
Gospel/Religious Version

This is a book consists of lyrics written by an underground and former gospel rap artist known as 'Deo' and poems that have not been released to the world until now. These heartfelt poems and/or lyrics are to reach and touch the souls of our youth and people across the nation on a spiritual level. Publisher: Author House (www.authorhouse.com), September 2005. Currently writing the sequels: *From the Depths of My Soul: Collection of Spiritual Poems and Songbook II.*

Unleashing The Spirit

This book covers various spirits throughout the Bible. In addition, the book elaborates further on worldliness issues, Book of Life, and God's purpose. There are real, sincere, and heartfelt testimonies confessing their struggles and overcoming them. Activities: Moments of Reflection. Blue Planet Publishing: http://www.bppbooks.com (for updates).

Counsel Me Lord To Be A Vessel For Christ

This book will focus on spiritual counsel: what are good counsel and bad counsel? It will also cover friendship, mentoring other believers, and purpose of being a chosen generation is the *joint heirs* of Jesus Christ. Moreover, we are to be seeking godly counsel from our Heavenly Father, which God speaks through evangelists, apostles, pastors-teachers, spiritual counseling, and other believers. This book will also cover wise counsel from judges, lawyers, leaders, and other lifestyles to press on with what God called us to become. *No date set.*

Desire At Will: Giving All The Glory To God Through Prayer, Praise, and Worship
-- Let It Overflow

This book will focus on pleasing God through our prayers, praise, and worship. We are to glorify the Lord in everything we do. *To be released December 2009.*

Miss the Mark Series is an inspirational suspense-drama novel, plans to write seven series. I am working on Book 4. Book 1: *Dream's Reality.* March/April 2010.

Resources Used

Betty Crocker's New Eat And Lose Weight: Three Steps to Lose Weight And Feel Great! Minneapolis: General Mills, Inc., 1996.

Life Application Study Bible, New King James Version. Wheaton: Tyndale House Publishers Inc., 1996.

Webster's New World College Dictionary. 3rd ed. MacMillan, 1996.

Women's Devotional Bible: A New Collection Of Daily Devotions From Godly Women. New International Version. Grand Rapids: Zondervan Publishing House, 1995.

Anonymous. Bible Quizzes, "Sex." http://www.christianet.com.

Anonymous. *Operation Timothy*. Chattanooga: CBMC, 1985.

Anonymous. *Praying God's Promises.* Tulsa: Victory House, Inc., 1998.

Anonymous. "Work A Blessing Or A Curse?" *The Watchtower,* 15 June 2005, 3-7, 18-31.

Abanes, Richard. *Harry Potter And The Bible: The Menace Behind The Magick.* CampHill: Horizon Books, 2001.

Anderson, Ken. *Where To Find It In The Bible: The Ultimate A to Z Resource.* Nashville: Thomas Nelson, Inc., 1996.

Bacchiocchi, Samuele. *The Sabbath in John.* Website: http://www.biblicalperspectives.com/endtimesissues/eti_110.html

Batchelor, Doug. *The Christian And Alcohol.* Roseville: Amazing Facts, Inc., 2002.

Braybrooke, Marcus. *The Wisdom Of Jesus.* New York: Readers Digest Association, Inc., 1997.

Cloud, Dr. Henry and Dr. John Townsend. *Boundaries In Marriage.* Grand Rapids: Zondervan Publishing House, 1999.

Crews, Joe. *The Surrender Of Self.* Roseville: Amazing Facts, Inc., 1992.

Elliot, Elisabeth. *Loneliness.* Nashville: Thomas Nelson Publishing, 1988.

Evans, Anthony T. *The Philosophy Of Church Ministry.* Dallas: The Urban Alternative, 2000.

Evans, Tony. *The Battle Is The Lord's: Waging Victorious Spiritual Warfare.* Chicago: Moody Press, 1998.

Falcon, Chuck T. *Family Desk Reference to Psychology: Practical, Expert, And Counseling Advice At Your Fingertips!* Lafeyette: Sensible Psychology Press, 2002.

Gray, John. *Mars & Venus On A Date: A Guide For Navigating The 5 Stages Of Dating To Create A Loving & Lasting Relationship.* New York: Harper Collins Publishers, 1997.

Hammond McKinney, Michelle. *The Power Of Feminity: Rediscovering The Art Of Being A Woman.* EuGenesise: Harvest House Publishers, 1999.

Jameson, Judy. *Fat Burning Foods And Other Weight-Loss Secrets.* Owings Mills: Ottenheimer Publishers, Inc., 1994.

King, J.L. *On The Down Low: A Journey Into The Lives Of 'Straight' Black Men Who Sleep With Men.* New York: Broadway Books, 2004.

Kipfer, Barbara Ann. *Roget's 21st Century Thesaurus In Dictionary Form.* New York: Dell Publishing, 1993.

Malone, Julius. *Introduction To The Ten Commandments.* Sermon at New Testament Church Milwaukee, WI, 2004.

Ministerial Association. *Seventh-Day Adventist Believe: A Biblical Exposition of 27 Fundamental Doctrines.* Hagerstown: Review and Herald Publishing Association, 1988.

Omartian, Stormie. *Lord, I Want To Be Whole: The Power Of Prayer And Scripture In Emotional Healing.* Nashville: Thomas Nelson Publishers, 2000.

Omartian, Stormie. *The Power of a Praying Woman.* Waterville: Thorndike Press, 2002.

Radmacher, Earl D., Ronald B. Allen, and H. Wayne House. *Nelson Study Bible: New King James Version.* Nashville: Thomas Nelson Publishers, 1997.

Rannibar, Don. *Choosing God's Best: Wisdom for Lifelong Romance.* New York: Multnomah Publishing Inc., 1998.

Rosberg, Gary and Barbara Rosberg. *Healing The Hurt In Your Marriage.* Wheaton: Tyndale House Publishers, Inc., 2004.

Shelton, Danny. *The Forgotten Commandment: A Battle For Our Loyalty To Christ Or Man.* Nampa: Pacific Press Publishing Association, 2001.

Sper, David. *How Do You Live The Christian Life?* Grand Rapids: RBC Ministries, 1986.

Vander Lugt, Herb. *How Can I Break the Silence?* Grand Rapids: RBC Ministries, 1988.

Viden, Holly and Michelle McKinney Hammond. *If Singleness Is A Gift What's The Return Policy?* Nashville: Thomas Nelson Publishers, 2003.

Water, Mark. *Sharing Your Faith Made Easy.* Peabody: Hendrickson Publishers, Inc., 1999.

Walsch, Donald Neale. *Questions And Answers On Conversations With God.* Charlohesville: Hampton Roads, 1999.

Whitelaw, Daniel. *Biblical Reasons To Wait For Sexual Fulfillment.* Wisconsin Dells: 2001.

Whitelaw, Daniel. *Health And Emotional Reasons For Waiting For Sexual Fulfillment.* Wisconsin Dells: 2001.

Printed in the United States
By Bookmasters